Hope and Vanquished Reality

Hope

and

Vanquished Reality

Nguyen Xuan Phong

A
publication
of
Center for A Science of Hope

Worldwide rights assigned by author
to
Center for A Science of Hope
121 Avenue of the Americas
New York, NY 10013

Library of Congress Number:		2001117746
ISBN #:	Hardcover	1-4010-2103-4
	Softcover	1-4010-2102-6

This book was printed in the United States of America.

To order additional copies of this book, contact:
Xlibris Corporation
1-888-7-XLIBRIS
www.Xlibris.com
Orders@Xlibris.com

CONTENTS

PART ONE

PART TWO

With my deep love and gratitude

To my mother and father

Le thi Man and Nguyen van Thach

and

with my profound respect

to my **teachers**

who gave me guidance and affection
during my young days in Ben Tre,
Saigon, Paris, London and Oxford

representative at the Paris peace talks from 1968 to 1973 that he met and forged a lasting connection with Nguyen Xuan Phong, the then Deputy Leader of the Republic of Vietnam's delegation who later became Minister of State in charge of negotiations for ending the war in Viet-Nam.

In 1986-87, while Howard Schomer and I were working on our fiftieth Harvard class reunion, he introduced me to his colleagues on the Board of Directors of ICIS. ICIS had already begun to look into the nature and dynamics of human hope as a worthwhile subject for intensive study, having been prompted to do so in an earlier eventful exchange that included Howard, the Swiss futurist Robert Jungk, the founder of organization development, Herbert A. Shepard, Lamar Carter, biologist Janis Roze and others. Jungk argued strongly that ICIS undertake to pursue a "science of hope." In due course, Lamar Carter, President of ICIS, encouraged Howard, me and a few others to draw up a prospectus for a Center for A Science of Hope. The Center came into being in 1989 with me as Chairman.

Since 1989 the ICIS Center for A Science of Hope has built a
mprehensive database on hope, developed world-wide contacts
h scholars and practitioners seeking to understand the nature
dynamics of hope, convened a conference on hope in 1991,
roceedings of which were published in 1993 by the Center as
TS OF HOPE, supported the production of a two-part videotape
n "Hope and the Helping Relationship," and publishes an
al newsletter, ***HopeWATCH***.

the fall of Saigon at the end of April, 1975, Howard lost
ith Phong despite continuing to try, through numerous
contacts, to learn what had happened to him as a
of the fall of South Vietnam to forces from the North.
n long years later, in the spring of 1988, when these
warded. There arrived in Howard's mailbox a seven-
n letter in fluent Oxford English with three detailed
e of which was on hope as a factor in Phong's
f his experiences as a Minister in South Vietnam's

INTRODUCTION

How has it happened that a remembrance of events over the past thirty years in Viet-Nam, recalled by Nguyen Xuan Phong, descended from many generations of Indochinese in the Mekor Delta of South Vietnam reflecting Buddhist and Confucian tr tions, should be published by the Center for A Science of Hc was an idea that emerged out of the work of ICIS (Inter Center for Integrative Studies), founded in New York (early 1960s by Erling Thunberg, a Swedish humanist of ICIS, the Center's form was guided to its cu Howard Schomer, a theologian and Minister of th of Christ, Lamar Carter, descendant of dirt-po ers, and David R. Schwarz, a German-Jewis

None of these persons were known t into their maturity. What brought th common belief in the potential of the a deep commitment to communit attributes nurtured a shared realiz is a powerful factor in shaping survival. At the Center, a genetically linked to humar central to all religious tr

Howard Schomer' for the underprivileg assigned by the W

government as well as in his subsequent survival during the reeducation program required by the conquerors from North Vietnam.

Thus, Howard and Phong were brought back into contact with each other. The Center benefited from their re-connection by Phong agreeing to join its Advisory Council and add his hoping practicality and historical and philosophical insights to the work of the Center. He was urged to expand his 1988 comments on hope into an article which the Center might publish. Over time, an article became a book.

This volume, ***Hope and Vanquished Reality***, has been in development for twelve years. I believe it has unique qualities which will be useful to those seeking to understand the nature and power of hope as well as those who wish to have a refreshingly different view of the impact of the presence of the United States in Viet-Nam from 1961 to 1975. Nguyen Xuan Phong brings deep understanding of Southeast Asian traditions and modern European culture to the telling of the story of experiences among the leadership of South Vietnam and the personal outcome for him from five years of reeducation in a North Vietnamese prison.

David R. Schwarz
Larchmont, New York
2001

11185-CART

FOREWORD

In about 1988, I was asked by my colleagues Howard Schomer, David R. Schwarz and Lamar Carter at The Center for A Science of Hope in New York if I could put on paper my thoughts about hope as I might have experienced it through all the years of turmoil during and after the war in Viet-Nam. For various reasons, I was at first reluctant to do it. There has already been so much written by so many people on the war in Viet-Nam. I have found it repugnant and, frankly, boring to talk about wars. Nevertheless, wars continue to be horrifying realities, and the question as to hope as a factor in historic events and in my own life led me to begin to write in the summer of 1996. But I locked the beginning manuscript away in a drawer for almost four years before tackling it again and surrendering it to my friends. The third millennium may be a good time for more determined resolutions and new hopes. What better way for me to depict it than through my experiences with hope in the anxiety and the aftermath of the war?

We have all experienced *hope*, some of us more than others, each of us using this wonderful inborn ability in his or her own way. Hope is very personal, yet also so communicative. It is to be found by each and all, individually and collectively. It appears to be omnipresent, and is able to help us make life better, more bearable. While it is a thing so real, it is also so evasive, so slippery for us to reach, comprehend and use more effectively in dealing with the so-called vicissitudes of life. We must all live with our

11185-CART

pasts, presents and futures, and experience the joys and sorrows of the human condition. We are fortunate to have this wonderful gift called hope to help us travel this mysterious journey of ours on Earth.

The title, ***Hope and Vanquished Reality***, refers to events concerning my moments of hopefulness and hopelessness, as I am best able to recall them, over a period of more than thirty years from the 1960s through the 1980s and their aftermath. In many ways, I tried to bury the memory and significance of these events irretrievably deep down inside me, particularly after the dramatic fall of Saigon in April, 1975.

This volume is the only writing I have done in the past twenty-five years about the War in Viet-Nam, breaking a long and self-imposed silence on that sad and painful episode of my life and the history of the Vietnamese people. I have written it as a simple witness, one along with untold numbers of others, to express my moments of hopelessness and hopefulness as I experienced them. I have also wanted to present situations which would provoke reactions in other people about this phenomenon called hope. Each person reacts in his or her own way to situations in life, and hope is before anything else very personal.

My telling of the story is one of hope. But, sadly, the story has to be at the same time and to some extent a story of war. I have tried not to judge too much the rights and wrongs of things, but recall the details of everyday life during this sad episode of death and devastation that befell the Vietnamese people and others, one of the countless human tragedies of the twentieth century. Wars, of any kind and for any reason, are not to be rejoiced in and must always be regretted. But wars are also great generators of despair and hope.

Hope is in some ways a sentiment very much concerned with emotions. The terrible horrors during those long years of war in Viet-Nam were for me the source of many feelings and emotions, including those of hope in various ways. I would prefer to talk about hope in less painful situations but, as I have found out, hope is not only joyfulness and happiness but is also connected with sorrow and desolation. I have come to understand hope as a continuing and tremendous human challenge. It can be a heartbreaking struggle with my own individual self as well as a sometimes seemingly impossible battle with the whole universe. Hope carries the difficult task of coming to terms not only with myself but also with the world around me.

I consider *hope* to be a precious God-given gift, or, if you prefer, a gift from Mother Nature or the universe. Hope obviously comes to each person in different ways and does not mean the same things to different people. I became aware of hope in times of hardship, both physical and mental, and hope was "revealed"—if I may so say it—to me through an evolving and a very trying process over several long years. Hope came to me as an unwanted and dreadful adventure thirty-five years ago. But since then it has become a welcoming and constant companion ever present by my side, for better or for worse, for good or bad, with aspects which still are not yet quite clear to me!

I am not motivated or driven to give a universal definition of hope or proclaim a magic formula for instant hope for everybody. Throughout this book I have tried to understand what hope meant to me in various circumstances and in the ups and downs of my adult life. I have welcomed the opportunity to share this history and experience with friends at the Center for A Science of Hope and many others. The journey of hope emerged in me through great adversity, acute anguish and moments of despair. In relating the events in their chronology of time, I have tried to respect and bring out another chronology, that of the emotions, feelings and sentiments in their manifestations and expressions of hope provoked by different situations and at different stages. Thus, I have taken the fall of Saigon and collapse of the government in South Vietnam in 1975, an extremely dramatic event in my life and for many others, to be my story's point of departure. In the telling of the story, I have tried to make some sense out of a very bewildering and confusing journey.

11185-CART

To hope is an undeniable human ability which is basically individual and ignited by an emotional rather than rational response by a person to his or her environment. This initial and emotional reaction concerns itself with the rejection of adversity, both present and future, with desired expectations, wishes, aspirations and aims for survival and betterment in the act of being and becoming. Hope may or may not concern itself with despair but is often mingled with despair or a sense of helplessness. In its initial stage, hope is a search for purpose, whether vague or specific, which requires meaning and involves values. There cannot be hope without purpose and meaning but hope is also quickly confronted with reason and reality. Irrational and unrealistic hope cannot prevail. Hopes are, therefore, invariably drowned in illusions and disillusions, mixtures of myths and realities, conflicts between the true and the false, the right and the wrong, the good and the bad. I gradually became aware of these aspects of hope during events which are related in Chapters One to Seven, and have come to consider them as parameters of hope. They provide a practical way, or methodology, for me to understand and follow-up on, or continually pursue understanding of, the evolution of the hopes in me. Each person has his or her own way to hope.

Besides its process and working mechanism in function of its parameters of *Purpose, Meaning, Reason* and *Reality,* hope goes through another chronology of evolution. I was able to identify *grosso modo* four main stages, namely, *Latent Hope, Passive Hope, Active Hope* and *Communicative Hope,* which found their contexts in time through events related in Chapters Eight to Eleven. I have come to certain conclusions in the Epilogue but can only say to myself that the search for hope and understanding of hope is an endless human endeavor, and the journey of hope in each and all of us will remain a wonderful mystery.

I have tried to summarize and remind myself about various aspects and stages of hope in the **Codas** at the end of each chapter, borrowing the word from the world of music in which the coda is a concluding section that is formally distinct from the main structure. The dictionary also defines a coda as something that serves to round out, conclude, or summarize, and has interest in its own right. The codas emerged as reflections—even meditations—which became of great help to me as I disciplined myself and little by little learned how to use the ability to hope. I put them in a format that allows me to browse through them whenever I feel downhearted or try to forget the sad moments of the past fifty years. And I feel much better.

Nguyen Xuan Phong
Spring 2001
Giong Trom Village,
Ben Tre Province,
Viet-Nam

11185-CART

ACKNOWLEDGEMENTS

With my great appreciation and affection to Howard Schomer, David Schwarz and Lamar Carter of the Center for A Science of Hope, who have excelled in their professional activities in the fields of science and industry, international relations and development, human resources development and management, as well as in their humanitarian, educational and social endeavors, for their unfailing encouragement and valuable support without which the present piece of writing would not have seen the light and come to be. Howard, David and Lamar know much more than I do about *hope* but have preferred to let me search for it by myself. I assume, therefore, full responsibility for the views expressed herein on the matter of *hope* which are in no way the official positions of the Center for A Science of Hope or any of its members.

I am indebted to Joseph Mancini, a true New Yorker with such a happy *savoir-vivre* about his wonderful hometown, for taking on the very challenging and tedious work of bringing order to my very disparate and sometimes chaotic ideas and their presentation. To the extent that the stories flow easily for the reader, it's the result of Joe's contribution.

I also wish to express my appreciation to Linda M. DeVore, editor *extraordinaire*, who has performed a very challenging task not only in correcting grammar, punctuation, and everything that makes for good writing in English but also for raising insightful questions about unclear points and offering thoughtful ways of making the points that needed to be made.

I am particularly and happily indebted to Rhoda Nguyen T. Bich Hop, who took endless notes, typed and retyped the many drafts, battled with files, computers and printers, struggled with data banks, records, names and dates. But I owe Rhoda much more than the administrative chores. During the last two decades, she has stood by my side, always reminding me if only by her silence that the most precious things in life are simple. Rhoda also went through profound grief and sorrow, and endured unbelievable hardships caused by the war in Viet-Nam. In my efforts to deal with the problems of *hope*, Rhoda has become my alter-ego and never failed to help me, simply by her presence, not to forget the most basic human values, the true and simple people with their common sense. I have come to think that Rhoda is the most precious thing I now have on Earth and a merciful gift from my Creator.

N.X.P.

PRONUNCIATIONS OF AUTHOR'S NAME

Nguyen—Noo-én (common dynastic family name)

Xuan—Se-an (means "spring")

Phong—Fong (means "wind")

11185-CART

SPELLINGS OF THE COUNTRY NAME: VIET-NAM

The name of the country, Viet-Nam, is written as two words with their first letters capitalized and linked by a hyphen. The language of Viet-Nam is monosyllabic. It does not link syllables, or two words, into one. The hyphen is not needed or necessary in written Vietnamese to link words but is used in written English, French or other foreign languages which have the Latinized alphabet. Thus spelled and written, Viet-Nam refers to the entire country from the north to the south, the whole nation with its peoples' common historical origins, traditions and customs, language, and their social, economic and political past since at least the Third Century B.C. of recorded history.

While Viet-Nam is written "Vietnam," as one word, with its first letter capitalized, in English, French and many other languages, the author wishes to maintain the historical, traditional and cultural meaning of the name, Viet-Nam, in this book.

It is common practice, however, to write the name as "Vietnam" when writing, for example, South or North Vietnam, the Democratic Republic of Vietnam, or the Vietnam War. In this book, it is written as "Viet-Nam," however, when referring to the War in Viet-Nam or the American War in Viet-Nam.

Vietnamese words in both their noun and adjective forms do not decline or vary in spelling. Therefore, the adjective form of

11185-CART

Viet-Nam is strictly an English grammatical construct which is much better spelled "Vietnamese" rather than "Viet-Namese." Thus, expressions such as, the "Vietnamese people" means the people of Viet-Nam. The "South Vietnamese people" means the Vietnamese in the south of Viet-Nam, and the "North Vietnamese," the Vietnamese in the north of Viet-Nam. Similarly, the "South Vietnamese government" refers to the government in South Vietnam (or the south of Viet-Nam) and the North Vietnamese government refers to the government in North Vietnam (or the north of Viet-Nam), etc.

HISTORICAL BACKGROUND ON THE COUNTRY NAME: VIET-NAM

During the legendary period called the Hong Bang, from 2897 to 258 B.C. under the Hung kings—who are traditionally considered to be the ancestors of the Vietnamese people—the country was called Van Lang. For a period of fifty years after that, it was called Au Lac. Then, during the very long millennium of Chinese domination, the country was called by different names including Giao Chi, Giao Chau and An Nam Colony. After regaining national independence from Chinese rule in the tenth century A.D., the Vietnamese kings renamed the country Dai Co Viet in about 968 A.D. (Dinh dynasty), and Dai Viet in 1010 A.D. (Ly dynasty). At the beginning of the twelfth century A.D. under King Ly Anh Tong (1138-1175 A.D.), the powerful Chinese Imperial Court granted and recognized for the first time the appellation An Nam Quoc, which literally means An Nam Country instead of An Nam District, Protectorate or Colony, as has been the case in the past. When Nguyen Anh was able to reunite the country and proclaimed himself Emperor Gia Long in 1802, the name of the country became Viet-Nam for the first time in its history.

After Gia Long's death in 1819, his son and successor, Emperor Minh Mang (1819-1840) changed the name to Dai Nam (meaning

Great South). Emperor Tu Duc, who occupied the Vietnamese throne from 1840 until his death in 1883, went through a painful time and witnessed, during his reign, the colonization of his country under French rule. The French colonization did not end until 1955. The colonial administration lasted more than a century as the *Indochine* (the French Union of Indochina), set up in 1887. The *Indochine* eventually included: Cambodia, already a French protectorate from the time of 1863; Laos (a part of Siam) in 1893; the northern part of Viet-Nam called Tonkin (ruled as a "French protectorate"); and the southern part of Viet-Nam called *Cochinchine* ruled as a formal colony. There was also a token "Kingdom of Annam" in the central part of Viet-Nam (with its capital city of Hue) that had the same status of protectorate as Tonkin, the northern part of Viet-Nam. For over a century of French colonial rule from the mid 1850s to the mid of 1950s, the name Viet-Nam, which had been used only during the short reign of Gia Long from 1802 to 1819, was ignored, forgotten, and erased from the maps of the world.

There were no longer Vietnamese but only *annamite(s)*, not only in the so-called Kingdom of Annam but in Tonkin and in *Cochinchine* as well. Many generations of Vietnamese referred to themselves and among themselves as "nguoi an nam" (without a capital A) to mean "Annam people," not "Vietnamese people," and never "Viet-Nam people." Under a century of French colonial rule, the term *annamite* acquired the connotation of "second class humans," as in any colonized country or nation in the world.

After Emperor Gia Long's death in 1819, the name Viet-Nam reappeared officially again on September 2, 1945 when used by Ho Chi Minh in his Declaration of Independence to refer to the country as "Viet Nam Dan Chu Cong Hoa" which means the "Democratic Republic of Vietnam." In 1949, Emperor Bao Dai signed the Elysees Agreement with the French on March 8, and on July 1, declared the formation of "Quoc gia Viet Nam," which means the "State of Viet-Nam" or State of Vietnam within the "Union Francaise" (French Union). It was during the long years of the two French Indochinese wars and the American War in Viet-Nam that the name of the country came up officially again, with the creation of "Viet Nam Cong Hoa" ("Viet-Nam Republic" or "Republic of Vietnam") which began on October 23, 1955 when Ngo Dinh Diem deposed Emperor Bao Dai by a referendum, then on March 4, 1956 proclaimed the Constitution of the Republic of Vietnam and instituted the political regime in Viet-Nam south of the seventeenth parallel (the Ben Hai river). From then on, it was variously called the government of the Republic of Vietnam in the south of Viet-Nam, the government of South Vietnam or the South Vietnamese government, and the Saigon government (to distinguish it from the government in the north of Viet-Nam—or the North Vietnamese government, the Hanoi government, or the government of the Democratic Republic of Vietnam).

After the fall of Saigon and collapse of the government of the Republic of Vietnam or of the country called Viet Nam Cong Hoa—which had prevailed from October, 1955 to April, 1975—the notions of North Vietnam and South Vietnam faded away and were replaced by the expressions "the north of Viet-Nam" and "the south of Viet-Nam." The name of the country and people came up again officially as Viet-Nam in its current use on July 2, 1976 when the country was reunified formally to become the present Cong Hoa Xa Hoi Chu Nghia Viet Nam which means the Socialist Republic of Vietnam (SRV or SRVN) as written in English or "Republique Socialiste du Vietnam" (RSV or RSVN) in the French language.

The author finds the English or French spelling of the name as Vietnam instead of Viet-Nam to be totally acceptable when those from other countries follow their customary practice, writing it as Vietnam. As a Vietnamese, however, he chooses in this book to follow the practice in his home country and write it as Viet-Nam.

PART ONE

PROLOGUE

Are there many people around today who can easily recall what happened in the country known as Viet-Nam in that fateful spring of a little more than a quarter-century ago? Yes, Viet-Nam, a radiant but star-crossed locale somewhere in the Far East. The name is not totally unfamiliar, is it? Americans had something to do with the place, didn't they? But don't search the almanacs or history books. Bringing back those memories would compel us to evoke all the horrors of a war that dragged on for decades, with millions of troops who battled, millions of bombs and rockets detonated, billions of dollars wasted, millions of lives lost, and immeasurable human suffering endured on both sides of the bloody conflict. Yes, for many long years, there was a dreadful war in that country called Viet-Nam, a strange war that Vietnamese call "The American War" and that Americans are in the habit of calling "The Vietnam War." But whatever it is called, it was a conflict that left profound wounds in both nations.

More than twenty-five years after the war's end, scholars and pundits continue their studies and ruminations about the American War in Viet-Nam. Americans still fail to comprehend how and why their great nation, the world's one and only superpower, possessor of the most formidable war machine on earth, champion of the weak and oppressed, land of the rich and free, home of the strong and brave, could be defeated in any war, even a war with powerful nations. But with Viet-Nam, you ask? Utterly ridiculous. Sheer nonsense.

How, then, did this historical defeat come about? There must be some misunderstanding. No, surely it was not an American defeat. It was a sad, bad, and maddening experience, but not a defeat. No war had been declared and no defeat proclaimed. No, sir, you must be dreaming. The United States of America cannot be defeated in any war. The Stars and Stripes waves proud and high in the wind, declaring that it can't be true. An American "defeat" would simply be a matter of terminology, a face-saving philosophical debate.

It would be inaccurate, even odd, to call the American failure in Viet-Nam an ignominious defeat merely because of the lamentable way Washington evacuated the last Americans out of Saigon before the arrival of the North Vietnamese troops. Nevertheless, the dramatic events in Viet-Nam in the spring of 1975 clearly expressed the enormous and painful failure of the U.S. government—for more than two decades and through the tenures of five successive American presidents—to achieve its aims in the names of freedom and democracy. Would it be fair, then, to call this regrettable episode in American history the collective failure of five U.S. presidents? It certainly would be very unjust for American history books to record the fall of Saigon as a defeat for President Gerald Ford simply because he happened to be in the White House in that spring of 1975. Nor would it be accurate to call it the failure of five successive U.S. presidents. Rather, the ignominious term "defeat" should be reserved for the Saigon government, also called the Republic of Vietnam, privileged "Outpost of the Free World" in South Vietnam and long-time ally of the powerful U.S. government. During twenty continuous years of conflict there, realities were created, nurtured, entertained and destroyed. Yes, realities were vanquished in Viet-Nam in the spring of 1975.

Realities come and go, and some realities are truer than others. There are evident and virtual realities. There are apparent and presumed realities, which need to be proven beyond any possible doubt. Realities can be anything that people are able to think of, and realities are also very much present in our world of illusions and disillusions. All kinds of realities make up the facts of life, and they always bring with them their trail of unavoidable hopes, whether true or false, which equally play an important role in our human existence, individually and collectively. Often mingled with and similar to realities, hopes are created, nurtured, entertained, destroyed, and vanquished.

The human ability to hope is so helpful and yet so frightening at the same time, capable of dispensing joy and sorrow alike, a tremendous challenge for the mind and the heart, but it is undeniable that hope is a wonderful gift to be thankful for. Hope is constantly there, latent in each and all of us, conscious or unconscious, welcomed or repressed, passive or active, and for good or bad, depending on each of us, who is still able to have his or her own say in spite of everything. Hope is the very essence of the human condition itself.

11185-CART

CHAPTER ONE

THE FALL OF SAIGON: HOPE AND DESPAIR

When Heaven and Earth have turned upside down.
Vietnamese proverb

I had returned to Saigon from my post as head of the Republic of Vietnam's delegation to the Paris peace talks five days before the North Vietnamese tanks crushed the gates of the South Vietnamese presidential palace on April 30, 1975. That cataclysmic episode shattered for some and released for others all kinds of hope for millions of people in both North and South Vietnam and elsewhere around the world. The latent anxiety and indiscernible fear that had surrounded me during the preceding months were to be replaced by profound anguish and hopelessness when the troops of Uncle Ho began to wander the streets of my hometown, from then on proclaimed Ho Chi Minh City. Heaven and earth had, indeed, turned upside down.

After deplaning at Saigon's Tan Son Nhut airport, I was dismayed by an apocalyptic scene of thousands of people in the airport compound and endless lines on the road vying for access to flights out of the country. The official escort that came to drive me to the presidential palace had to force its way through these waves of humanity. The security agents, to whom I was a familiar figure,

11185-CART

did not greet me with joy as on previous occasions, and the fifteen-minute ride into the city was endured in complete silence. The streets of Saigon were unusually quiet, shrouded with a sense of foreboding and an atmosphere of oppression.

As I arrived at the presidential palace at about six o'clock in the evening, one of the first people I encountered was U.S. Ambassador Graham Martin. He was coming out of a meeting with the Republic of Vietnam's president of one week, Tran Van Huong, whom I also was about to see. I had met briefly with Ambassador Martin when he had passed through Paris a few weeks earlier on his way back to Saigon, after having tried in vain once again to obtain support from the U.S. Congress for the South Vietnamese government. After brief courtesy exchanges, we quickly found ourselves agreeing that the military situation had clearly reached the point of disaster.

"Mr. Ambassador," I asked, "is there still some way for us to avoid the 'Battle of Saigon'?"

There was no need for me or anyone else to go into what such a battle would involve. We both knew well what the likely consequences would be, what devastation and bloodshed would ensue if there were fighting in the streets of Saigon. He also understood that our most immediate concern was for the safety of the innocent civilian population.

Ambassador Martin seemed to be at a loss to reply, trying to speak several times, with the words getting stuck in his throat. In a gesture of desperation, he simply waved his hand in the direction of the thunder of mortars and rockets outside the city. Then he collected himself, took my hand in a farewell gesture, and intoned slowly and solemnly, "President Huong must act very quickly."

On that enigmatic note, we parted. His struggle to find words, his wave of the hand conveyed more than any speeches could a poignant sense of helplessness—his own, and that of the U.S. government as well. Left hanging, however, was any explanation of what "act very quickly" signified.

A few minutes later, I put similar questions to our Defense Minister, General Tran Van Don, and to General Cao Van Vien of our Joint Chiefs of Staff, who had appeared in the hallway. After working together for ten years in the Saigon government, these two and I had become trusted friends who could speak plainly and freely to each other. Most people in Saigon, Washington, and Paris had come to consider Generals Don and Vien exceptional among the Saigon military establishment, not only as army officers but also as people to be respected for their moderation, integrity, honesty, and dignity in the midst of local corruption.

With them, I could dispense with the courtesies required with Ambassador Martin and fire a volley of blunt questions, including: "What has really happened here at home? How could you let the situation degenerate so fast? How could you let President Thieu do what he's done? Were the Americans that bad in the field, after all? What's happened to the ARVN (Armed Forces of the Republic of Vietnam)?"

Only Vien replied. "The troops are trying to do their best," he said. General Don just looked out into the invading darkness of the Saigon sunset as if expecting some miracle to happen in the palace gardens while I hurled such embarrassing questions at them.

So, there was not much hope then, not much hope of any kind—not from the U.S. ambassador or our generals. Earlier, all three of them must have had some hope to inspire them to come to see and press pitiful old President Huong to rapidly hand over his so-called presidential powers to fifty-nine-year-old General Duong Van Minh, whose stature made him known to everybody as "Big" Minh.

Yet, at that crucial time, was I trying to generate hope for myself by asking these questions? Did I really think the U.S. ambassador or our generals were in a position to give anyone in Saigon any kind of hope at this eleventh hour? To this day, it is difficult to say precisely. That evening in the presidential palace of the South Vietnamese government, my greatest anguish was not over the survival of the Saigon political regime but over how to

11185-CART

avoid the death and devastation that would come to the people of Saigon, including my old parents and relatives, from a much-feared "Battle of Saigon."

I asked these questions because they were the ones filling my mind. I was fully aware that the final agony of Saigon had, in fact, begun, and there was not much left to do except witness the withdrawal of our great American ally. I didn't have much hope, but there was a compelling need in me to seek it, even if for an obviously desperate situation. Though there was not much left for me to hope for, I nevertheless clearly felt a natural compulsion to hope. Was it hope to remain alive somehow? Was it simply the basic human instinct for survival that gave me the urge to hope? Hope may or may not concern itself with survival, but survival must have hope among its components.

* * *

Waiting to see President Huong, my attention certainly was not directed to Vietnamese history, which has been engulfed with wars. But there was an historical context that both Huong and I could not fail to bear in mind that evening. Furthermore, we and most other Vietnamese would have been aware of the distinction between "The Vietnam War" and "The American War" in the land of our ancestors—distinctions not made by many elsewhere in the world. Could anyone really sort out what "The Vietnam War" had been all about? Fighting and killing had been so much a part of Vietnamese history for so long a time; many of us had lost track of events and circumstances. Now, for the first time in nearly two centuries of disputes, conflicts, and wars, we, the Vietnamese people, were about to be face-to-face with ourselves alone. It was disconcerting. No more Chinese, French, Japanese, British, or Americans. Just Vietnamese face-to-face with Vietnamese.

There had been so many wars of so many kinds in this tiny nation: colonial wars, fascist wars, imperialist wars, wars of liberation, wars of aggression, wars for freedom, wars for independence, wars for democracy, wars for progress and prosperity, conventional wars, protracted wars, localized wars, internationalized wars. They were fought for all of the philosophies, ideologies, and theories humans propagate to justify wars. They left a trail of history and a legacy of myths.

But the twentieth century war in Viet-Nam was different. It created devastatingly stark realities. It is undisputed that more bombs and rockets were dropped on Viet-Nam than the entire tonnage detonated in World War II. Eventually, consolidated data from official statistics from all parties involved will provide the exact total figures on human losses. But conservative estimates by the international press, specialized agencies, and others put the figure at more than three million dead from the war's three continuous decades. Add over fifteen million maimed and wounded, plus countless victims suffering numerous side effects in the years that followed, and you have a disastrous total indeed.

Now, suddenly, the Vietnamese would face themselves alone for the first time in nearly two hundred years of French and American occupation and influence. How had it been possible for brothers, cousins, fathers, and sons to keep on killing one another, generation after generation? They had had plenty of help from near and far. That cannot be used as an alibi or excuse, but the agendas of other nations were often dominant.

The historical backdrop had been long and intricate. My mind could click down through the list of major events that I learned as a schoolboy. The roots of the Vietnamese people went back to the Bronze Age, but the country first got its name about 4,000 years ago when the "Viets" of the Hong Bang era (2879-258 B.C.) made up the Kingdom of Van Lang along the borders of ancient China. No wonder that the Viets were dominated by their powerful neighbor during almost the entire first millennium of the Christian era.

It was the Vietnamese national hero, General Ngo Quyen, who was able to put the final end to Chinese rule with his historic and resounding victory in the year 938 A.D., against the formidable

11185-CART

armada of the T'ang Dynasty on the Bach Dang River. By most accounts, the first independent, united, and formally organized Vietnamese state took shape with Dinh Bo Linh, who defeated the twelve insurrecting lords in 968 A.D. and proclaimed himself king. He founded the Dinh Dynasty and named the country Dai Co Viet. The Le Dynasty succeeded the Dinh in 980 A.D. It was replaced by the Ly Dynasty in 1009 A.D., during which reign the country acquired the new name of Dai Viet (Great Viet) in the year 1054, with its capital city established in Thang Long (now Hanoi). The Viet people then went on to build their nation with one dynasty after another, the main ones being the Ly, Tran, and Le. By the sixteenth century, the Mac Le/Trinh Nguyen dispute over the Vietnamese throne had resulted in a fierce Vietnamese thrust southward, expanding the country's borders into the Champa and Khmer kingdoms.

A Viet-Nam house, divided for nearly three hundred years, was eventually reunited in 1802 with Emperor Gia Long as the Nguyen Dynasty—with help from the French. It was then that the name Viet-Nam appeared for the first time in Vietnamese history. This Nguyen dynasty was to be the last line of Vietnamese monarchs whose demise was sealed with the arrival of the French colonists in the mid-nineteenth century. Nguyen Vinh Thuy inherited the crown and was enthroned as Emperor Bao Dai in 1932 by French authority. He was the last of the Nguyen emperors, managing to linger on and off as circumstances permitted, in one function or another with Mother France, the Japanese, Uncle Ho, and again the French Union until 1955, when he was finally brought down by one of his subjects, Ngo Dinh Diem, the first president of the Republic of Vietnam (South Vietnam).

The Vietnamese had had their family quarrels and had fought against one another for over three centuries, but they had never forgotten their common roots and history, even during the thousand years of Chinese domination. In their prolonged fighting as brother-enemies from the sixteenth to nineteenth centuries, they had come to call themselves the Nguyen "inner family" in the south, and the

Trinh "outer family" in the north—both named after outstanding generals of the Le Dynasty—but they always felt they were one people in one Vietnamese nation. Vietnamese differences sometimes exploded into heated arguments and occasionally bloody fighting, but the people invariably banded together to push back foreign invaders and defend the land of their ancestors.

Then in 1847, France fired its first cannonballs into Da Nang in the central part of Viet-Nam, a town that in the 1960s became known worldwide for the huge American air and naval base there. The Vietnamese tried to put up a bloody resistance in a very unequal fight against French colonization, but they were ultimately crushed. "Mother" France came to what it called *Indochine* (Indochina) in the name of civilization and progress. It brought lots of good things—*foie gras* and champagne, chateaubriand and bordeaux, Victor Hugo and Molière, steam engines and railroads, cars and planes, the French language and refined *savoir-vivre.* Mother knew what was best for her adopted children in not only Viet-Nam, but also in Laos and Cambodia for more than one hundred years.

Then "Uncle Sam" came in the name of freedom and democracy, to replace Marianne's French cuisine with hamburgers and hotdogs, blue jeans and bourbon, B-52s and M-16s, GIs, and American slang. And cash—lots of cash. The Saigon shoeshine boys were also able to make their small contributions to the language of Hemingway and Mailer with colloquial expressions such as, "You number one me, I number one you. But you number ten me, I number ten you." (Easy to learn and remember, "number one" means "the best" as in almost any language, and "number ten" in Viet-Nam means "the worst." These expressions can be used as either noun or adjective, as well as in the verb form, to make someone or something the best or the worst.)

Over fifteen centuries, patterns and modalities of accommodation had been relatively easy and clearly drawn in Vietnamese-Chinese wars and disputes. In good times, the Vietnamese had been intermittently successful in pushing back their God-given big neighbor. In bad times, the "Sons-of-Heaven"

(Chinese) had been quite satisfied with tributes in goods (especially the succulent litchis [or lychees]) and girls. The female tribute could not be too ugly, of course, so as not to offend ancient Chinese tastes.

But with the contrasting culture brought by Mother France, life and conditions were more complicated. When Uncle Sam came, it became even more so—it was a "pea soup," as Londoners call their fog. The Vietnamese had always fought over very understandable things like land and crops. But to go to war over ideologies? That was something new and obscure to the peasants in the countryside.

The French presence and colonial rule lasted from 1850 to 1955. The American intervention from 1955 to 1975 was far shorter in comparison, but had a profound impact because of its intensity and the indescribable horror of the events that accompanied it. What really happened in that century and a quarter of French and American presence? The Vietnamese will have to sort it all out for themselves, someday, by themselves. It will have to be accomplished by future generations. We surely could not do it on those last days of April in 1975.

* * *

If my conversation with the U.S. ambassador in the hallway of the presidential palace that fateful evening was marked by helplessness and hopelessness, I had a powerfully moving and poignant meeting with our old, ailing, and almost blind President Tran Van Huong. He obviously was trying to salvage a final few moments of decorum and dignity for an office he had neither sought nor wanted, even for the single week he occupied it. As vice-president of the Republic of Vietnam, he was thrust into the office when President Thieu summarily resigned nine days before Saigon was to fall. Many were shocked that Thieu had resigned and left the chaotic situation in the hands of his feeble vice-president. Had it not been for the onerous inevitability of relinquishing South Vietnam to the North

Vietnamese military forces that were on the verge of entering Saigon, Tran Van Huong would have been made to measure for that time and place in the history of the Vietnamese people.

It was incomprehensible to him that he would have to play such a shameful role. It was totally against his nature. His government had been the ally of the number one superpower in the world and had been formally recognized by the governments of over one hundred other countries, yet here he was, desolate and abandoned. Exacerbating his shame was the pressure he was being subjected to from all sides, including from the U.S. ambassador, to resign so that "Big" Minh could take over and negotiate—and perhaps come to some agreement—with the communist victors.

Huong felt he had to stand for the Constitution of the Republic of Vietnam—the will of the South Vietnamese people as expressed in general elections. No other possible point for him to hang onto presented itself. He had hoped that this point of international law and decency would induce the U.S. to intervene again with its military might to save Saigon. Or perhaps the point could provoke the United Nations or the so-called international community to take some action to prevent the illegal advance of the North Vietnamese troops. So, Huong clung to the position that it would be unconstitutional for him to relinquish his job to "Big" Minh. Having been forced into this predicament, he was surely torn between his long-held hope for a free and democratic South Vietnam and his sickening despair in the face of the rapidly deteriorating situation resulting from the complete refusal of the U.S. government to prevent the fall of Saigon to the Vietnamese communists.

President Huong was a very sensitive man. He could burst into tears over issues affecting his people and country. He had done so in cabinet meetings. The last time I witnessed this display of emotion had been when I returned to Saigon in January 1973 to attend a National Security Council (NSC) meeting just a few days before the signing of the Paris Accords. Then-President Nguyen Van Thieu had announced that negotiations had reached a point

11185-CART

where the Republic of Vietnam had no choice but to sign the accords (Saigon had very strongly refused to do so until then), because the U.S. government would go ahead and sign alone if necessary. That eventuality would signal a clear parting of old friends and allies. Thieu and the South Vietnamese government would have to find another ally. Old Huong had not been able to repress a sob at that time; unfortunately, he would soon find cause to weep again.

There had been no need for Thieu to explain to his NSC colleagues that the Paris Accords would put an end to American military intervention in Vietnam—and to the anti-communist Saigon government. The accords contained provisions that the Saigon government would eventually be replaced by a "non-communist" coalition, a crude disguise of communist rule by Hanoi. Thus had Washington finally decided to abandon the notion of South Vietnam as the "Outpost of the Free World" in Southeast Asia, a notion it had once so convincingly created. For the United States of America, an anti-communist South Vietnam simply ceased to have any value. All his life, Huong had been known as a patriot, nationalist, democrat, and liberal. He had struggled endlessly for what he believed was his country, and for the Free World. He had been in and out of prisons repeatedly, relentlessly fighting French rule and President Ngo Dinh Diem's dictatorial regime, and had lived poorly and simply all his life. He was respected for his integrity and honesty. A schoolteacher turned politician, he was an amiable grandfather figure for the South Vietnamese. Huong was already seventy-two at that time. He had been mayor of Saigon in 1954, and prime minister twice, just for a few weeks each time in 1964-1965 and 1968-1969, in the so-called civilian Saigon governments. As with many in South Vietnam and elsewhere at that time, Huong could not imagine that Thieu would resign and leave to him the collapse of the Saigon government. Furthermore, as with most people in Saigon, Huong found it hard to believe that the U.S., with all its wealth and military might, could forsake its diminutive South Vietnamese friend and ally.

Was there some semblance of a hope on the part of those pressuring him to turn power over to "Big" Minh, that doing so would provide a basis of hope for the survival of South Vietnam? That by surrendering to North Vietnam with pretended "national reconciliation" and "self-determination," disguised as "non-communist" for the sake of so-called freedom and democracy, it would make it easier for the Vietnamese in South Vietnam? For Huong, it was impossible to entertain such a hope. It was beyond his comprehension and imagination. The only hope left to him and many others in Saigon was simply the "hope to hope" without knowing what to hope for, a "hope against all hope."

Was there anything left for Huong except despair? "Big" Minh made no statements that would instill any sort of specific or concrete hope. He emphasized his professed ability to "talk" (a euphemism for "make deals") with the brother-enemies who were already closing in around Saigon. To be able to "talk" to Hanoi was the "in" thing for Saigonese politicians, who presented themselves as acceptable interlocutors to Hanoi. One slight indication from Hanoi attesting to that effect, and the designated man would hit the jackpot. Hanoi had never said outright that the communist side would accept "Big" Minh, but it craftily implied that he could be such a person—and, incidentally, might get an appointment with Madame Binh's National Liberation Front (NLF). The French and American ambassadors in Saigon were dead sure "Big" Minh could do just that. They knew very well that Hanoi would not accept any negotiated settlement with Thieu still in power—even if it were just an agreement to sit down and have tea—and it was even less likely with Huong, who was way out of his league.

Old Huong may have thought that whatever "Big" Minh could do, he could do, too—and do it better, for that matter. He was not an army general who had engaged the brother-enemies on the battlefield as "Big" Minh had. His purposes and ideals and hopes for the Vietnamese nation and its peoples had always been honorable and worthy by any decent, civilized standard. He believed a peaceful and negotiated solution should be possible, and felt there was no reason he should be disqualified from the contest.

A sick and penniless old man, Huong had no motivation to hope much for himself. But he held ideals he had cherished dearly all his life, ideals of freedom, democracy, and progress. These were abstract concepts, perhaps, more than experienced realities, coming as they had from reading and study that had prepared him as a teacher. He had not actually known or even seen *de visu*—with his own eyes—these things in other lands, since he had not traveled much because of bad eyesight and precarious health. But cherish them he nevertheless did.

* * *

When I entered President Huong's office, he was not sitting at Thieu's former desk in the Saigon "Oval Office," but alone at a conference table in an adjacent NSC room with map-covered walls. He leaned heavily on the edge of the long and empty table. His meeting with Ambassador Martin had just ended—in fact, it would be the last time they ever talked to each other. Martin's message had left Huong in a near state of shock. He had been made to understand unequivocally by the ambassador that he should not expect any intervention by the Americans to save Saigon, and that the only thing left for him to do would be to resign immediately in favor of "Big" Minh.

Hearing my footsteps and my voice perked him up. "Are you well?" I asked. "I have just arrived from Paris and have come directly from the airport."

Huong responded in a very tired voice: "Oh, Phong, how are you? How are your parents? I haven't seen them for such a long time. Please, transmit to them my best regards." He extended a wavering hand, and I took it in both of mine, in deep affection, trying to convey through the physical human touch some comfort and encouragement.

Two days earlier in Paris, I had received a telex asking me to return to Saigon. It was an unusual communication, not a request by the president asking the minister of state to come back for consultation. It said simply, "Huong needs to see Phong." Huong had sent me the telex just a day after he had formed his government—as soon as Nguyen Van Thieu had resigned—with Nguyen Ba Can as Prime Minister. Can, a professional civil servant trained under President Diem, had been Speaker of the Saigon National Assembly under Thieu's tenure. Coincidentally, I had already come to my own decision to return and had booked my flight a week before. One of the people I called to tell I was going home was my long-time friend David Anderson, the Australian ambassador to France. We had known each other since he had been ambassador in Saigon in 1965. He rushed to my office and urged me to reconsider, while at the same time expressing sympathy and compassion for the situation.

My main motivation to go home was to be with my old parents and family. Since he was a close family friend, Huong was also in my thoughts. He had been a dear friend of my parents for over fifty years.

Now that I was with him, and since I was one of the few to have returned while many others were leaving, "Old" Huong seemed to feel a need to ask me, "Well, is there any hope anywhere?"

And I had to say what he surely expected to hear: "No, no hope of any kind."

Then we talked a bit *du coq à l'âne*—jumping from one subject to another. Reflecting on having just seen the U.S. ambassador, he began to talk about the Americans. Then we went on to the Soviets, the Chinese, and the French—he had much to say about the French. He was clearly annoyed with the unconstitutional idea of "transferring" his presidential powers to "Big" Minh.

He said scornfully, "The presidency is not a handkerchief to be handed around for anyone to blow his nose . . . ."

I resisted the temptation to reply that his so-called "constitutional" concern was the least of anyone's worries, given the crisis situation.

Our topics of conversation were, of course, solemn and the issues vital, but they would not make the history books. Those books would record what had been said and done in Washington, Moscow, Beijing, Hanoi, and Paris—least of all in Saigon. South Vietnam would fade like a myth from the exalted realms of high diplomacy. Such is reality in world politics. As if on cue to our musings, an aide came in with a telex from our embassy in Taipei. Unable to read it with his bad eyesight, Huong tossed it to me without comment. It said that our foreign minister, Vuong Van Bac, had arrived there and was tendering his resignation. Was it a gesture of courtesy or an ironic joke? Whichever, it was surely symbolic of the unfolding débâcle and the mass ship-jumping to . . . where? Anywhere overseas, of course.

As the meeting continued, Huong repeated the same question several times, almost to himself, audibly but in a sort of sigh, "No more hope of any kind, is there?"

Again, so as not to let him feel too alone, I also repeated each time, "No, no hope whatsoever."

When he mumbled the question a fourth time, I decided to help him put an end to the litany by replying very slowly and in a more forceful tone, "No. There is no hope whatsoever. But there are still a few little things to be done. But it is not for you or me to do them, nor is it for the Americans, either. It's for somebody else to do. Don't bother. Go get a good rest. Others will take on these tasks gladly."

Of course, at once I regretted saying this. I knew well that the specter of defeat and surrender would be distressing to the dear old man. I became aware that he was sobbing softly, withdrawn heavily into his chair. There was not much left for him to do. His fading hope was clearly exacerbated by helplessness. His tears could have been of frustration, indignation, disgust, betrayal, or simply despair. Nevertheless, he desperately clung to shreds of hope, knowing there was no basis whatsoever for any hope to prevail. Like many people in Saigon, dear old Huong was blindly and stubbornly driven by the hope to save and maintain the "constitutional" government of the Republic of Vietnam. He was not interested in anything less or thinking of anything else to hope for.

For two decades, many in South Vietnam had been encouraged to understand and believe that freedom was a matter of life and death, something to fight and die for. But Old Huong was no longer very sure about that, because the government of the United States of America, leader of the Free World, did not seem to think that way any longer. It was cutting its last moorings to the outpost.

Finally, I felt it was time for me to leave. It had been a meeting both bittersweet and painful. We both knew very well that further conversation was fruitless. The ultimate source of hope for Huong that historic evening could only be the American ambassador, Graham Martin, from whom nothing would be forthcoming. Before closing the door on my way out, I looked long at him, achingly wanting to help him but knowing there was nothing more I could do. I did not see the president of a country, just a motionless, lonely old man with a visage of utter despair and shoulders bowed in sadness. That was the last time I saw Tran Van Huong.

I knew Huong did not really expect hope from me. The thing he needed from me most was a friend's comfort to fill the great void that surrounded him. That I could give. I had not returned to Saigon that day to be with him, particularly, but I could easily share his feelings, like those I was able to share with my old parents later that evening—my parents who were joyful to have me back home by their side at a time when many people preferred to go into exile.

President Huong did not see how the government of the Republic of Vietnam could be saved, with or without U.S. help. He did not believe that "Big" Minh could save it, either, but faced with no other choices, President Huong succumbed to the pressures to resign, and General "Big" Minh assumed the leadership role in South Vietnam's final hours.

* * *

Hope . . . . I remember actually feeling a high level of hope about two years earlier, hope that had been infused in me by the same U.S. government that was abandoning us now. It was at Orly Airport in mid-January 1973, with Henry Kissinger, when he was still National Security Advisor. He was leaving for Washington to confer with President Nixon after having once again met with Hanoi's politburo member Le Duc Tho. The meeting had followed the twelve-day-and-night bombing of Hanoi by the U.S. around Christmas 1972, a strategy intended to press Hanoi to accept the Paris Accords (which were eventually signed about two weeks later, on January 27, 1973).

Before boarding his special plane at the VIP lounge, Dr. Kissinger had to face the press, all of whom knew both him and me very well, since they had been covering the Paris peace talks for years. Approaching the microphones, Dr. Kissinger was in one of his jolly moods and jokingly introduced me to the reporters by saying, "You all know Mr. Phong, my Special Assistant for Latin America," alluding to then-current tensions between the U.S. and certain of its Latin neighbors.

The reporters were aware that the "secret talks" in Paris between Kissinger and Tho were reaching their final stages and would soon result in an agreement. My remarks, therefore, included these words, "We have resumed the Paris peace talks with the other side in the spirit of 'renewed hope,' in order to reach an acceptable solution to the war in Viet-Nam." Later, Kissinger incorporated the expression "renewed hope" in his own declarations.

Did Kissinger really did share in a renewed hope, or was it just a handy catch-phrase for media consumption. I suppose even the mighty of this world must sometimes hope, when things get out of hand. I also suppose powerful leaders must be able to formulate and articulate hope more easily than the ordinary persons on the street. I nurtured a strong and realistic hope at that time for the signing of the Paris Accords. One of the reasons for this was Dr. Kissinger's presence at my side, representing as he did the most formidable war machine on earth. President Nixon badly needed the Paris Accords for domestic consumption in his run for re-election, if for no other reason. My particular hope was not to be long-lived. It evaporated with Nixon's Watergate-induced resignation on August 9, 1974, an event that was the *coup de grâce* for American intervention in Vietnam and the fate of South Vietnam. Hope, reality, and destiny.

* * *

Hope is endless struggle, with realities not always very evident, but often evasive and unpredictable. Hope is also the battle of illusions and, therefore, hope requires logic and rationality. But reason is not always at hand. Hope must be meaningful and make sense, but is most of the time drowned in passions and uncontrollable emotions. Everybody hoped for an end to the killing and for the restoration of peace in Viet-Nam. Presidents Johnson and Nixon did search for "peace" which meant, above all, an honorable end to the painful and costly American intervention in Viet-Nam; and American honor was more or less related somehow to the survival of a South Vietnamese political regime not under communist rule. It would be insane for the Hanoi politburo to say that they did not want "peace," but "peace" was not an end in itself for Ho Chi Minh and his disciples, who firmly believed that they would surely obtain their own kind of "peace" from their crafty mixture of independence and nationalism without American presence and intervention, social justice with socialism, instead of the cruel capitalistic way of life: that is to say, "peace" under the leadership of the Communist Party of Viet-Nam.

It was, of course, unfair to play the game of words and have ordinary people hope for "peace" in those years of the dreadful

11185-CART

Vietnam War, or American War in Viet-Nam. Peace in Viet-Nam simply boiled down to American honor and/or communist rule. Peace is not just the absence of war. There are all kinds of deadly and devastating forms of warfare in times of so-called "peace." There were, therefore, hopes for American honor and/or communist rule in Viet-Nam but there were no grounds, in terms of purpose, meaning, reason, or reality of any sort, for the Saigon anti-communist regime to have hope.

* * *

On that fateful evening of April 25, 1975, was U.S. Ambassador Graham Martin in any better position than South Vietnamese President Tran Van Huong to bring about hope of any sort for the survival of the Saigon government? Or hope for the ambitions of the Saigonese politicians? Or hope for the safety of the innocent people in that old capital city of the Republic of Vietnam? Probably not. The U.S. ambassador was aware of what was going on concerning the fall of the Saigon regime. There was no doubt that he had done everything in his power to save not only the anti-communist "Outpost of the Free World," but also the notion of some sort of a non-communist South Vietnam for the people to inhabit without further killing and destruction.

Martin, on-site representative of the number one superpower of the world, found himself in a position of total helplessness to influence events. He was compelled to perform an historical part in a drama far more onerous than the part being painfully played out by South Vietnam's President Tran Van Huong. There was no way for others to know what the American ambassador's inner thoughts and feelings were. But the scene at the U.S. Embassy spoke for him. It was utter chaos, with the rooftop evacuation setting the tone. Such a visible display of hurried escape by U.S. government officials provided no hope—except of course for those who succeeded in boarding the choppers. It was a scene that contributed to the despair of many Saigonese.

Graham Martin and Tran Van Huong were very good people. Both were honest public servants impelled by goodwill and the best of intentions for the well being of others. But they were caught in a hinge of history, in which the good guys got the bad parts to play and the bad guys mostly managed to avoid consequences they had helped to create.

Ambassador Martin and President Huong surely tried to forge strategies that would provide threads of hope, but despair was the dominant state they had doggedly to work through. Knowing both their characters, I can only imagine the shame that cloaked them as they played out the roles that history and the actions of others over many years had relegated them to. Unlike Huong, Graham Martin knew very well why the U.S. government was abandoning South Vietnam's anti-communist government. But I believe that Martin, personally, in the closing months, weeks, and then hours, increasingly experienced a state of disgust and despair. It was something new and strange to him. In a way, it may have been even more profound than Huong's despair, since Martin knew much more than Huong how bad the situation had become, and that there was nothing he could do to save Saigon. He held on as long as he could—longer, in fact, than it was safe for him to do so.

During those two days, Monday and Tuesday, April 28 and 29, Dr. Kissinger and President Ford repeatedly called on Ambassador Martin to get out of Saigon, saying that even heroes were needed at home. But Martin tried all the tricks he could think of with Washington and the U.S. Seventh Fleet Command in an attempt to get in as many helicopters as possible to rescue the last Americans and hundreds of Vietnamese still stranded in his embassy. Martin himself was forced to board one of the very last choppers, because the pilot refused to take off without him, shouting over and over again that he had received President Ford's strict orders to get the U.S. ambassador out. That was about 5 a.m. on Wednesday, April 30, 1975, and the first few North Vietnamese troops had just crossed the Saigon Bridge, less than a ten minutes' drive from the U.S. Embassy.

11185-CART

I believe that even as he flew out of Saigon that early morning, Graham Martin clung to the hope that a peaceful solution to the bloody conflict might be negotiated if "Big" Minh was the South Vietnamese president seeking a peaceful compromise with Hanoi's arriving North Vietnamese troops. Ambassador Martin might or might not have had good grounds to consider his hope realistic, but it was at least a desperate attempt on his part to try to bring to an impossible situation a "hope against all hope" with strategies and actions, not simply desperate maneuverings.

With both Huong and Martin, despair and hope co-existed side by side in those critical and final moments of South Vietnam as a nation. Time had run out, however, for hope to outdistance despair. The spring of 1975 was a time in which hope and despair both operated intensely and simultaneously in everyone touched by "The Vietnam War." The sudden, swift, and distressing collapse of the Saigon government was beyond anything imaginable, a striking surprise to the Vietnamese peoples, both North and South. Was it possibly and truly a surprise to the U.S. administration? Could U.S. intelligence resources have missed something? Or were they being duplicitous? By all appearances, the experts and leaders in Washington were caught by surprise by the rapidity of deteriorating events. But weren't Washington's decisions and actions a major impetus for the disastrous consequences? Over two decades, Washington had propagated all kinds of high hopes about "The Vietnam War," but never had they presented a scenario that at the close of April 1975, it would all end with the deplorable scenes so dramatically symbolized by the helicopter evacuations from the rooftop of the U.S. Embassy in Saigon.

In all fairness, it should be said that it was totally beyond the ability of any expert, prophet, fortune-teller, robot, or the most brilliant minds in Washington D.C., to foresee or predict the course of events in Viet-Nam at the beginning of 1975. It was, obviously and nevertheless, a time that marked a major turning point in the history of Viet-Nam. "Man proposes and God disposes," goes the universal saying. The Vietnamese say it slightly differently, a rough translation being, "Things are conceived by Man but realized by Heaven." Was it fate and destiny that decided it was high time for Vietnamese brother-enemies to reach decisions and take actions that one way or the other would halt their prolonged dispute and sad, fratricidal killing?

Nothing really unusual or serious had happened at the start of 1975. Communist troops had launched their annual winter-spring offensive as they had done over the previous twenty years, in what they looked upon as their sacred war for independence and liberty. They were, however, somewhat surprised that their attacks this time in Phuoc Long Province near the Cambodian border, not very far from Saigon, were not met with the expected resistance of the ARVN forces. The communist troops were able to occupy some governmental positions, as they had done on and off so many times in the previous two decades. They then waited and prepared for the Saigon elite units to come and recapture these outposts as had always happened in the past. During twenty years of fighting, the communist troops had always had the capability to strike whenever and wherever on their initiative and at their discretion, but they had never had the forces to occupy and hold territory for long—an inherent characteristic of guerrilla warfare.

Guerrilla warfare was the post-World War II big headache of former colonial mother countries like France, Great Britain, the Netherlands, and even Portugal. Guerrilla warfare spread everywhere like bushfires in the Far East from China to Viet-Nam, Laos, Cambodia, Thailand, Malaysia, Indonesia, the Philippines, and many other parts of the globe. The western military academies began to study this new form of warfare. The Americans and the British had their so-called counter-insurgency experts in the persons of Edward Landsdale and Robert Thompson, who had done very good jobs in the Philippines and Malaysia, and who were rushed to South Vietnam to help President Diem and then-President Thieu. Unfortunately, guerrilla warfare in South Vietnam was nothing like that in Malaysia and the Philippines, or, for that matter, in Latin America, the Middle East, the Balkans, or Africa.

Guerrilla warfare was one of the most misunderstood and misconceived aspects of the armed conflicts in Viet-Nam, from the time of the French "Indochina War" to the period of the "American War." Western military and political experts completely failed to comprehend or refused to take into consideration the basic historical, cultural, and social factors of those wars in Viet-Nam over a period of three decades. The communist leaders in Hanoi did not invent the guerrilla form of fighting. The Vietnamese had used it off and on during fifteen centuries against Chinese occupation. People all over the world had used it. Guerrilla fighting was the natural, logical, and only realistic form of armed struggle by the weaker against the stronger, by the poorer against the richer, by the destitute oppressed against the plentiful oppressor.

With all the successive wars in Viet-Nam, guerrilla fighting was not a full-fledged strategy, but simply a small tactical element in the so-called "people's warfare," an element that required two fundamental conditions to prevail: first, the presence of a foreign intruder on national soil, and second, the active participation of the native population in fighting against that foreign presence for the liberation and independence of their nation. The best brains in Washington stubbornly discarded such fundamental considerations in their conduct of the war. Some Vietnamese see an analogy in the American Revolution. That glorious war of liberation and independence proudly and forcefully expressed the formidable explosion of the new sense of American nationalism, even before the French Revolution. Those first citizens of the American nation at the end of the eighteenth century did not have the thousand years of history, culture, and sense of nationalism that the Vietnamese had by the twentieth century, but they bravely stood up, fought fiercely during moments of despair, and, in the end, escaped from the chains of colonialism and oppression. The American Revolution and the victory of the American War of Liberation and Independence were much more the doing of the American people than of any American government or administration.

The Viet Cong's Tet Mau Than general offensive in the spring of 1968 clearly demonstrated the complete fiasco of General Westmoreland's "search and destroy" strategy. Westmoreland was allowed to go home at last to become the U.S. Army Chief of Staff and was replaced in Viet-Nam by his deputy, General Creighton W. Abrams. A well-known World War II hero, General Abrams then rapidly changed the American strategy to "ambush and destroy". General Abrams was famous in his honorable profession for his tanks, but for him to play "guerrilla" was like having an elephant in a china shop. In a so-called "people's war," strictly concerned with self-defense and not invasion, guerrilla forces fight not for pretended occupation of territories and liberated zones, but actually for feelings and sentiments of nationalism and independence. That was the field on which Washington was made to play its game. It could never know how the nightmare would really end.

It should have been obvious to the leaders and experts in Washington that guerrilla fighting used by the communist side in Viet-Nam would not have a leg to stand on without the people's support and participation. The challenge was an enormous piece of puzzle to be assembled by the minds and hearts of people—not a scientific equation to be resolved by computers, laws of physics and chemistry, with aircraft carriers, jet planes, bombs, defoliant agents, tanks, electronic detectors, troops, and dollars. Even in the late 1950s and early 1960s, Pentagon generals and other military experts were aware of this aspect of the war in Viet-Nam, and declared that Washington was conducting the bloody conflict on the terms dictated by the adversary. Not one single American general thought that bombing North Vietnam would bring Hanoi to its knees. American GIs, however numerous, faced an unending fight in the battles in South Vietnam.

President Johnson was an intelligent man who did not fail to see this dilemma, but had no other choice but to opt for escalation of the war, not to destroy the enemy, but to annoy Hanoi and its allies. The frustration in Washington was utterly heartbreaking. It was like trying to kill mosquitoes with elephant guns. Very soon, LBJ noticed that his Secretary of Defense had become so disgusted with his soldiering job that he acted like a diplomat instead, hoping to have talks with the enemy. The president also realized that all his repeated attempts during three long years from 1965 to 1967 to get Hanoi to the negotiating table had not led anywhere, and his diplomats at the State Department, and not the Pentagon generals, were in fact conducting the Vietnam War.

There were some attempts, however, to deal with the immaterial aspects of the American War in Viet-Nam. President Johnson sincerely thought that plentiful consumer goods in South Vietnam would deprive the Viet Cong of the Vietnamese people's support. He might better have taken the lesson of the American Revolution. It was said that the Viet Cong were like fish in water, with the guerrilla fighters being the fish and the people the water. Unfortunately, when President Johnson found out that putting butter in the water could not kill the fish, his commanding generals in South Vietnam, General Westmoreland and his successor, General Abrams, had no other option but to try to pump out the water to catch the fish. They soon realized that their efforts to separate the Viet Cong guerrillas from the population simply resulted in continuously displacing hundreds of thousands of people in South Vietnam, while the Viet Cong guerrillas turned out to be more active than before. The fish just followed the flow of water—the millions of displaced persons during those long years of war in South Vietnam.

Throughout two decades of armed conflicts in Viet-Nam, from the time of President Ngo Dinh Diem in 1955 to Presidents Thieu, Huong and "Big" Minh in 1975, the Saigon leaders and politicians knew very well what guerrilla warfare meant to them and the Vietnamese people, even if the Americans didn't understand or preferred to ignore it and cried out instead for freedom and democracy, with the hope to win the minds and hearts of the Vietnamese people. It was not difficult for the experts in Washington to see that it would be ridiculous for the American GIs to search, find, ambush, and destroy the Viet Cong guerrillas by themselves. How could you expect those country boys from the Far West to identify those "Gooks" and "Charlies" of the Far East? The U.S. forces were there only to "assist" the anti-communist Vietnamese in South Vietnam to identify and kill the communist Vietnamese who were there.

That was the fundamental premise. Did those great American minds helping LBJ in the Oval Office in the 1960s honestly think that it would be easy for the Vietnamese in South Vietnam to recognize and kill the faceless Viet Cong guerrillas? It was "no sweat" to identify them, since all the Vietnamese families in South Vietnam had relatives on both sides. But to kill their brother-enemies was a completely different story, even for the sake of the "Free World." Some Saigon security agents, some policemen, some ARVN troops, and some Vietnamese anti-communist politicians might do just that, but not the majority of the Vietnamese in South Vietnam, especially the overwhelming peasant population in the countryside. If asked or ordered to undertake an anti-communist crusade, would they really help foreign troops and use guns and bombs against their own flesh and blood?

That premise contained the fatal flaw that led to the deadly error of demanding the impossible from the South Vietnamese. Sure, there was corruption in the Saigon administration, just as there was even more lucrative corruption among some Americans during those long years of the Vietnam War. But even without the eternal sins of humankind, the whole thing was doomed and a "mission impossible" right from the start, however hard some people sincerely tried in Saigon. You could throw insults at those Saigon leaders if that somehow relieved you of anger, frustration, or a guilt complex. It did not matter, really. The actual hardship, shame, pain, and sorrow were borne not by the so-called Saigon leaders but by those who did not run away, the millions of ARVN troops, Saigon civil servants, and many others who happened to believe very candidly in American ideals, promises, and policies. They did not believe for a moment in the Saigon leaders, but they believed in the "Leader of the Free World." So, some more or less blaming, mud-throwing, and name-calling at those South Vietnamese bums would not make much difference. "Defeats are always orphans and victories have many fathers," but many millions of people on that day of April 30, 1975, were willing to accept paternity for the fall of Saigon and the passing away of the "Outpost of the Free World."

"East is East and West is West, and never the twain shall meet," the saying goes, and never was it more evident than in this situation. But, by the end of the day, the more important refrain became, "We are all the same, Brother."

It was not only Saigon leaders like Diem, Thieu, Huong, and "Big" Minh, but also most of the ordinary people of South Vietnam who knew that the anti-communist Vietnamese would not have a dog's chance to win in any general elections with Ho Chi Minh. It was not only better but also vital for them to keep silent on that particular reality of the bloody conflict with their brother-enemies in Viet-Nam. They did not prefer it, but they had no choice but to welcome the American tiger in and climb onto its back.

Neither did Ho Chi Minh and his disciples have any other choice but to watch President Diem do just that. Diem, a former Mandarin of the Imperial Court of Annam, devout Catholic and friend of President Dwight D. Eisenhower, Secretary of State John Foster Dulles and Francis Cardinal Spellman of New York, mounted the American tiger's back in 1955, and the Far East circus act continued until that spring of 1975, with Presidents Thieu, Huong, and "Big" Minh. It was a great conspiracy, largely unspoken, but it was how a reality was created, then silenced, and finally vanquished in the American War in Viet-Nam.

Guerrilla tactics in the so-called "people's war" invariably entailed the so-called "leopard skin" concept in making claims for military victories, liberated zones, and political control of the population. It was a real headache and major item of discussion and negotiations between Kissinger and the Hanoi politburo's Le Duc Tho. The Viet Cong could always claim they had liberated zones, but they were never able to hold and defend these zones when American and ARVN troops moved in to recapture them. Furthermore, in the use of guerrilla tactics, it would have been plain stupid to indicate the positions of your troops and locations of your bases. But the situation was very different for Hanoi and the Viet Cong in South Vietnam by 1975, because for the first time in twenty years of bloody wars, large chunks of territory and "liberated zones" became available to them through Thieu's refusal to have the ARVN recapture South Vietnam's posts lost in Phuoc Long Province, then in the Highlands, and in Central Vietnam.

In his resignation TV-radio address on April 21, Thieu blamed the U.S. government, saying the primary cause of the situation's deterioration was the U.S. decision to end its military intervention in and stop further assistance to the Republic of Vietnam. The Saigon government knew well that it could never survive by itself without American aid, both military and economic. It never had the capability to compensate for this vital shortcoming. How could the anti-communist Vietnamese in South Vietnam fight the American War in Viet-Nam without the Americans? Even with all the plentiful, sophisticated, and conventional means of war, American bombs, over a half million American GIs, 1.2 millions ARVN troops and billions of U.S. dollars, they barely managed over twenty years "not to lose." The North knew what was happening and accelerated its military, political, and propaganda machines to exploit the God-given situation. It was ever more evident that Washington was cutting its last moorings with the "Outpost of the Free World."

The results were that by the end of April 1975, President Huong was in a situation of helplessness, first because the U.S. was no longer committed to an anti-communist South Vietnam, and second, because the "presidential powers" he inherited did not even have the weight of the paper on which they were written. He was in a situation of despair because the only role left for him to play was to relinquish his constitutional power to the person chosen by the U.S. and others in governmental leadership roles in South Vietnam.

* * *

I saw what I had hoped not to see, but what I had inoculated myself to be prepared for upon landing in Saigon: the helplessness of the U.S. ambassador, the hopelessness of our generals, and the despair of President Huong. My words to Huong were designed to help him carry out his resignation without further delay. For different reasons and purposes, I also set about to help everyone else that I could—the French, Chinese, Russians, and Americans, the Saigonese politicians, and even the other side.

The inability to overcome the adverse situation provoked in me a deep sense of helplessness, but not despair. I didn't think the collapse of the Republic of Vietnam would lead to my immediate execution by communist and Viet Cong troops, but the specter of defeat did cause profound anxiety in me. What I felt was similar to the state of mind of the majority of ARVN troops—they would simply discard their uniforms and go home to their families. That's what they did in the last few days of April 1975. There were no scenes of significant panic anywhere among the military units in South Vietnam. I had the impression that Saigon civil servants were much more nervous than the military. Maybe this was because, for decades, the civil servants had been responsible for so much anti-communist propaganda, they convinced themselves to be scared. After all, hadn't they forecast the much-publicized scenario of the inevitable "blood bath" that would take place when invading North Vietnamese troops arrived in the city of Saigon?

I didn't notice any particular manifestation of despair around me in the general population of Saigon. People continued to go about their business, and the streets of the city remained calm, except for a few locations downtown where foreigners gathered around the big hotels, in the appalling scenes of exodus at the airport, and at the rendezvous points for helicopter pickups. The most chaotic of such places, of course, was the American Embassy, where thousands of people converged at the gates, yelling and fighting to get in. They were mostly the wealthy Saigon upper class, high-ranking officials, army officers, and others who had managed to amass fortunes thanks to the American presence. Many of them were able to catch the continuous shuttle service from the embassy rooftop.

As noted before, Ambassador Martin was among the last to go as North Vietnamese tanks entered the Saigon suburbs on the morning of Wednesday, April 30, 1975. He was the only high-ranking American official in the field at that dramatic, historic, and terminal moment of the American War in Viet-Nam. I'm sure he felt despair when, from his helicopter, he watched Viet-Nam's beaches fade into the distance. I am sure, too, that he felt profound sadness in his heart and could not, would not, have avoided thinking about the son he had given to the war that had raged in our country.

President Nguyen Van Thieu had not reached the point of despair when he agreed to resign on April 21. Thieu and his Saigon military establishment were reduced to a state of helplessness, but did they not still cling to some hope for a last-minute, massive military American intervention to stop the advance of the North Vietnamese tanks and permit the survival of an anti-communist South Vietnam? Taking the road of exile on April 25, did Thieu and the Saigon generals feel hopelessness, despair, a mixture of outrage, and deceit? As for Tran Van Huong, who had lived all his life with helplessness, never having acquired real power at any time, even during one week as president of the Republic of Vietnam, could he have entertained any form or kind of hope? Would hope be compatible with the conflicting feelings of frustration, bitterness, anger, and profound sadness for his own fate, which was also that of his poor and powerless country, people, and nation? How about "Big" Minh? With less than forty-eight hours in office as South Vietnamese president, he did not have much time to hope or despair in any meaningful, rational, and realistic manner.

I have not been able to figure out clearly whether I experienced despair or hope during those last days of Saigon because I did not really know at that time what those two human sentiments were. If despair meant hopelessness, I was not in despair, because I did not feel hopelessness. If despair meant helplessness, I must then have experienced despair, but still not hopelessness. Furthermore, events happened so fast that I did not have time to ask myself what kinds of emotions and sentiments filled me during those dramatic days.

As time goes on, various thoughts and feelings emerge in our consciousness. We try automatically to express them in words, but our words do not always reflect accurately or convey fully our thoughts and sentiments. The dramatic events of the end of April 1975 in Saigon generated all sorts of hope and despair for people in all walks of life and on all sides of the war. The dreadful conflict had dragged on for such a long time and caused such untold suffering, not only to the Vietnamese but also to many other people in the world.

"The Vietnam War" left profound and still vivid wounds in the American nation, just as "The American War" filled the Vietnamese people with unspeakable sorrow and horror. But the bloody conflict, whatever it's called, reminds us that human beings are very much alike everywhere in regard to two very common sentiments—hope and despair—which demonstrate how we react to situations, but are not always very clear-cut notions for us to comprehend.

CODA

Reflections on Hope and Despair

Hope and despair—
two common states of mind
associated with the human ability
to respond to circumstances
involving projections into the future
that may be beneficial
or detrimental
to the person concerned.
Hope—
an expectation
with a desired object,
intention, or purpose.
Despair—
the feeling of inability
to overcome an adverse situation.

><

Hope and despair—
two opposite conditions
often mingled together
in confusing ways,
having common features and similarities
in their cause-and-effect relationship
and in responding to circumstances.

><

11185-CART

Despair—
often considered
the opposite or absence of hope,
or loss of hope,
the rejection or repression of hope.
Despair—
can lead to a state of resignation,
abandon, indifference, or apathy.
Yet despair
does not cause
the annihilation of hope.
It may include
the condition of latent hope.

><

Despair—
can generate formidable driving forces
to rebel and revolt
against an unwanted outcome
in disregard of consequences.
Despair—
can accept the "hope to hope"
or the "hope against all hope."
It can spark active hope
with meaning and purpose,
despite situational reality
and logical reason.

><

Despair—
a natural but negative human sentiment
found in both passive and active forms,
can be neutralized

in its passive form
of apathy or resignation
by overcoming the denial,
rejection, or repression of hope.
Despair—
is essentially helplessness
but not hopelessness.
Despair—
in its active form
requires the presence of the elements
of reality and reason
if it is to be turned to positive hope.
Despair
is the denial of hope.
Passive despair is zero-level hope.
Active despair
may be meaningful hope,
however unrealistic it appears.

CHAPTER TWO

FORTY-EIGHT HOURS: HOPE AND PURPOSE

When there is a problem, there is a solution.
English saying

On Monday, April 28, 1975, at three o'clock in the afternoon, Saigon, which usually basked under a blazing tropical sun, was suddenly plunged into Stygian darkness. The worst winds and stormiest rains the city had ever witnessed shrouded the landscape, creating a fittingly oppressive, yet mystical, Faustian atmosphere. Fittingly, I say, because this was the hour of the so-called "power transfer" ceremony. Against that tempestuous backdrop, Republic of Vietnam president Tran Van Huong was to convey the title he had held for seven short days—and what little (if any) powers that honorific entailed—to Duong Van Minh, leader of South Vietnam's so-called "Third Force." It was a presidency General "Big" Minh would hold for less than forty-eight hours.

The road leading to this tragi-comic, storm-ridden ritual had been long and serpentine. South Vietnam had strived mightily since 1955 to fulfill its role as the Far East "Outpost of the Free World," a legacy of President Eisenhower and his Secretary of State, John Foster Dulles. Their strategy was intended to check the spread of international communism in that far-flung region and in the world at large. The war in Viet-Nam had haunted the terms of five U.S. presidents, who held onto their Western ideals that liberty, democracy, and even the American way of life could be introduced and preserved in that obscure Southeast Asian corner of the world. With Presidents Eisenhower and Kennedy, the American public shared these ideals without really delving into what the war was all about. By the time of Presidents Johnson and Nixon, however, the American people began to demonstrate their serious and historic misgivings about U.S. intervention in that far-away country.

The war in Viet-Nam had, after all, failed to deliver to anyone the benefits all those presidents had hoped for. On the contrary, two decades of American intervention in Viet-Nam had brought ineffable death and destruction, consumed outrageous sums of tax dollars and—worst of all—generated a profound division in the American psyche. The American public felt immense relief when all U.S. troops had been withdrawn from Viet-Nam by the end of March 1973, thanks to Nixon, Kissinger, and the Paris Accords. After that, the United State's greatest priority under President Ford was to banish the war in Viet-Nam from America's collective memory as quickly and expeditiously as possible, without too much bitterness and recrimination.

In the spring of 1975, the only person center-stage in Washington who might have been keenly attuned to South Vietnam's ordeal of despair was, of course, Henry Kissinger, who was still Secretary of State. I have wondered whether Dr. Kissinger had glimmerings of hope during the Paris peace talks. Now another bout of curiosity strikes me: Did he ever experience despair over American involvement in Vietnam? I find it hard to imagine that he did. I had opportunities to work with Kissinger in those four years between 1969 and 1973 at the Paris peace talks, mostly in group meetings, but in private one-on-one sessions as well. Like many, I found Kissinger a dynamic man with a tremendous force of intellectual attraction.

If it were a high-class and frighteningly formidable challenge you were looking for, you might accept an evening out with him. I was deeply impressed by Kissinger's lucidity, rationality, historical perspective and, above all, his pragmatism. People liked or disliked him with equal intensity. He was a very effective Secretary of State, and, certainly, his utmost concern was for the interests of the American people. He did try his best to help the Saigon regime, but his principal objectives were to end the massive U.S. military intervention in Vietnam, stop American casualties, return all the boys home honorably, and terminate the insane spending. I could not think of anything that would cause despair in Kissinger over Vietnam.

He might have come close to despair, however, in October 1972. He had gone to Saigon with what he thought was a swell deal in his pocket, a draft of the Paris Accords agreement that he had forged painstakingly and painfully in secret negotiations with Le Duc Tho of Hanoi's Politburo (Washington and Hanoi had agreed to sign the accords on October 24). But to his surprise and some anger, during his five-day stay from October 17 to 22, Dr. Kissinger ran into a solid wall of resistance in the bastions from the Outpost of the Free World. Thieu refused to go along with the pact, leaving Kissinger in an embarrassing diplomatic and personal position.

On the flight back to Washington after his meetings with the stone-deaf leaders in Saigon, members of Kissinger's retinue clearly sensed that the good doctor was furious at the patient's refusal to swallow his medicine. How dare those characters demand twenty-three changes in the draft? Even one change would surely upset North Vietnam's Tho, who would start calling him names again back in Paris. The Saigon clique could go to hell, he may very well have grumbled.

The doctor was to face further frustration. In less than a week's time, the twenty-three changes became sixty-nine. But Dr. Kissinger's reputation for dealing with difficult situations carried the day. Nothing was too difficult for him. He took to heart the saying, "When there is a problem, there is a solution," which may as well go together with, "There are no stupid questions but only stupid answers."

Right after that lamentable encounter in Saigon, President Nixon gave the Saigon regime a last-gasp effort with the spectacular and dramatic bombing of Hanoi over the twelve days and nights—December 18 to 30—of the 1972 Christmas season. Sadly, the French Consul General who was in Hanoi was one of the first fatalities. Militarily, the bombing did not change anything one way or the other for either side. As for any psychological effect in terms of persuasion or dissuasion, the bombing also came up short on results. It served as a momentary placebo for the egos of the Saigon leaders and a short-term sleeping pill for the Saigon regime. It was a brief nap.

After the bombing of Hanoi, Le Duc Tho and Kissinger resumed their secret talks in Paris on January 8, 1973. This was to be their last round of negotiations for the Paris Accords. Raising the stakes, Nixon sent Thieu a double-edged letter on January 16. It was delivered by U.S. presidential special envoy General Alexander Haig, escorted by Ambassador Ellsworth Bunker (nicknamed "The Fridge" in Saigon for his cool appearance). It was, on the one hand, a moving letter between friends. On the other, it gave Thieu a very clear ultimatum: Sign the Paris Accords, or the time had come for good friends to part. In other words, the Saigon regime would have to jump into the Saigon River and fish for another Number One Superpower to support it. I had a look at the letter within minutes of Thieu receiving it—a copy was telexed to me in Paris. I had also been given a copy by the American delegation, who had asked me to help Thieu swallow the bitter pill for his own sake.

President Nixon made his intentions crystal clear in this letter to President Thieu, which stated, "I have irrevocably decided to initial the agreement on January 23 and sign it on January 27 in Paris. I will do so, if necessary, alone."

11185-CART

President Nixon's letter continued, "In that case, I shall have to explain publicly that your government obstructs peace. The result will be an inevitable and immediate termination of U.S. economic and military assistance, which cannot be forestalled by a change of personnel in your government. I hope, however, that after all our two countries have shared and suffered together in conflict, we will stay together to preserve peace and reap its benefits . . . ."

I was summoned back to Saigon immediately to attend a special meeting of the National Security Council (NSC). When I arrived directly from the airport, Thieu was waiting for me in his office, and we spent about an hour together before joining the NSC meeting. There were just the two us, and we were able to speak quite openly. Our ability to be frank with each other went back to 1967 when Thieu, then a powerless army general, Chairman of the National Leadership Committee and nominal Head of State of the Republic of Vietnam, had defied everyone by running for president. At that time, I had been responsible for planning, organizing, and setting in motion the administrative machinery for the so-called general elections in South Vietnam in September 1967. These general elections were crucial to Washington's effort to demonstrate to the American people and to the whole world that freedom and democracy had been born in South Vietnam and must be defended there.

Now, again, I felt compassion for Thieu, but had to tell him there wasn't the slightest doubt in my mind that the U.S. was serious about dumping him if he refused to sign the Paris Accords. He responded that it would be suicidal—catastrophic—for the Saigon government to do that. I needed no convincing on that score. A Saigon pedicab driver could have come up with that particular piece of political analysis.

Thieu considered the agreement a sellout of South Vietnam to the Soviets. I tried to console him by explaining that the contents of the accords were just so many words, and what really mattered was whether the Americans were willing and able to support the survival of the Republic of Vietnam. Since the 1966 Manila Summit, I had been completely convinced that—despite the symbolic "Outpost of the Free World" lingo—the U.S. would not be able to justify playing Big Brother in Southeast Asia forever. Sooner or later, Washington would have to come to terms not with Hanoi, Moscow, or Beijing, but with the American people. It would become a dreadful family quarrel, no longer having anything to do with world politics or world peace or saving the world. Family quarrels, as we all know, can be appalling. Long-standing arguments in favor of the war in Viet-Nam had lost their persuasiveness. Relative global stability had been achieved since 1953 at the thirty-eighth parallel in Korea, and there was really no need to maintain any other major U.S. military presence in East Asia in terms of the interests of the American people and world peace. I had never been impressed by the so-called Domino Theory that raised the specter of total communist domination of Southeast Asia by sheer force of arms—including "guerrilla warfare"—requiring massive conventional military intervention by the U.S. to prevent it.

I thought of the time President Nixon had paid his state visit to China and of how we in Saigon began calling him "Peking Dick" after that bold diplomatic move. I went on to remind Thieu that there were only three major and meaningful military protagonists who could actually pay the bills in the Viet-Nam conflict, and if the U.S. had no alternative but to jettison South Vietnam to resolve its own interests and internal problems, South Vietnam had no choice left but to find another ally. Thieu knew the only alternative left to him was to "play ping pong" with the People's Republic. By the prolonged look he gave me at that moment, I knew he wanted to tell me again what he had already said to me at the end of 1970: that such a choice would be much worse than not having a U.S. military presence in South Vietnam. So I repeated my contention that Saigon had no other option but to play ball with the Americans.

"You'd be a sitting 'Peking Dick' for the CIA chefs' oven before you could hit your first serve to Chairman Mao," I suggested, mixing my figures of speech a bit in appreciation of the British black humor I'd picked up in my Oxford days.

Thieu bade me join him for the NSC meeting in the adjoining room, where the members had already gathered. It was there that I witnessed Vice-President Huong breaking down in tears when Thieu explained that the Saigon government had no choice but to sign the Paris Accords as drafted by Hanoi and Washington.

Sad moment though it was, there was no compelling reason for Saigon to despair in that spring of 1973. After all, Nixon and Kissinger had been good enough to provide Thieu with an American presidential "written guarantee" that the U.S. would ensure the security of the Republic of Vietnam if Saigon agreed to sign the Paris Accords.

Everything went well that spring. The Paris peace talks (for the doves), the Christmas bombing (for the hawks), and the eventual accords (for everybody except Saigon) had served Nixon and his Grand Old Party well. With more than sixty percent of the popular vote, he had scored a resounding re-election victory over Democrat George McGovern, a much more convincing mandate than his slim 1968 victory over Vice-President Hubert Humphrey. All the torments of secret talks and the prosaic contents of the Paris Accords were rendered academic in that realistic and pragmatic context. In all good conscience, Nixon and Kissinger had surely assured themselves that the terms of the accords would allow the U.S. to end with honor its military intervention in Viet-Nam. And they pursued the rationalization that the accords would give the Saigon regime a viable chance to fend for itself without the massive presence of U.S. troops.

With the Paris Accords, Kissinger achieved the total withdrawal of U.S. troops from Viet-Nam, a nominal cease-fire that at least would reduce the level of fighting between Vietnamese, and a limit—at least in principle—on the shipping of additional war supplies to Viet-Nam. The much-disputed and much-discussed expression "replacing used weapons" had been a sticking point for

Tho and Kissinger in the last moments of their negotiations in Paris.

Kissinger also succeeded in including provisions to help the Vietnamese resolve their internal political problems: The people in South Vietnam would enjoy "national reconciliation" and "self-determination" through "free general elections," with the eventual reunification of Viet-Nam by democratic processes at an appropriate time in the future. As far as South Vietnam was concerned, these issues were to be thrashed out in the subsequent phase of the Paris peace talks in the Conference of La Celle Saint Cloud between the two South Vietnamese parties (Saigon, aka the Republic of Vietnam, and the National Liberation Front, aka the Republic of South Vietnam), from April 1973 until the collapse of the Saigon government in April 1975.

There were enough concrete elements in the Paris Accords to inspire hope for everyone. Concerning the military aspects, Kissinger deserves high marks for enabling Washington to "pick up its marbles and go home" with its dignity intact. As for the political issues between the Vietnamese, they were long-shots with lots of room for maneuvering, and the Saigon regime had all the time in the world to take care of itself. Thieu had to try to pull the blanket to his side as much as he could, but Nixon's 1973 ultimatum was not at all cause for despair for the Saigon regime. So what really was the cause for the lamentable rout of the ARVN and Thieu's resignation on April 21, 1975, which inspired his military brass to follow his example and join him in exile rather than put up a decent fight against their brother-enemies in South Vietnam?

It had never been popular sport in Viet-Nam for political leaders to resign from high office, and Thieu had never shown signs that he was the kind of soldier to run away from his post while almost all of his one million ARVN troops were still manning theirs. Thieu could have remained president of the RVN in defiance of the whole world if he had wanted to. He could have led his troops into the final battles with honor and fought the fights worth

11185-CART

fighting. Why didn't he do that? The generals were still behind him; the troops were there with thousands of planes and tanks; the ammo he needed was still piling up in the warehouses. The situation was not yet hopeless on the battlefields in South Vietnam at the beginning of 1975. Then-U.S. Secretary of Defense, James Schlesinger, declared that the Viet Cong attacks in Phuoc Long province were of minor magnitude and not a major offensive. But it clearly appeared to Thieu and many other people that the situation in Washington demonstrated a lack of determination and will to carry on with the American War in Viet-Nam. The show was over. "Take good care of yourself, brother" was the message to the Saigon leaders, despite Richard Nixon's letter of guarantee, promise, and pledge by the government of the United States of America to ensure the security of the Republic of Vietnam.

President Nixon gave his word in all sincerity and good faith. He was committed to preserve an anti-communist South Vietnam and was confident that he could do just that with the Paris Accords, as long as he remained President of the United States and had all the might of the Number One Superpower of the world behind him. Nixon had various options open to him. As for Thieu, he did not have much choice except to perform *hara kiri* (the traditional Japanese form of honorable suicide) if he and his anti-communist followers were to live up to their ideal and conscience.

Nguyen Van Thieu had been a typically good representative figure in the South Vietnamese armed forces for over thirty years. He was one of the better generals by Saigon standards, very meticulous, hard working, a good manager and administrator. He occasionally kicked up his heels as army guys do, but he was by no means a playboy. My feelings about Thieu at that time were that he was a not-so-bad general who had become a not-so-bad president, given the circumstances. It wasn't easy holding together the military establishment in South Vietnam. He didn't trust anyone, and no one trusted him, but he was fair and square enough. He was more of a chess aficionado than a poker player.

Until the very end, Thieu sincerely believed that no Saigonese but he could convince the U.S. to save South Vietnam. In that way, he had created hope for himself. He was not in a helpless situation, and did not have to resign in despair. But he finally agreed to do so because his sole and long-time ally, the number one superpower of the world, said he had to go. By resigning, he supposedly might allow a better set of conditions for South Vietnam's survival through a negotiated solution between "Big" Minh and Hanoi. For Thieu, that was just for the birds.

Thieu resigned, seemingly holding to the conviction of *après moi le déluge*, as the French would say: "After me the great flood." But was it what psychiatrists would call a "free act"? Not very likely, given the circumstances. Presidents do not do something for nothing, and it would have been regrettable if people in Washington had entertained such thoughts about Thieu. Even U.S. ambassador Graham Martin did not forget to remind Thieu as late as on April 20 to make his decision in the best interests of the Vietnamese people. This was a case of Martin speaking as a friend and not from his position as ambassador. He was aware that President Ford had repeatedly declared to the press that the U.S. government could not demand that an elected president of an ally country resign, much less overthrow him by a *coup*. Ultimately, it took Thieu only twenty-four hours of pondering to come to the painful decision at last to resign. I am inclined to think that Thieu, in good conscience, did make his decision in the interests of his people, but it was certainly with a nod to Ambassador Graham Martin and his friends in Washington.

Until April 20, 1975, how could Thieu not have held on to the view that the situation was not really hopeless? How could it be hopeless with South Vietnam having the world's fourth largest army, fourth largest air force with nearly two thousand planes, the seventh largest navy, and billions of U.S. dollars' worth of war supplies and sophisticated equipment? But even with an atomic bomb to entirely destroy North Vietnam, it would not have made the slightest difference, because the issue was not there. Thieu was finally persuaded that the urgent issue was to no longer continue to fight and continue the war, but to structure pacts for the people of South Vietnam to survive and avoid the terrible catastrophe of a murderous fight between the two Vietnamese armies of North and South Vietnam. He was told that the situation for the South Vietnamese anti-communist regime was hopeless and that he, Nguyen Van Thieu, was the cause of this hopelessness. He was relentlessly bombarded with the perspective that he was the obstacle to efforts to bring some measure of salvation and hope to the Vietnamese in South Vietnam with a "non-anti-communist" political government. Quite a good cocktail, wouldn't you think? What more could you expect? That same "rock 'n roll" number had been played repetitively to Thieu from 1967 to 1975, very forcefully by Washington and its ambassadors, Ellsworth Bunker and Graham Martin.

With the Paris Accords and the resulting adverse effect on the balance of forces caused by the end of U.S. assistance and intervention, the continued presence of the North Vietnamese regular divisions, and the free flow of arms and ammunitions to Hanoi from the Soviet Union and China, it was impossible for South Vietnam to survive as a State. Yet everyone honestly continued to concoct various ways and means for hope. Unable to find anything better anywhere, people became willing—*faute de mieux,* as the French would say—to pick up on Hanoi's suggestion that Thieu resign. In the spring of 1975, the order-of-the-day to the Saigon troops was, therefore, not to fight, but to hope for a peaceful way out of the whole mess. Paris joined with Washington in convincing Thieu to quickly pass the buck to his Vice-President, the old and ailing Tran Van Huong. Huong, of course, would have no other duty but to re-enact the scenario seven days later, when "Big" Minh would inherit the mantle and become the sole personification of the only hope possible. Despair had to be neutralized and hope had to be found for the Vietnamese in South Vietnam.

In practical terms, President Thieu's resignation on April 21, 1975, was in fact a clear message to the one million ARVN troops that there was no more fight worth fighting. French president Giscard d'Estaing had made his contribution on April 22 by calling on everyone to observe a cease-fire and sit down again at the negotiating table (that famous large round table in Paris would again be ready for immediate use).

Thieu did not resign in the hope that "Big" Minh would be able to save South Vietnam. The only player with an ace up his sleeve was still Uncle Sam. Chess player Thieu was compelled, in the short time left to him, to go for a quick and decisive poker-bluff showdown with Washington, and he had to shuffle the deck in search of a card to play. He had made his anti-communist position very clear by his total refusal to co-exist with anything remotely related to communism in his South Vietnam. Had he not said that without Nguyen Van Thieu, there would not be a South Vietnam? It was quite clear in his mind that Ngo Dinh Diem would not have been able to create the anti-communist South Vietnam without the might of the United States of America. South Vietnam had been made to depend solely on the U.S. So, whether under a presidency of Thieu, Huong, or "Big" Minh, it would boil down to the same thing: no more South Vietnam.

After his resignation on April 21, Thieu continued to cling desperately to a "hope against all hope" for a last-minute massive military intervention by Washington to prevent the imminent fall of Saigon into the hands of the North Vietnamese troops. Even after the "wooden face" declaration by President Ford on April 23 at Tulane University of New Orleans, asking the American people to put the Vietnam War behind them, forget the past and look toward the future (easier said than done), Thieu waited and waited in vain, and only agreed to leave the country on the evening of April 25 after being repeatedly summoned by Ambassador Graham Martin to get on a waiting, special U.S. Air Force C118 to take him and his former Prime Minister, four-star General Tran Thien Khiem, to Taipei. Just before boarding the plane, Thieu took the time to make a half-minute phone call to me to say goodbye, and to tell me to take care of myself and friends still in Saigon.

In concrete terms, Thieu's schemes, manipulations, and hopes were three-pronged: First, he tried to link American honor again to the survival of South Vietnam's anti-communist political regime; second, he intentionally let the military situation degenerate in such a way as to put Washington in an utterly shameful position unless forceful U.S. military intervention was taken; and third, should the U.S. decide not to stop the advancing North Vietnamese forces, the ARVN would not be left in the position to clash with the communist troops—in other words, there would be no point for the ARVN to prolong the war without Thieu being backed by U.S. presence and support. Without further American aid and the will to resist eventual communist rule in South Vietnam by North Vietnam, it would make no sense for the ARVN to prolong the fighting and killing for a few more months just for "Big" Minh. Thieu put these ideas into action in January 1975. Upon his departure in April of that year, he left the consequences to be dealt with by Old Huong and "Big" Minh. It was thus up to them to make the historical kowtow, or take the final bow, whichever act depending on whether or not, and how, Washington dropped the curtain.

Furthermore, the refusal of the ARVN to put up a fight with the North Vietnamese troops would greatly reduce the possibility of a bloodbath in Saigon and other major cities in South Vietnam, and it would surely avoid bloodshed of the innocent civilian population.

During those last days of the Saigon political regime, President Huong and many Saigonese surely asked themselves again and again why the U.S. would do nothing more to help them. Twenty years earlier, the Americans had infused hope in them and made them believe in the ideals of freedom and democracy. It had become a way of life for many in South Vietnam. Huong had grown up during the French colonial period, spoke fluent French, and had fought against both French colonialism and Ngo Dinh Diem's dictatorial regime. He didn't know much English and did not particularly like the Americans. The United States had been the only ally available in the conflict with the communist brother-enemies, and he had accepted that reality. It was not so much a matter of choice for Huong and others in South Vietnam. Many of them just happened to be south of the seventeenth parallel in 1954, and were born into the "Outpost of the Free World." Even if they had had a choice, it would have been between remaining in a burning building or jumping out the window. A choice to join the "Yankees" or the "Commies" would simply be "Chinese" to my mother and aunts in our native village—or as the Americans say, it would be "Greek" to them.

So when it was no longer possible for Huong to hope, no longer possible for him to give hope to others, no longer possible for others to have hope in him and with him—when there was no hope at all for the Vietnamese in South Vietnam—it was necessary to invent hope. It was necessary to invent hope for everyone's benefit. For the high and mighty, it was a matter of honor; for ordinary people, a matter of survival.

This invented hope was the proclamation made on Monday, April 28, 1975, throughout the land and beyond, of the "power transfer" from Huong to "Big" Minh. Nobody knew or was told exactly the reason and purpose of this ritual, except that there was no more hope with Huong and there might be some with "Big" Minh. The ceremony was the concrete realization of a plausible hope, the hope of all hopes, the hope that was supposed to save Saigon, South Vietnam, freedom, progress, and democracy. It was hope for almost everything, and yet nothing. It was no one's fault, of course. Everyone did their best.

Huong's resignation and the long-awaited "power transfer" were acclaimed as diplomatic win-wins, easy to implement and without cost. Why hadn't we thought of it before \$150 billion were spent? Or was it \$230 billion? It had been about \$20 billion a year. But these were now immaterial considerations. In the end, the money had not paid for victory, nor even for a "not-to-lose/not-to-win" policy. It paid simply for honor, a priceless commodity to the American people and to their leaders, from President

Eisenhower down to Ford, from Secretary of State Dulles down to Kissinger.

At such a price, it would be an aberration to say the Vietnam War was Vietnamese—the total populations of both North and South Vietnam could not have robbed their piggy banks for a hundred years to pay for the right to call the shots. The War in Viet-Nam was many other things, but it was a war by proxy—or franchise.

So, under pressure from almost everyone, including the French and the Americans, old Huong agreed to perform the "power transfer" exactly one week after Thieu's resignation. He could have chosen to do nothing, stayed home for a good nap, and that would not have changed the situation one iota. A conscientious schoolteacher, he played the role bestowed on him by history. Twenty years earlier, Huong had witnessed the creation of the Republic of Vietnam by Diem, with the help of Eisenhower and Dulles. In his classrooms, Huong would have explained many times to his young pupils that nations and countries under different colors often come and go on the maps of the world. Now, with no longer any help from Ford and Kissinger, he was to perform the act that would erase the Republic of Vietnam from the face of the earth.

It was just a role to play, but why should fate have foisted this disgrace upon a harmless, poor old man? The most obvious reason was the simple fact that Huong had never possessed one single U.S. dollar in all his life and, therefore, had no reason whatsoever to flee as many were doing. Casting directors could not have found a better actor for this desperate part, even though there were only a few lines to mumble. What Huong actually did was to surrender not to the other side, but to "Big" Minh, who considered it necessary to officially end the Republic of Vietnam's existence. He replaced its symbols and standards with Buddha's lotus flower, an emblem of peace, love, and mercy for Buddhists, as the sole hope possible for the South Vietnamese at that time. It was man-made hope, without spirit or soul, invented and set into motion with no specific purpose except to muster hope in other's hopes—however false they were. To ignite this feeble hope, it was sadly necessary to compel an old invalid to go through the motions of transferring hypothetical powers to another utterly helpless man to achieve an impossible unknown.

In those darkest hours of the Saigon regime, there were surely contrasts of despair and hope. Among the people who hoped were those who did so because they needed to, those who hoped because they were made to hope by others, those who tried to share hope with others, and those who had the duty to create the mirage of hope when they knew there was none. No one knew what hope "Big" Minh harbored or wanted to provide to others. But most people in Saigon were surely hoping for all things possible under the sun. They had one overriding common hope at that time: that nothing too drastic would affect their simple lives. In the absence of a hope with a clear purpose, people in Saigon could have simply hoped somehow that "Heaven and Earth would not turn upside down," that their miserable lives could continue without further pain and sorrow. And no doubt, there were many people over the land from north to south who simply hoped that the war might end soon, very soon, and for good. No more death and devastation. And, for the first time, that the Vietnamese would no longer have to kill one another.

Huong personified despair, "Big" Minh hope. I could find neither in me when I attended the "power transfer" ceremony at the presidential palace. I had two simple reasons for being there. One was to be with the lonely old man who did not have even a proper aide left at his side. The second was my wish to publicly assume full responsibility for my function at the Paris peace talks, as the so-called "Minister-of-State in Charge of Negotiations/Chief of the Republic of Vietnam Delegation at the Two South Vietnamese Parties Conference of La Celle Saint Cloud." That conference between the Vietnamese brother-enemies had dragged on and off for two years from 1973 to 1975. It became one of those small historical legends set up for purposes that included all the hopes that peace talks could generate for the Vietnamese and others. It, in part, resulted in Tho and Kissinger sharing the 1973

Nobel Peace Prize. Maybe a Nobel Hope Prize should have been created as well.

* * *

The "power transfer" ceremony was disorderly and unexpectedly theatrical, due to nature's assistance with the *mise en scène* that plunged Saigon into a daytime darkness for about an hour. As I have said, that deft touch was beautifully timed for Buddha's lotus flower. The sky cleared immediately after the ritual transfer was complete. The palace's Big Hall was filled mostly with the international media and members of "Big" Minh's "Third Force." A few acquaintances came to shake my hand and did not fail to ask quickly, "Any hope?" One of them even said to me, "To see you back in Saigon today means it's not hopeless, is it?" I could respond only with a stupid smile. A long-time friend, Francois Nivolon of the French daily, *Le Figaro*, also elbowed his way to me to say hello with an uplifted eyebrow of surprise and dismay, clearly concerned for my personal safety.

Many friends and relatives thought I was completely out of my mind to have returned to Saigon while thousands and thousands were trying by all means to get out. Didn't it occur to me that with the imminent fall of Saigon, I would be captured by communist troops and very likely executed? Did I have no concern for the safety of my parents and family by posing a real threat for them with my presence by their side in Saigon? Didn't I see the urgency and hopelessness of the situation with the chaotic evacuation of the remaining Americans, which meant beyond a shadow of a doubt that there was nothing left but to get out as quickly as possible? These considerations were in my mind but did not enter into my decision to return to Saigon. No one in my family had asked me to return or not to return. The choice was mine. I simply wanted to be by my parents' side, and I was sure that was what they wanted, too, in the last days of Saigon. That was probably the most meaningful purpose for me and my family to have and hope for during those critical and dramatic moments. We all knew there was real danger now, but it was more important for us to be together. Many species of animals also do just that instead of running in all directions separately. The natural instinct is to cluster together and accept together their fate and destiny.

All kinds of hope, individual and collective, existed at the presidential palace that day. The international media must have clearly seen the tremendous urge for a demonstration of hope, but no one clear, overriding hope could have predominated. The Saigonese politicians could not accept the idea of the collapse of the Saigon regime. With Thieu's resignation and now that of Huong, the "Third Force," personified by "Big" Minh, had what it had been anticipating for the past twenty years: to be "in power," to take residence in the beautiful "Independence Palace," built by Diem with U.S. aid and the help of architect Ngo Viet Thu who had won the Rome Prize in architecture. So what more could the "Third Force" have hoped for? A military solution was totally out of reach. The ARVN troops no longer had a fight to fight, having been unable to do what half a million U.S. troops had failed to accomplish in a decade. They could hope for a political solution, of course—but what sort and how? The prospect of talking politics with Hanoi didn't seem much different from "talking to your knee," another Vietnamese saying. "Big" Minh's negotiating position was not an advantageous one, to say the least.

There was no use asking for the continuation of a country called the Republic of Vietnam. There might be a slight possibility to hope for a non-communist rather than anti-communist political regime in Saigon, but that would be like announcing a miserable one club in a bridge game. Would it be unrealistic and too late for "Big" Minh's "Third Force" to say it was willing to accept any form of government Hanoi considered fit, provided that "Big" Minh's group be given some sort of recognition, even a kind of *strapontin* (folding chair) at the cabinet meetings? Not much hope for that either.

The Saigonese politicians had to reject despair and seek hope, but hope without a coherent and meaningful purpose, except perhaps one: to avoid death and destruction from the expected "Battle of Saigon." Many might have mistaken the basic survival instinct for hope. However, in the extreme tension of the transfer ceremony, I suddenly felt a sort of relief, not that it brought me any hope, but because, for me, it marked officially the end of my now-useless function and responsibility of "Minister-of-State in charge of Negotiations and Head of the Republic of Vietnam at the Conference Between the Two South Vietnamese Parties at La Celle Saint Cloud." Hope, as it is wont to do, would usually come and go without one thinking about it. I knew there was a thing called hope, but I did not really know what hope was. Hope was, at that time, rather a vague feeling for me, but it seemed to be very contagious and a much-needed thing for people to have.

Hope was present during the Paris peace talks and filled the hearts of millions of people at the signing of the Paris Accords. Hope brought some reconciliation to the Americans and some relief to the Vietnamese, with less death and devastation in their country, both in the north and south of Viet-Nam. Hope was felt by everybody one way or another in those last days of that month of April, 1975. But hope was entertained at that time by different people for different purposes in a big confusion of aims from Saigon to Washington, for Thieu, Huong, and "Big" Minh, for Gerald Ford and Henry Kissinger, for Mao tse-tung and Chou en-lai, Leonid Brezhnev, Giscard d'Estaing, and many more who were instrumental in the fate of the government of a country in the south of Viet-Nam labeled the Republic of Vietnam. Hope was concerned then, first of all, with purpose, and there were so many different purposes of the different parties.

In that spring of 1975, the foremost purpose, which really mattered and counted, was the purpose of the United States—not that of the doves or hawks, the generals or politicians, the President or Congress, the learned university professors or financial tycoons. It finally and truly was the will and purpose for, of, and by the

American people themselves. There was an American War in Viet-Nam but there was neither American defeat nor victory in Viet-Nam. There was, in fact, a Vietnam War in the United States, which was vanquished, not yet entirely, but almost, by the American people.

Purposes of hopes are very personal and individual, but hopes with meaningful and rational purposes are also communicative. They require their collective contexts in order that they may be searched for and sustained, and that they may prevail, acquire, and give meaning to hope's purposes.

CODA

Reflections on Hope and Purpose

Life has hope.
Hope—
is inherent in the condition of being
and the act of becoming.
Thus life and hope
are not separable.
Life requires hope
because life without hope
is despair.
Being and becoming
constantly generate intentions
and purposes to reach for.
Life is change and evolution.
Change and evolution with *purpose*
is hope, and
life without hope is life unfulfilled.

><

Humans hope
consciously or unconsciously,
positively or negatively,
influenced by genes and environment.
Humans need to generate hope
to sustain the act of being and becoming.
Despair—
is the absence of hope.
Hope is the negation of despair.
Hope is survival.
Hope is intertwined
in the ***to be*** and the ***to become***.
Hope—
is the source of meaningful life.

><

Awareness
of ***the becoming***
is the starter of hope.
Awareness
provokes the genesis of hope,
disregarding reality,
reason, desperation, despair.
It liberates the "hope to hope"
without yet knowing a purpose
for which to hope.
The will to hope
enables us to draw
on unique human resources and abilities,
make use of reason
and find meaningful purpose
in the face of realities.

><

The hope to hope—
rejection and denial of despair—
is the ignition key, the genesis,
for hope to start.
It helps us human beings
become conscious
of our own being and place
in the vast universe.
The natural human ability to hope
is the fundamental element
in our search for a better tomorrow,
the very essence of
our being and becoming.

><

The primordial function of hope
is purpose—
both cause and finality.
The struggle for hope
is meaning—
accompanied by confusion and heartbreak.
The disconcerting
and daring challenge
of hope
is reality.
Hope enters the mind and heart
of human beings
by intention, desire,
wish, and expectation.
Hope—
is provoked by purpose
and harvests meaning of purpose.

CHAPTER THREE
"GET LOST" AND "DROP DEAD":
HOPE AND MEANING

Plus çà change, plus c'est la même chose.
French saying

In the beginning of 1975, it was really difficult for many to comprehend that no one in Washington could find a way to save the Republic of Vietnam, to say nothing of avoiding the much-feared "Battle of Saigon." It was, after all, a city that had seen much less fighting with the enemy than in the many *coups d'état* of the Saigon regime itself. The helplessness to prevent the fall of Saigon was not really due to the paucity of ARVN troops or ordnance—both of which were more than sufficient to last comfortably for many months. Nevertheless, history's hour of reckoning came upon that spring of 1975. It became a time for the experts on both sides of the war in Viet-Nam to confront the realities and discover the validity of their concepts and theories about freedom and democracy, nationalism and independence, sovereignty and world peace.

Closing the war out was a terrible dilemma, of course, for the hierarchies in both Washington and Saigon. But it caused sheer astonishment among members of the Hanoi politburo, who had been yearning for two decades for an end to U.S. intervention in Viet-Nam. Hanoi had never been very much concerned by the million-man armed forces of the Republic of Vietnam, and the communist troops soon discovered that there was not much of a will to fight anymore at the beginning of 1975. Most of the ARVN was made up of young recruits forced into military service. Their highest priority was to find a way to avoid fighting of any kind. The overwhelming majority of Saigon troops really had not been recruited for fighting battles anyway. They were seen more as patrol cops on-the-beat, or civil service security guards, whose main mission was to provide "territorial security" for the population, mostly in the rural areas. From the time of Diem, the rural population had found itself in so-called "strategic hamlets," never really knowing whether they were locked in or out of the rest of the country. Conscripted youngsters of the ARVN infantry were, therefore, of little interest or problem to Hanoi and the communist troops in South Vietnam. Their concern was with the U.S. intervention there.

But Saigon and Washington did consider the ARVN an essential element for inclusion in important reports and debates about guerrilla warfare, troop levels, rapport of forces, firepower, pacification, and body counts. In other words, they helped to provide statistical window dressing for the "Four O'Clock Follies," the boring dog-and-pony show staged daily for the international press corps in Saigon. President Johnson also insisted that the same act be performed daily at the State Department to keep the American public informed of the good progress of his crusade for freedom and democracy in South Vietnam. Thankfully, the 1973 Paris Accords had dropped the curtain on these spectacles, and the American public no longer had to listen to the dreadful stories they entailed. The American people continued to believe in their precious ideals of freedom and progress, of course, but they were being sold less and less on the idea of South Vietnam as the "Outpost of the Free World" in Southeast Asia. The U.S. had returned to President Kennedy's original, but not simple, hope for

1185-CART

the South Vietnamese to be able to defend themselves without the assistance of U.S. troops.

People still wonder whether John F. Kennedy would have sent U.S. combat troops to South Vietnam in 1962 instead of "advisers," as the Viet-Cong seriously intensified the war with North Vietnam's participation. President Nixon later tried to put the blame on President Kennedy for having started the whole Vietnamese mess, and for doing nothing to prevent the assassination of President Diem. I am more inclined to think that JFK would not have committed the United States to spend billions of U.S. dollars and put a half million U.S. troops in South Vietnam, and very likely would have tried to find a negotiated way out with Ho Chi Minh—even thought it might have been at the expense of a so-called "non-communist" instead of "anti-communist" Saigon government. Hanoi might or might not have gone along with that possibility, since the fighting was not yet very intense at that time. It would very likely have gone for a military resolution, and the dilemma would have remained the same for Washington.

A peaceful arrangement with Ho Chi Minh would also have put President Kennedy against the hawks and the CIA, which was instrumental in making and very keen in keeping Ngo Dinh Diem president of the Republic of Vietnam. Nevertheless, credit must be given to President Nixon, who was able to return home all the U.S. troops in South Vietnam (541,000 in March 1969, as reported by the U.S. Defense Department) during his first term of office and, by his policy of "Vietnamization" of the Vietnam War, reduce American casualties to a minimum. By the time of the Paris Accords in January 1973, there were only about 25,000 U.S. troops left in South Vietnam to be withdrawn. In January 1975, Washington was reduced to pursuing John F. Kennedy's hope for a "non-communist" South Vietnam that could defend itself by itself without U.S. military intervention. But that idea was rapidly fading away by March 1975, with the inability or refusal of the South Vietnamese ARVN to fight back the North Vietnamese troops.

For nearly two decades, Hanoi had used guerrilla tactics against the U.S., but in its final confrontation with the ARVN, it employed traditional and classical conventional warfare. It would have been ludicrous for Vietnamese to wage guerrilla warfare against other Vietnamese. Guerrilla warfare, with no foreign troops remaining in South Vietnam, would be just a nonsensical waste of time. Generals Giap and Dung were, therefore, only too happy to unleash the full force of their conventional military power against Saigon in March 1975, in the best traditions of West Point. Unfortunately, Generals Maxwell D. Taylor, William C. Westmoreland and Creighton W. Abrams were no longer there. Real opposition might have been expected from Saigon's crack units—the marines, air force, tanks, rangers and special forces, Saigon's elite professionals with chests full of medals, all privileged and well-compensated warriors for more than a generation. In more than three decades of fighting under all kinds of flags, they neither understood nor cared much about the political issues behind the conflicts. They had chosen the army as a career, concerning themselves little about the origins or endings of war. They simply put their trust in their commanding officers, carried out orders to the best of their abilities, and did their jobs year in and year out. They fought to support not the politicians but their families.

What happened to these elite Saigon units in the spring of 1975? In March, a few of them were half-heartedly sent into relatively small battles in the central Vietnam highlands, where their performance was decidedly sub-par. These battles were just minor skirmishes. Saigon's elite troops had emerged victorious from much deadlier encounters. Why not now? Even the civilian population became aware of a lack of spirit, will, and readiness among the ARVN. Furthermore, the performance of these troops usually reflected the thinking, attitude, and behavior of their commanding officers. What had happened to the military leaders?

Since the January 1973 signing of the Paris Accords, Saigon's military brass had enjoyed a favored position. Thieu could point out to them that the president of the United States of America had provided a solemn, written "guarantee" ensuring the security of the Republic of Vietnam. The sleeping pill had been working quite nicely for nearly two years. But now it was time to wake up to realities. With the situation degenerating rapidly in the highlands and other areas, Thieu repeatedly appealed to Washington for military support, even if just from the air. Saigon's generals were at their wits' end over Washington's refusal to act. Was it really that difficult to send in a few planes from the Seventh Fleet, if only for psychological effect, or any other kind of signal to Hanoi that the U.S. was not giving up their long held idea of defending an anti-communist "Outpost of the Free World" in South Vietnam? It would have gone a long way toward helping the Saigon government hold the lines for a little while. President Ford did send a nice message to Thieu on March 25, reiterating the U.S. government's continued support for the Republic of Vietnam—but sorry, no American planes would be available from the U.S. Congress.

As a placebo, on March 28, Washington sent U.S. Army Chief of Staff Frederick Carlton Weyand, a four-star general, to Saigon. Weyand had been at the Paris peace talks and subsequently had become commander of U.S. forces in South Vietnam, a post he held until the complete withdrawal of the U.S. troops by the end of March 1973. I had known Fred Weyand for many years, and we had become good friends. Fred sincerely believed in South Vietnam as the "Outpost of the Free World." After his visit to Saigon, in an April 4 meeting with Ford and Kissinger under the California sun of Palm Springs, I am sure he did his eloquent best to describe South Vietnam's dark and desperate military situation and wholeheartedly pleaded for South Vietnam's cause. It was in vain, of course, because there was nothing much left for the president of the United States of America to do in face of a categorical "No" by the U.S. Congress for any additional aid to the Republic of Vietnam for continuation of the war, not to mention the $720 million suggested by General Weyand or even the $300 million in strictly economic assistance that the White House aides were thinking of. President Ford was told clearly by his Senate friends that he would not get one single American dime for anything military in Viet-Nam, but could have whatever money he might need to get all the Americans out of South Vietnam.

So, it was decided that it would not cost anybody anything for President Ford to ask Congress for $720 million to save the Saigon government. The legal and moral responsibilities for the kill would fall on Capitol Hill and not the White House. Furthermore, everybody knew well that even with $1 billion, it had become physically and humanely impossible for Washington to send more "guns and butter" to South Vietnam in time for the ARVN to stop the advance of the North Vietnamese troops. The only effective, but insane and outrageous, thing left for President Ford to do in that month of April 1975 was a massive military intervention by the U.S.

Since the little battles in Phuoc Long province in the beginning of 1975, Thieu had set the stage for his final showdown with Washington and had made dead sure that President Ford would have to face no other choice but to throw in the only chip left in the game for the Americans. Thieu might have been encouraged by remembering the impulsive bouts of escalation of the American war in Viet-Nam by President Johnson. Thieu might also have hoped someone in Washington might perform a "madman" act (in reference to stories that circulated that Nixon had gone crazy enough at one point to push the nuclear button to end the Vietnam war). But Thieu, of course, knew very little about President Ford, and badly overestimated American willingness to continue to pour its assets into South Vietnam.

The incredibly rapid breakdown of the ARVN and the irresistible advance of North Vietnamese troops southward undeniably saw hope rise in Hanoi while despair rose in Saigon's leaders. It caused no despair in Washington's Oval Office, just resignation. President Johnson might have felt desperate in 1968 in his fruitless attempts to achieve either victory or an honorable way out. The imminent demise of the anti-communist Saigon regime might also have raised some dismay—if not despair—for

President Nixon. (Nixon had sincerely done his utmost to help, but his concerns over hope or despair for Viet-Nam were overwhelmed by Watergate in 1974.)

As for President Ford in 1975, South Vietnam had long since become a satellite lost in space and, by then, billions of light-years away. In the view of many—a prophetic view, it turned out—Ford's was just a caretaker presidency anyway. So South Vietnam's forces fell like dominoes in a row from the highlands down to Saigon in just fifty-five days of incoherent, almost fanciful battles, a development that defied imagination and logic.

The only public justification Thieu gave for his resignation was the refusal of the U.S. to provide further military assistance. That did not explain the complete and immediate collapse of the ARVN and the Republic of Vietnam. There was still plenty of time to save the Saigon political regime, but it became clearer and clearer with every passing day that Washington had already decided otherwise.

It was imperative, then, for "Big" Minh to provide a concrete and meaningful purpose to sustain his forlorn hopes. He surely had some hope when he took over from Huong. He might have interpreted the information at hand, to either know or believe, in a way that helped him hope that the situation was not beyond rescue. He wouldn't have tried to take over if he'd had no trust in anything or anyone. Who could have provided that confidence? Surely not the Americans. The French? The Chinese? The Soviets? Hanoi? The NLF? It was, of course, from Madame Binh, the NLF, and the "Third Force." How confident could he have been with the long columns of tanks rolling past the South Vietnamese forces and closing in on Saigon? "Big" Minh's only hope was to effect a *rapprochement* with another side, but with whom? Great leaders had tried and failed. Hanoi no longer answered the phone except for social chats. There were just a few days left for all Americans to be evacuated. One thing became clear to "Big" Minh: the *sine qua non* for him to be able to do anything at all was the immediate and complete removal of all American presence in South Vietnam. At the very end, Hanoi's major concern remained that there would be a surprise intervention of some sort by the U.S.

It had come to the point that it no longer mattered much anymore whether "Big" Minh had a meaningful, reasonable, and realistic hope. He personified hope for his "Third Force," for others in South Vietnam, and even for some officials in Washington and Paris who entertained some vague hope by pushing "Big" Minh to take over from Huong. The "Third Force" earnestly tried to create and propagate this much-needed hope. The Buddha's lotus flower, hurriedly affixed to the lectern by "Big" Minh's aides as soon as old Huong had said his few formal words of resignation, represented hope in its highest symbolism, combining, as it did, poetic and mystical forms. It would, of course, be blasphemous to consider Buddha's lotus flower a political symbol (How many sins have been committed in Thy Name!).

I have always believed strongly in destiny. I found it exemplified in the events of the times. Irreversible reality and fate had set in, and the die was cast by April's end, 1975. In almost half a century, Ho Chi Minh had indeed established a well-oiled team. Uncle Ho had done his homework and, even after his death in 1969, his disciples were able to finish the task. "Big" Minh would not present any particular problem and was the least of Hanoi's worries. The North's most basic and long-awaited objective of the war in Vietnam had been to break the American will and determination to fight. That had been achieved, not on the battlefield, but on Capitol Hill in America. Ho Chi Minh had accomplished the same thing twenty years before in 1954 with the French Expeditionary Forces in Paris at the Palais Bourbon. Yet, with North Vietnamese tanks at the gates of Saigon, with the ARVN unwilling to put up a fight, and with Washington's determination never again to intervene, "Big" Minh still managed to hope and try to give hope to others.

Hope, for what reason and purpose?

For one, he hoped to avoid bloodshed by proclaiming Saigon an "open city" and welcoming Vietnamese of any and all political stripes. That would allow anyone to come in, without any invitation or proclamation of any sort by anybody. Make the offer, "I don't shoot, you don't shoot." That was what "Big" Minh's entourage was advocating. It wasn't possible for him to direct the ARVN to stop the snowballing advance of the North Vietnamese troops. Even with his enduring reputation and prestige in the South Vietnamese army, "Big" Minh could only, at best, call on the Saigon soldiers to lay down their arms rather than to take them up. That was what he was expected to do and was able to do.

How about proposing shared power with the other side? That would prove a bit difficult, if not be ridiculous. The Saigon government no longer had anything powerful to share, not even an ally, and the Hanoi politburo had nothing it cared to share with us.

What was apparently hoped for was a coalition between 'Big" Minh's "Third Force" and Madam Binh's NLF—a modest hope, indeed. Actually, it was a pathetic hope. But it sounded good and honorable. In fact, it was much better than Ngo Dinh Nhu's proposal in 1963 to invoke an outright act of allegiance of South Vietnam to Ho Chi Minh in a unified and federal Viet-Nam. Nhu's idea, together with the desperately poor performance of the Saigon government at that time, simply prompted the rapid overthrow of his elder brother Diem by a military coup in the best "banana-republic" tradition. Both Diem and Nhu were massacred by Captain Nhung, a well-known close aide of "Big" Minh, after the two brothers had agreed to surrender. "An unfortunate accident by submachine gun inside an M-113 vehicle," it was claimed. The term used at the time by "Big" Minh, when asked about the dreadful killing by then-Colonel Nguyen Van Thieu (who had led the attacks against Diem's Independence Palace), was "accidental suicide." That was not under Buddha's lotus flower, of course, but under the military junta. Nhung got promoted to major for his deed, and was later reported to have hanged himself with his battle-boot laces. Anyway, he provided a good scapegoat to calm down the Kennedy brothers, who were extremely annoyed by Diem's death. Unlike what had occurred in 1963, the 1975 situation was hopeless for South Vietnam and did not present a difficult choice or problem to the Hanoi politburo: It would be either a disguised defeat of Saigon or a full-fledged, historical, and glorious victory. The temptation to choose the second was only natural.

The Saigon government's demise and the mirage of "national reconciliation" between the NLF and other forces opposed to the Saigon regime had always been the politburo's immutable strategy and objective. It was a simple but effective concept that turned out to be quite successful (thanks to all players for reading the script so well, both the local and foreign casts). Throughout the four years of the Paris peace talks, Hanoi's position had always been clear and simple with regard to the governments of the U.S. ("get lost") and Saigon ("drop dead"). Now that the "get-lost and drop-dead" goal had been attained, the objectives of "coalition" and "national reconciliation" had also become obsolete. But it wouldn't cost anything to let everybody think that Saigon's "Third Force" and the NFL could get together for "national reconciliation."

So hope, with "Big" Minh as bait, was given to "Big" Minh himself, and anyone else who wished to believe in it, including those in Paris and Washington. Both those nations' ambassadors were really eager to get "Big" Minh into the presidential chair as quickly as possible. So "Big" Minh's big hope had the value of somehow permitting people to believe that Saigon might be saved through "national reconciliation," thereby softening the terrible shock of South Vietnam's defeat, particularly for Saigon's troops and for the pragmatic purpose of getting them to lay down their arms. It was outstanding Machiavellian craftsmanship.

What else could "Big" Minh's presidency hope for? That with some international intervention, it might be possible to unite the South Vietnamese parties with the NLF as leader and preserve some sort of South Vietnamese entity (without the Saigon government, of course) to placate the pro-Soviet North Vietnam? That notion would be even harder to swallow than national reconciliation, but it did sound grandiose and noble. The NLF would be strictly South Vietnamese to counterbalance Moscow. Many in "Big" Minh's entourage actually believed in this epic scheme. "You never know," they might have been thinking. Clever international diplomacy can work wonders sometimes.

Many people could still remember that we had gone through this exercise in 1971, and had missed the opportunity. We should have played ping-pong better. Nevertheless, Nixon and Kissinger had tried hard, with limited but encouraging results, to achieve this unlikely coalition, to the great displeasure of Hanoi's politburo members, who had been even more disturbed that Moscow had joined the game. The objects of their displeasure were the budding good relations and cooperation between China and the U.S. The years 1971 and 1972 were milestones in international relations, with Kissinger in the diplomatic driver's seat. In July 1971, Kissinger went to China to prepare the Sino-American summit. In February 1972, Nixon paid a warm visit to Chairman Mao in Beijing, resulting in the signing of the so-called Shanghai Declaration on February 28. It was time for China to remind the U.S. that their two countries should be very good friends, because Beijing's number one enemy had always been Moscow and not the United States. Did you not get the message in 1953 in Korea? While the Cultural Revolution had ended, China was still facing serious internal power struggles and unrest, and needed to catch its breath. Therefore, a friend in need would be, of course, a friend in deed. Richard Nixon would be most happy to sponsor Chairman Mao for membership to the plush and very "in" club called the United Nations. And that was quickly said and quickly done.

In May 1972, three months after his visit to Beijing, Nixon traveled to Moscow and offered the Soviet Union a chance to outdo China, with a U.S.-Soviet declaration of good intentions to reduce tensions between the two superpowers and to begin friendly discussions about problems having to do with Germany, European security, and other important items. One was the first Strategic Arms Limitation Treaty (SALT), which really helped many people sleep better, although everybody still continued to produce nuclear weapons like mad, with the popular game of two steps forward and one step backward.

It was, indeed, a new era in world diplomacy, thanks to the wonderful U.S. policy of *détente,* as it was called, an unfortunate choice of a French word which means either "relaxation" or "pulling the trigger of a gun"—take your choice. In his secret talks in Paris, Kissinger did not fail to use his new Chinese and Soviet friendships to improve his credentials with the Hanoi politburo's Le Duc Tho.

The Iron Curtain had somehow been smelted into an aluminum one, while North Vietnam's Bamboo Curtain remained as thick as ever. Kissinger's theory of "The Three Kingdoms" in world politics had finally turned out to be productive, workable, and very effective. Everyone had come to agree that it would be less dangerous and much easier for all the protagonists to sit, talk, and do their balancing acts on a three-legged stool rather than on a two-legged shelf. In fact, Beijing had had experience with this "Three Kingdoms" idea more than three thousand years before and, through a modernized version, had put it back in circulation again in 1953 with the thirty-eighth parallel in Korea. Beijing simply wanted a U.S. military presence by its side in case of an attack by the Soviet Union. Moscow and Beijing had for years massed about a million troops at their common borders. It took the U.S. a long time to learn what those Peking men were up to, as always. The "Three Kingdoms" had been working quite well since the 1950s (thanks also to the two homesick Chinese-American nuclear physicists who helped the People's Republic develop the bomb). The theory is a bit outdated now, but you never know. As the French say, "*plus çà change, plus c'est la même chose,*" reminding us that "the more things change, the more they stay the same."

* * *

Back to the spring of 1975 and hope for the "Third Force" in Saigon—hope to be able to claim some credit for having opposed the Saigon regime, hope to be able to impress the brother-enemies with the notion that the "Third Force" had never been anti-communist and would live happily ever after with the NLF and Hanoi. National reconciliation would save face and look good for both domestic and foreign consumption. Well, the social games were over. "If you're not with me, you're against me." No time, no need for anything now, except the hard fact of those columns of tanks rolling full speed southward, some already at Saigon's gates. They would be in town before you got the words national reconciliation spelled properly. The hour of truth and history had come—there was only the advancing First Force. No Second Force, no "Third Force" or any other forces required.

Fate has always been determined on the battlefield, never at the conference tables. Negotiations and agreements should only express realities and be used only to sign surrenders and victories. Otherwise, they are just blah-blah declarations of good intentions. Negotiations deal in hard facts, not hopes. International agreements work only when they fit the reality, which means the balance or rapport of forces. Sadly enough, the 1973 Paris Accords were full of good intentions and hopes rather than facts.

National reconciliation and self-determination could mean anything under the sun, and were mentioned in the Paris Accords. No one could deny the validity of the basic principles of brotherly love, freedom, and democracy. When it becomes impossible to say anything more, anyone can declare, "I love you very much and always respect your will as you respect mine." At the La Celle Saint Cloud conference between the two South Vietnamese parties, national reconciliation and self determination were my cup-of-tea for more than two years. Brotherly love, like any kind of love, was hard to express in concrete terms and in action. The meaning of national reconciliation and self-determination could range from proportional representation in the legislative branch to power-sharing in the executive branch of a coalition government. It might well require years for the parties to work out free and democratic elections. Hope for national reconciliation and self-determination was not very bright, but they were very appealing topics of endless discussions.

With the North Vietnamese tanks arriving in the suburbs of Saigon, one could have hoped for at least a formal surrender ceremony, with signing pens, international guarantees and supervision, and the presence of superpower representatives. One also could have hoped to be declared a POW under the Geneva Convention. That hope, however, would have really been only a long shot; it more likely would have been an issue under the aegis of Amnesty International and the International Committee of the Red Cross, rather than between Vietnamese.

We had been "traitors to the Fatherland" during the more than one hundred years of French colonialism and, before that, "puppets" of the Chinese invaders during the whole of the first millennium. The other side had told us so again and again. So any hope to be re-baptized Geneva Convention POWs was a ludicrous one. We were free to call ourselves anything we wished—freedom fighters, defenders of democracy, economic miracle workers, humanity's elite—but not POWs. We were simply "traitors to the fatherland." The only hope left for our people and our nation was to reunite as a family. There was the hope to surrender as brothers, cousins, uncles, but to claim the international status of POWs among Vietnamese relatives would have been ridiculous and laughable to both sides.

Of course, there was at least the hope of "the last wish," if you will—the hope not to be taken to the wall. Unfortunately, this is a matter between each person and his or her conscience. No one can help us here. No one is going to take millions of "puppets" to the wall, but there are people being taken to the wall every day all over the world. Small hope, but big anguish. The list could go on *ad infinitum*. Everyone had the ability to hope for anything, good or evil, fancifully or reasonably, for oneself or for others, or for everyone. For hope to occur and prevail, "Big" Minh had to substantiate his "hope to hope" with purpose, meaning, reason, and reality, or even a semblance of these. That was his dilemma. He forced himself to hope, without any of those elements.

The war in Viet-Nam was a great tragedy for many people in many ways, but it was also a strange war. It was a first of sorts for the American people and their presidents. There was nothing in the books from West Point or Wall Street to help Lyndon Johnson know what kind of U.S. security he was dealing with. LBJ sincerely thought he was acting in the interests of the American people and that his concrete job in South Vietnam was to check the spread of international communism, which his experts considered synonymous with guerrilla warfare. It took LBJ a lot of time and money to learn it was not that simple. If LBJ's concept had not been a very rich and militarily powerful Great Society, it would have taken much less time and taxpayer dollars to learn the lesson.

Yes, Washington viewed the war as a fight against the spread of international communism, but the best minds in the Oval Office ignored a most fundamental and decisive factor: That communist contagion was skillfully mingled with a tremendous surge of nationalism against a background of worldwide de-colonization, calling for an end to foreign presence, rule, and domination, and for the restoration of independence and dignity. These things had nothing to do with guns. Uncle Ho's fight for national independence would not have had a leg to stand on had it not been backed by international communism against Paris and later Washington. There was no other choice possible for Ho Chi Minh but to equate international communism with Vietnamese nationalism. That had been evident to President Eisenhower, who advised his French ally that Paris should abandon its old fashioned colonial war in Indochina and replace it by a war against international communism for freedom and democracy. Easily said but not easily done.

Paris was completely bankrupt and out of breath. How could they ask an apparently ugly, former colonist to suddenly become a shining knight on a white horse? So, it was a bit unfair later on, when Richard Nixon complained that the Vietnam War was John F. Kennedy's baby and the responsibility of the Democrats to save

American honor. Richard Nixon did attempt and somehow succeeded in saving American honor to the best of his abilities till the last minutes of his presidency.

* * *

In practical terms and with all the help of President Eisenhower, it must be recognized that President Diem started the whole game with a severe handicap: Equate Vietnamese nationalism with the American presence in South Vietnam and be the Outpost of the Free World. It was a very hard, if not impossible, task compared with that of Uncle Ho, who had the much easier job of explaining to the ordinary men in the streets of Saigon and the poor population in the countryside of South Vietnam about being a "patriot" with the sacred duty to fight against any foreign rule and presence on national soil. It was not difficult for Uncle Ho to link this tremendous urge for nationalism to communism and to propagate the Marxist-Leninist line as being the best way to defend the legitimate interests of the destitute and oppressed against the rich and powerful. He could demonstrate through simple syllogism that the Communist Vietnamese were the personification of the truest Vietnamese patriots and most genuine Vietnamese nationalists. How could anyone convince anyone that the opulent rich were defending the interests of the poor? It would have been as ridiculous asking the miserable poor to fight for the ways of life of the rich.

As with many people in South Vietnam, my confusion was caused by other aspects of the conflict: its horror and blind violence. Once the thunders of war were unleashed, everyone began putting the blame on everyone else for having started the bloody fight. There was undeniably the same confusion and dilemma in the minds of many others as I experienced at the time. A raging and bloody war was going on. Everyone wanted to see it end as quickly as possible, but no one knew how to achieve that end. Like many others, I strongly wished for an early end to the violence, death, and devastation. But how? How? LBJ must have asked himself that same question a million times, not knowing exactly what to do with his troops in South Vietnam, except to continue the escalation process.

There in the spring of 1975, I couldn't help remembering a 1968 evening's candid discussion about the strange American war in Viet-Nam. It was in Saigon, during a dinner at the residence of South Korean ambassador Soo Young Lee, who later was the ROK ambassador in Paris. He and I were chatting with General William C. Westmoreland, then-commander of U.S. forces in South Vietnam. I reminded them what Korean president Park had said to us at the 1966 Manila Summit: "When you go to war it is to-win and not not-to-lose."

Ambassador Lee, a former air force general, then joked, "Yes, it's also like playing soccer on only your own half of the field!"

General Westmoreland did not comment on our remarks but gave us one of his famously broad and crisp smiles. The dinner, if I am not mistaken, was a farewell to Westy (as he was familiarly known). Well, in its "no-win-no-lose" strategy, the U.S. did at one time bomb up to the twentieth parallel, mined Hai Phong Port, and air-raided Hanoi during those twelve days and nights around Christmas 1972. What did it accomplish? Disruption of supply lines? Threat of escalation? A psychological impact on the enemy? Was it, on principle, a gradual, limited, proportional response in self-defense against aggression?

* * *

One week after the spectacular 1972 Christmas bombing of Hanoi, Henry Kissinger and Le Duc Tho resumed their negotiations in Paris. President Nixon declared then that it was "a marvelous surrender of the enemy on our conditions." So, the U.S. bombing of Hanoi was for psychological effect, not on the North Vietnamese Communists but on the American Congress and people. Was it purpose versus reality, and hope in function of purpose? If not at the time, certainly in retrospect it was not the hope-to-win, but the hope not-to-lose, or rather the hope to get out of the horrible mess with honor at all costs. Heaven and Earth had again turned upside down. We can all be grateful to President Richard Nixon, National Security Advisor Henry Kissinger, and Admiral Thomas H. Moorer, Chairman of the Joint Chiefs of Staff, for shortening considerably the American war in Viet-Nam with the 1972 Christmas bombing of Hanoi. The longest war (albeit undeclared) in the history of the United Sates of America should be renamed "the unique American War in Vietnam." This might help people forget quicker this sad and dreadful episode in American history.

* * *

It was, of course, unbelievable in the spring of 1975 that the American government, ally of the Saigon regime, leader of the free world, with its formidable war machine, could let the communist troops of North Vietnam arrive at the gates of Saigon. As soon as everyone realized that the U.S. had removed its might from Viet-Nam, it seemed that the *raison d'être* of the Saigon administration also evaporated. And that was it: The realities, the inability to see a worthwhile outcome, to see a reason or purpose for the killing to go on, meant there was no point for the South Vietnamese to hope any longer, as they had been taught by the leader of the Free World to do for two decades. There had been a South Vietnam with the U.S. Without the U.S., there was no longer a South Vietnam. But was there really a loss of purpose in Washington?

There had been meaningful purpose in American policy for the Vietnam War during two decades, through five presidents in the White House, and yet that meaningful purpose was abandoned because it became so outrageously unreasonable, irrational, illogical, and nonsensical, by its insane spending, the magnitude of its devastation, the unbelievable death toll and untold suffering caused to all the parties in that American crusade for freedom and democracy in Viet-Nam. The loss of that meaningful purpose was

185-CART

actually and finally decided by the American people themselves and not by the five presidents of the United States involved in the Vietnam war.

As for the Saigon leaders and politicians, the human ability to hope seems to have been reduced to its basic contrasting element: the hope for survival, or facing fatality in despair with a "hope against all hope." It was not much of a hope in that case. Hope must be more than the natural and instinctive urge for survival. Survival is meaningful, but survival alone cannot be a meaningful purpose to hope. On the other hand, the "hope against all hope" does not provide any meaning or purpose to hope for something, but simply releases a vague "hope to hope," devoid of any rationality. Reason is clearly needed in hope. Washington had given reason for Saigon to hope for twenty years but was no longer able to provide to the American people any acceptable reason for freedom and democracy to be upheld anymore in South Vietnam at such high cost to American taxpayers' money and lives. As with anything in life, ideals of freedom and democracy also have their price. And hope must also have its own price of reason.

CODA

Reflections On Hope And Meaning

Life without purpose
cannot generate hope.
Life without meaning
cannot acquire purpose.
Hope—
requires purpose and meaning,
as life
requires purpose and meaning.

Hope—
without meaningful purpose
cannot prevail.

><

Meaning and purpose in hope
are interrelated and interactive.
The emerging impact of hope
into human beings' awareness
is provoked by purpose
and substantiated by meaning.
The initial effects of hope
are subjective.

><

Hope—
energizes with purpose,
its driving force
and meaning,
its source of combustion.
Meaning,
in the context of hope,
is initially emotional,
subsequently intellectual.
Meaning and purpose in hope,
at the start of its operational process,
concern more the heart
than the mind.

><

The search for meaning
in hope's purpose

constitutes the complex exercise
for the activation phase
of hope.
Hope—
cannot be sustained
without meaningful purpose.
To give meaning
to the purpose of hope
is the exalting challenge
of providing meaning and purpose
to life itself.

><

Hope—
driven by purpose without meaning
is not hope,
but gratuitous behavior.
Purpose,
without meaning is not purpose,
but whimsy.
A meaningful purpose of hope
begins with the heart,
then needs to be sustained
by the mind.
Human ability to will
and to think
are God-given natural gifts
enabling us to search
for meaning and purpose
throughout our existence,
helping us make use
of the wonderful gift of hope
to shape and express
our individuality, humanity and destiny.

><

Hope—
can take any facet
that life can.
Hope—
requires humans
to seek for the good in our heart
as well as
look for and accept
the truth with our mind.
The task
is to find out what we are,
what we want,
what we should become and mean
to the vast universe
that surrounds us.
Hope—
is concerned with humankind's
sentiments and intellect.
Meaning,
in the context of hope,
is altogether involved and confusing,
abounding and distressing,
alluring and terrifying,
exciting and compelling.

><

Meaning, situationally, in hope
is both individual and collective,
subjective or objective in perspective,
vague or specific in expectation,
broad or limited in response,
gradual or integral in progression,

185-CART

uncompromising or flexible in adaptability,
irrational or realistic in concept,
relative or absolute in value.
Hope—
is activated by purpose and meaning
but also requires
reason and reality
in its operational process and evolution.

CHAPTER FOUR

THOSE WHO LEFT AND THOSE WHO STAYED: HOPE AND REASON

I do not seek to convince my adversary of his error but to unite with him in a higher truth.
Jean Baptiste Henri Lacordere (1802-1861)

Reason is always employed to justify arguments, armed conflict, and particularly epic wars, but in the final analysis, the death and sorrow that war entails cannot really be assigned to the realm of reason. It would be too easy to say that humankind is driven by passion—as if human passions were devoid of reason—and fueled by tremendous energies born of powerful emotions. Surely someday humans will be able to agree about what to do with their DNA and not just formulate how it works. The road to perfection remains long, and, for the time being, we must all make the best of what we have, including our passions, often the companions of hope and despair, and with no less force, power or energy.

More than twenty-five years after the fall of Saigon, the flames of hope, despair, and passion generated by the war in Viet-Nam have subsided or died out in most people. For the few who have

185-CART

not quite managed to heal their more deeply felt wounds, time and change will ultimately do that for them. The more intense human emotions, such as joy and pain, tend to linger longer than reason and logic in the aftermath of human conflict, especially the most dreadful and bloodiest ones. But we human beings can think and learn from even these terrible experiences. The War in Viet-Nam was a horror for all its protagonists, both near and far, but it left precious lessons.

It has been said that it is easier to start a war than end one. The war in Viet-Nam was no exception. It was also an example that proved the rule. Whether it's called "The American War in Viet-Nam" or "The Vietnam War," its greatest legacy has come from how it ended rather than how it began. Oddly, the people of America seem to have been much more traumatized by the war than the Vietnamese themselves, who have had to bear the direct and, by far, heavier physical consequences of that bloody conflict.

In the spring of 1975 when Saigon fell, hundreds of thousands of South Vietnamese chose, for various reasons, to leave the land of their ancestors. That was a first in the four thousand years of Vietnamese history. In 1955, about one million Vietnamese left the North for the South, but they didn't leave the country. Those who could have found ways to leave in 1975, but decided to remain, did so out of a sense of belonging and sharing with their families *and* with their fellow countrymen. Then, too, they stayed out of a sense of belonging to their homes, ways of life, habits, and all the old familiar places, not unlike New Yorkers who can't imagine living anywhere else or Parisians who would prefer to be in Paris, no matter what. Such a mix of motives provided rational justifications for those who did not flee. The French philosopher Blaise Pascal (1623-1662) said, "The heart has reasons that reason does not know."

Reason is obviously a determining factor in the conduct of our life and must not be ignored, but reason isn't everything in human existence, self-exploration, and the world around us. It's not the only way to understand our hopes, desires, and aspirations. In many ways, the war was the most dramatic event in the history of my people. Its devastation was unprecedented, even when compared to the thousand-year subjugation under the ancient Chinese Sons-of-Heaven, or even when compared to conflicts elsewhere in world history.

The war left long-lasting and far-reaching consequences for all Vietnamese, North and South, victors and vanquished. Nevertheless, Vietnamese on both sides of the conflict quickly set aside their differences and joined forces to face the new challenges of their common future on the land of their ancestors. But for the American people, the war continued to be a strange, almost unreal, undertaking, for many of them incompatible with the precepts set out by their Founding Fathers.

By the fateful spring of 1975, U.S. troop withdrawal had become a visceral reality—not the "drop-by-drop" process or "pretended" pull-out Madame Binh complained about during the Paris peace talks. Nor was it "Vietnamization," as President Nixon euphemistically put it in carrying out his gradual troop withdrawal. For the U.S., the time had come to improve relations and live in peace with the Soviet Union and the People's Republic, the world's two largest communist countries, and for the Vietnamese to live with each other by themselves and for themselves. The two billion dollars' worth of war machines the U.S. left behind had helped the Thieu regime be successful for a while, allowing it to "pacify" more territory in a relatively short time during 1973 and 1974 than in the previous ten years. But it soon became clear to everyone, including the Hanoi politburo, that the U.S. would not intervene again after the closing days of April 1975.

The painful American crusade for freedom and democracy in South Vietnam had actually ended. Thanks again to Henry Kissinger, American honor was somehow saved "par la peau de la dent . . . ," as the French would say (by the skin of the teeth). Thieu was made to resign and leave the country. There was no longer any purpose, meaning, and reason, of course, for the

Vietnamese to continue with The American War in Viet-Nam without the Americans.

The Vietnam War became even more ludicrous when everybody tried so hard in the end to have old Huong and "Big" Minh make a deal, any deal, with Hanoi for, among possibilities, the survival of the Saigon government, a coalition government with the communists, allegiance to Hanoi, mercy for the vanquished? Anything was possible but, surely, not honor for the corrupt and incompetent members of the anti-communist Saigon regime. Honor, shame, and death for the Vietnamese in South Vietnam was a very personal thing to be resolved by each individual to the best of his or her ability. No Vietnamese Kissinger was at hand to help us out there. About 150,000 people opted to leave South Vietnam within the short few days before the fall of Saigon, but the rest of the South Vietnamese population remained on the land of their ancestors, uncertain as to what would happen to them. Only less than two weeks earlier, the Khmer Rouges had occupied Phnom Penh, and many people knew what had happened there: savage bloodshed and sheer barbarity.

Many high-ranking civil servants of the Saigon government preferred the road of exile, but the overwhelming majority remained and waited for their fate. Only a handful of the Saigon military brass remained. The others had already fled the country with their families and savings. Among the few who decided to stay, some donned their ceremonial uniforms with their proud decorations and put a pistol to their heads in the best ancient tradition of their honorable craft. General Pham Van Phu, the commanding officer of the Army Corps II who had ordered the retreat of his troops from the highlands as instructed by Thieu, prefered poison in a room of the Saigon Dong Dat Hospital (formerly called Hospital Grall during one hundred years of French colonial rule). A former foreign minister also took poison in his own bathroom. In the command centers for the rest of the million Saigon troops scattered all over South Vietnam attending to "territorial security," there was no one to even answer the phone. Everyone went AWOL, from the joint chiefs of staff down to the battalion commanders. What became of the presidential palace or the Ministry of Defense was of little interest to them. They saw no need to go through the long, ritualistic surrender march, with hands over their heads as they had seen in films. The only thing left for them to do was lay down their arms, change into civilian clothes and go home to their loved ones.

Hanoi viewed these developments with satisfaction, its leaders' hopes and convictions supported by incredible realities. In only twenty days, two South Vietnamese army corps in Military Zones I and II, covering twelve provinces of the highlands and central Vietnam and representing forty percent of the ARVN, vanished. The most significant development was the surprisingly lamentable performance of Army Corps I under the command of General Ngo Quang Truong, considered by Washington to be the best of the Saigon generals. General Truong's First and Second Infantry divisions had always been considered crack fighting units and had scored many resounding victories against the regular North Vietnamese troops in the border provinces in central Vietnam, particularly during the communist large-scale offensive in March 1972. By the end of March 1975, the U.S. had to send in vessels for the emergency evacuation of both civilians and military personnel from central Vietnam. Truong was dismayed that his troops had failed to put up a decent fight. He tried his best, but when Thieu refused reinforcements, his soldiers lost the heart for fighting. It's easy to understand the desperate and impossible situation for General Truong: only one ARVN division faced three North Vietnamese divisions in the border province of Quang Tri. A frantic and very skinny man, General Truong could only run around aimlessly or watch thousands and thousands of his men seek cover by simply throwing themselves into the South China Sea. I can well imagine how Truong must have cursed his one-time comrade-in-arms, the former General Nguyen Van Thieu. On March 29, Truong was lucky enough to evacuate Da Nang under heavy shelling, in the company of the American consul general, aboard an HQ-404 vessel bound for Saigon. He went completely berserk, walking around and around from one room to another, continuously talking to himself like a madman in the following days and weeks at the ARVN General Headquarters, ignored and forgotten by his fellow-generals.

Army Corps II, operating in the Highlands, did not fare much better. From the beginning of March, the communist forces had launched offensives in Pleiku and Kontum provinces, occupied the districts of Thuan Man and Duc Lap, and—in three short days—occupied the provincial capital city of Buon Ma Thuot. On March 11, the Hanoi politburo released a communiqué saying that the victories at Duc Lap and Buon Ma Thuot "have demonstrated that we have the ability to win major victories much faster than expected." On March 14, Thieu traveled to Cam Ranh (instead of the originally designated city of Nha Trang, in an effort to fool everyone, including the CIA) to consult with General Pham Van Phu, commanding officer of Army Corps II. He instructed Phu to retreat from the highlands and organize defense lines along the coastal provinces leading to Saigon. The March 16 retreat of General Phu's troops was chaotic and anything but dignified. Army Corps II's retreat, combined with the collapse of Truong's Army Corps I, caused hundreds of thousands of civilians to panic and join the troops along the roads of exodus, with the hope of reaching safety in Saigon.

Washington was flabbergasted by the rapidity of events. A retired U.S. general-turned CIA agent rushed to his Vietnamese general contact at the presidential palace to complain furiously of not having being informed about such vital information. The source pointed out that, at the last minute, he preferred to be more loyal to his president than to the CIA. A rationalization was made that the ARVN's rout might turn out to be helpful, leading to Thieu's speedy resignation and a coalition at last with Madame Binh.

Hanoi's leaders were apparently incredulous as they watched the rapidly deteriorating situation in the South, but remained quite cautious in their predictions. In a March 25 meeting, the Hanoi politburo issued this statement:

> With the great victories in the highlands, our general offensive has begun. These continuous victories mark a major new phase in the military and political situation in South Vietnam . . . . The time has come for a strategic opportunity. During over twenty years of our fight against the U.S. for the safeguarding of our country, now is our greatest opportunity . . . . We must concentrate all our forces, act most rapidly . . . and liberate the South as soon as possible.

It was not until at its April 1 meeting that the politburo indicated its belief that final victory would be a possible and realistic object of hope by declaring, "Our revolutionary war in the South has not simply reached a point of sudden progress but also come to the ripe time for the general offensive and general uprising." On April 7, General Giap ordered his troops to proceed with the all-out "general offensive in the most expeditious way for final victory and the liberation of South Vietnam." However one might wish to look at the North's strategy, it followed a pattern that was consistent and determined, as well as meaningful and having rational purpose with the hope that things would work out, finally, according to their long-held goals.

* * *

I held no hope at the "power transfer" ceremony between Huong and "Big" Minh, because I had no reason or purpose to hope at that time. Submerged in the complexities of the situation, I couldn't even concoct something to hope for, as much as I might have wanted to. I didn't see anything coming out of Washington, Moscow, Beijing, Paris, Hanoi, or Saigon that could have provided grounds for hope. I felt no reason for hope within me, nor around me. "Heaven and Earth had turned upside down." In the midst of such mental turmoil, life itself lost almost all meaning and purpose. Nothing mattered anymore. Anyone could have done anything. At this point, the only alternative to despair was simply to try to take care of oneself. That was surely the hope that was the driving force for more than one hundred thousand Vietnamese who got out while the getting was good.

Many friends and relatives wondered why my family didn't join the millions who tried desperately to find space on a helicopter, plane, or boat in hopes of getting away and saving their lives and belongings. Both my brother and I could have taken our family out of the country without much effort. My brother was then the head of our national carrier, Air Vietnam, and was personally on the scene at the airport during the two frenetic weeks, getting hundreds of friends and staff members on departing planes. As for myself, my own plane was on standby, ready to take off any time of day or night, by order-of-mission signed by Huong. By my authorization, on Monday morning, April 28, the crew left with their families. A very close American friend of my family (Jim Eckes, now Managing Director of Indoswiss Aviation Ltd.), had repeatedly phoned and summoned us to leave with him, and had kept the engines of his plane running for hours on the tarmac, waiting for us until the very last moment, before taking off amidst the first shells falling on the runway—shelling that condemned for good Saigon's Tan Son Nhut airport. As his plane soared over the skies of Saigon that morning, Jim was torn between feelings of hope and despair—hope for himself, of course, yet despair for the Vietnamese friends he was leaving behind, whose fate was unknown.

Acute anguish, nearly unbearable, finally arose out of my inability to know or even imagine what retaliation, punishment, or revenge now awaited me, and when it would come. A persistent state of helplessness took hold of me. I was utterly unable to find an acceptable solution to my predicament. There was no plausible course of action, no plausible way out. There was no rational basis for hope; any would be unrealistic, meaningless. No matter how much I tried, I always found myself back to square one: I happened to be on the side of the vanquished in a long and bloody war, and still alive in the hands and at the mercy of the victors. That was what it came down to, a cruel and hard reality that had to be accepted. Just accept the distressing reality, with all its possible adverse consequences. Was this crushing helplessness a sort of hopelessness?

Then, as events unfolded, I realized that hope came to me instinctively in the form of a reaction to my state of helplessness and absence of hope. It was a basic reflex of rejecting an impossible situation, a natural urge to survive. But this hope needed to be salvaged from some semblance of reality and reason in order to be credible. Something sensible was needed to give hope both purpose and meaning. Without a minimum of such elements, there would be just despair. Even as I was helpless, I did not fall into despair. I gradually felt the need to hope, and it welled up in me as soon as it found a reason, an aim to feed on, and a meaningful, stable basis to prevail.

My mind knew that Saigon had reached the darkest hour of its history by April 28. On that date, the "power transfer" to "Big" Minh also relieved me of my public burden. All my mental torments about South Vietnam's fate did not seem to matter anymore. A mechanism had been triggered within me that permitted other values to set in, values much more basic to someone stripped of all his artifices, standing naked with the common denominators of his species. I came to realize that the ability to reduce the act of being to its simplest and most basic elements allowed me to shed many unnecessary artifices of existence and truly to value the essential aspects of life, which would help me search for and find something to hope for. Hope's rationale was no longer the stubborn and blind pursuit for the survival of the Republic of Vietnam or some form of political regime in Saigon. These causes now ceased to have any meaning for me. What filled the void was family, only family. I was down to fundamentals, nothing else. After a decade of running about day and night all over the world, busy with one thing or another, I was back home at last. It was a good feeling to be in the midst of those closest to me. Everyone was glad I was there with them. They hadn't seen me very often for such a long time.

I could feel that my parents were happy that I was there with the family. We didn't talk much about it. I had the impression that everyone wanted to leave me to myself, respect my privacy, as it were. They assumed that I was really distressed by the situation. As much as my intellect told me there was not a new set of fundamentals, I continued to be plagued with innumerable "what ifs." I was glad my parents were by my side, and I gradually became conscious of all the other relatives around me. My old parents brought me back not only to the immediate family, but also to our extended family, most of them simple farmers in the countryside, totally apolitical, too busy and absorbed in cultivating their paddy fields, which barely allowed them to feed their kids and left no time to think much of anything else.

There were also many other relatives on the other side of the war. All the uncles and cousins on my father's side had gone North in the 1940s to join Ho Chi Minh and the Viet Minh resistance fighters against French colonialism. Two reached the rank of army general, and others became superior officers or high government and Communist Party officials. Many of my kin living in the North became ordinary combatants, civil servants, and workers. On my mother's side, most of the relatives remained in the South as Viet Cong in their hamlets and villages, while some in Saigon became wealthy as medical doctors and capitalist rice merchants. All in three decades.

I suddenly realized that the whole family in the South was gathered for the first time in our family home, at this very crucial and historic moment of our country. My parents, in their late seventies, were surrounded by their children and grandchildren and countless cousins, nieces, nephews, and in-laws. There wasn't much disruption in daily activities, either before or after the communist troops arrived, but things seemed to slow down a bit in the house. The kids didn't make as much noise as usual and were in their rooms most of the time, rather than in the courtyard. The grown-ups gave the impression of going about their personal chores and, I sensed, all were hoping for something, a decision to be made, an action to be taken, to deal with a situation considered dramatic. I was certain all were entrusting their fate in the family and putting all their hopes in my parents, my sister, my brother, and me, who were considered the senior members of the clan. All of us were waiting for something to happen and, it could be said, hope was also waiting in us. It was a latent hope that hope was still possible, although we weren't exactly sure what to hope for. It was an understandable, simple, and natural reaction to the situation. We all felt fear and anxiety, too. Perhaps it was that fear and anxiety that led us to hope.

My parents' attitude and behavior were clearly different from that of the rest of the family. They carried on with their routines and conveyed the feeling that hope was not needed for the circumstance, especially my mother, an exceptional woman with a striking Cartesian frame of mind—hot-tempered for the little things in life, but always totally serene in times of great crisis. She had gone through the long years of her married life measuring existence by the sole yardstick of total devotion and concrete contributions to her parents, husband, and children—her Confucian upbringing having instilled the notion that to love her family was her unique mission and natural purpose on earth. Her hope at that time was, without any doubt, for the safety, well-being, and togetherness of her family.

My parents did everything they could to safeguard love and affection in their own original families. The war had divided the clan and sent relatives to opposing camps. This was true for most families in Viet-Nam, and hope must have had many different objects for members of the same family, who had fought for so long as brother-enemies on different sides of the bloody conflict. Both Huong and "Big" Minh also had relatives on the communist side, the former a son (a captain) and the latter a younger brother (a lieutenant colonel). A cousin of mine, Duong Dinh Thao,

185-CART

spokesman for the NLF, had sat opposite me at the Paris conference table for years. In three decades of war, these relatives from our native villages of the paternal and maternal sides (Giong Trom and Ba Tri) in Ben Tre province were in constant contact and came to visit us in Saigon regularly.

From my frequent talks with relatives on the "other side," it was clear that the deadly war had not severed family bonds and affection. There was a tacit agreement not to say anything that could ignite heated arguments. We came to accept that each side had its own way of life, and tried to make an abstraction of the suffering and death, things we had to endure, since it was beyond the family's abilities to end the killing and devastation. I felt that these relatives had a much harder life, and a more impossible task than mine, but that they were more devoted to victory for their cause. There was real and deep affection and love among us. I had not had much of an opportunity to get to know many of these relatives well. I had been sent to Europe for my studies in my early teens, and brought up in the West with Western values and notions of democracy and freedom. I had been busy simply trying to secure the kind of living I believed in and hoped for. I didn't agree with some of my relatives' values, but I sensed that their faith, belief, determination, and hope in their purpose and cause were much more intense than mine. They needed hope much more than I did, and I felt that they were much more desperate than we were on our side.

What I was able to learn from the visits by relatives from the "other side" was the strength of family bonds, even in the face of adversity and bloody conflict. Familial bonds are natural, God-ordained values in all living creatures, but particularly so in human beings. The ties are not just physical and material, but constitute an inherent part of humanity's metaphysical reality, individual and social, personal and collective, involving the entire process of life, including union, procreation, and continuity. Family bonds may not be powerful enough to overcome the forces of ideologies or violence, but neither can ideologies and violence annihilate family ties, for they express the most concrete, basic and immediate spiritual values in human existence.

We were deeply divided by the ideologies, either after being born into one side or the other or compelled at one point to choose. But deep down inside, the family bonds prevailed, as we all strived to live by what we had in common and set aside that which divided us. Now that the killing had stopped, we were all victorious in the fight to preserve the love and affection handed down to us by our forefathers, and which we will have the duty to transmit to our offspring.

Following our family reunion, never even once did anyone argue about—or even raise the question of—the rights and wrongs of the war. That didn't seem to matter much to us anymore. Right and wrong are very important things, of course, the stepping stones of civilization. But civilizations are made of more than just rights and wrongs. Humankind is made not only of mind, but also of heart. Another Vietnamese saying goes, "Resolve it with your heart and mind . . . ." Our ancestors did not say, "mind and heart." Both are important in human affairs but, with the most difficult issues, we try to let the heart speak first. I'm absolutely convinced that human progress has been, can be, and will be achieved from the heart much more than the mind. Of course, the heart can't ignore the mind's warnings, but it is rather the mind that serves the heart and not the other way around.

Hope, which is very personal and emotional, at first in terms of purpose and meaning, must then secure for itself a rational basis and logical process of reasoning. In fact, the real issue and challenge here is not a conflict between the heart and the mind, but the reconciliation and integration of the heart and the mind in the process of hope.

CODA

Reflections on Hope and Reason

Reason—
is inherent
in the human being's ability to think.
Reason—
is an endowment to mankind
to help us to know
and to understand.
Reason—
has its own rules
of rationality and logic.
Human beings draw on reason
as justification for hope,
as soon as purpose and meaning
emerge into our awareness.

><

Reason,
in context with hope,
comes into play with
and complements it.
Reason,
in concert with meaning,
is instrumental
for reconciliation
between the beautiful and the true,
between good and right.

><

Reason
is activated
to counter emotional states
caused by refusal
to accept detrimental situations,
or the expectation of
better future outcomes.
Reason
is the source of confrontation
between the impossible and the feasible,
between illusions and realities.
Reason in hope
is the battlefield
between the present and the future,
the conflict
between the heart and the mind.
Reason,
in concert with meaning,
is instrumental
in reconciliation
between the beautiful and the true,
between good and right.

><

With the wonderful gift
of hope,
human beings call on Reason
to match and merge
the two basic abilities—
to will and to think—
helping us come to terms
with our own self,
our fellow humans,

and the world around us,
allowing us to find out
what we are and should be.

CHAPTER FIVE

VICTORS AND VANQUISHED: HOPE AND REALITY

Call a spade a spade.
English saying

When Saigon fell, I gave no thought to leaving but stayed because my parents were there and my place was with them. During my last telephone contact with Ambassador Martin on Tuesday, April 29, I tried to pursue again the unfinished conversation I had started with him three days before at the presidential palace about avoiding the "Battle of Saigon." He did not respond to my questions. Instead, he kept on repeating that he would do his best to get me out of Saigon. I thanked him for his concern about my personal safety but again insisted that there should be some way to avoid the expected horrible bloodshed in the streets of Saigon. In the background sound on his end of the line I could hear what sounded like Secretary Kissinger's voice saying something over a loudspeaker. Hastily, Martin said he would call me back and rang off. He was never able to do so. That was the last contact I had with my American allies. This sad memory stayed with me during my subsequent long years of imprisonment. The next time I talked with an American was fourteen years later in Ho

Chi Minh City when a long-time American friend from Paris days, Howard Schomer, came to Viet-Nam for a visit. Ambassador Martin had personified hope for millions in South Vietnam—the many who refused to accept the reality that the U.S. could abandon South Vietnam and the many who expected their powerful American ally to keep them safe from the expected bloodbath if Saigon did fall into the hands of the communist troops.

In the brief telephone conversation with Ambassador Martin, I had hoped for nothing because there was nothing to hope for. I was, however, curious to know what he would do as an individual. I couldn't bring myself to imagine that he would simply run away as others were doing. I didn't care any more that the U.S. government could run away in such a dreadful manner in face of the enemy because such images had become totally abstract in my mind. But I was really concerned for Graham Martin, the person, who had lost a son in the war, and who had sincerely tried with all his might to help South Vietnam. It had occurred to me that he would not be able to bring himself to run and would prefer to sit in his office and wait for the communist troops to come. As I stayed behind, I feared Martin might decide to do the same. Quite a number of foreigners were still in Saigon. The thought of Hanoi taking Graham Martin to the wall was utterly unconceivable and pointless. They hadn't done it with the French General de Castries in 1954 at Dien Bien Phu. But for Martin to stay behind was a bad idea by any point of view and surely would have been vetoed by Kissinger. But after the phone went dead we never got to discuss the matter.

Ambassador Martin was an exceptional gentleman, among the very best ones I had the privilege to know and work with. Others included Ambassadors Averell Harriman, Cyrus Vance, Henry Cabot Lodge, David K. E. Bruce, Ellsworth Bunker, William Sullivan, Philip Habib, Robert Komer, and William Porter. Besides these elder statesmen, there were also many dedicated and brilliant young men including Richard Holbrooke, Robert Miller, John Negroponti, Winston Lord at the Paris peace talks, and John

Condon, David Lambertson, Charles Twining and Tom Weisner among the numerous Americans in Viet-Nam. Most of them went on to become U.S. ambassadors to various countries or occupy cabinet and other high ranking positions in the U.S. government.

I greatly appreciated Martin's concern for my personal safety but it was no longer my order-of-the-day. It was not that I didn't want to think about it but I had come to accept that it was a matter beyond my ability to deal with. I was able to set it aside because other considerations began to emerge in me—the sense or need to share with others a common lot, however detrimental. If there was hope in me at that time, it would have been a vague hope of being together with my loved ones in adversity and in the need to belong with my family, home and the country of my ancestors. With Saigon in communist hands, reality and reason put me in an impossibly detrimental situation, but meaning and purpose began to help me accept my lot. It was not hope, exactly, but the ability to accept an adverse reality. In whatever circumstances, life needs meaning and purpose for hope to reveal and manifest itself.

* * *

My father and mother had shared much meaning and purpose during their 70 years of marriage. They found good and viable reasons to make life worth enduring. They were in many ways very alike intellectually. I don't imagine my father hoping very much—he was mostly a practical man and if he hoped at all it would have been through a computer. He was a fervent adept of the ancestors' cult—it had nothing to do with religion, just traditions and customs and respect for the forefathers. I have come to understand that during half a century of building roads and bridges all over the south of Viet-Nam, mainly in the Mekong Delta, it didn't concern him much under what ruler or regime he did his job. In the end, as long as there was someone to pay for the roads and bridges, he simply built them for the people to use. His constant concern was finding the funds to build his roads and bridges, as many as possible and as quickly as possible.

From the 1930s to the 1960s, my father was widely known in his profession as the most economical of builders; that is to say, with the same amount of funds he was able to build twice to three times more roads and bridges than anyone else. Of course, doing that didn't make him rich but he collected all sorts of medals from all sorts of people: the ancient Kingdom of Annam (if that meant anything), the French regime (*Légion d'Honneur*), and all manner of orders and citations from the Republic of Vietnam. He received those decorations by courier because he never took the time to present himself to accept them. That was my father. To him, the money for his construction works was the people's money and he merely returned it to them in the form of roads and bridges. The endless complaining, nagging, soliciting and waiting for the funds to pass through the hands of bureaucrats and be awarded in the name of some emperor or president, or of freedom or some just cause, or of some sacred war or even some god—all that did not faze him as long as he could pay for his roads and bridges. His formula was that simple.

The unspoken decision by my parents to remain in Saigon in those dramatic days of April 1975 turned out to be the greatest and most cherished lesson of my life. We all stayed in our home because it had been home to five generations of us who had lived and died there, because we were all reunited there, gathered in a time of trial, joined in a sense of togetherness and sharing common purposes. I felt a part of something a bit unreal but worthwhile, part of a family that had provided love and warmth, part of a land that had always been ours. We were all there simply because God had made it for our people to live in. It was not a matter of choice, not something to reject or accept, but given to us like the colors of our skin, eyes and hair. That was probably how my mother felt, how millions of other ordinary women felt.

I wouldn't be surprised if in the simple mind of my beloved mother—who had endured hardship all her life and shared seven decades of our country's fate, from the French colonial period to the American War, who had gone through much more sorrow than joy, spent most of her time in her kitchen battling with the household chores, surrounded by scampering, boisterous children—all these successive and deadly conflicts and family quarrels were nothing more than nuisances that made it difficult to cook properly the kids' daily meals.

My mother seemed to have accepted wars and conflicts as an unavoidable state of affairs to be deplored and endured until the day when all members of the family at large could experience togetherness. With the passage of time, all wars and conflicts would be viewed as regrettable misunderstandings. Living by her side during the last ten years of her life, I came to see that she didn't bother much about wars and their causes. She considered them to be not much worse than other natural calamities like smallpox, cholera, bubonic plague, tornadoes or earthquakes.

The only hope worth having in my mother's way of thinking was for togetherness and love, for giving to, sharing with and caring for one another. That was the meaning and purpose of her life, and she willingly accepted all the sad realities of existence and endured all the hardships, supported by the conviction that her simple idea of hope for togetherness would prevail in the end. The togetherness she was able to give us was the same togetherness she had received from her own mother. What mattered most at these times of great crisis was the togetherness of her small family. She certainly hoped that "brothers" or "sons" would one day come to terms with each other, learn how to live in harmony and without bloodshed, set a better example for the children and share her aspirations for a togetherness that would be much more reality than hope for a reality.

By my parents' side, we all accepted our fate to stay and face the fall of Saigon. This "acceptance" was not resignation resulting from helplessness or a passive state of mind but rather from the sharing of togetherness and belonging in the family. It could be thought of as "joyful acceptance" or even "joyful abandon," but with meaning and purpose in the most adverse of situations. Hope may be characterized by joyful abandon but it cannot be meaningless or purposeless. At the time, I still had a long way to go to find such a hope for myself. The unspoken collective decision to stay did not permit much hope for survival, but fear of death, the anxiety that had lingered in the days preceding Saigon's fall, had subsided considerably.

I cannot say what the others were thinking but my decision to remain, while not plunging me into despair, reminded me of what U.S. Ambassador Philip Habib had said to me in jest one day in Paris during the talks: "You (the South Vietnamese) must have the lemming instinct."

* * *

The April 28 "power transfer" was followed in the evening by a sharp intensification of rocket and mortar shelling by the communists, mainly on Tan Son Nhut airport and its environs, which included the important ARVN general headquarters and high command of the joint chiefs-of-staffs. The civilian population didn't suffer much from these attacks but were certainly frightened by such thundering explosions they had not previously experienced in the three decades of war. The next day, life began to resume its normal patterns for the Saigonese. Nothing unusual happened except for "Big" Minh's repeated radio and TV broadcasts demanding the immediate removal of all American presence from South Vietnam, especially members of the Defense Attaché Office (DAO) at the U.S. Embassy in Saigon.

Many people were still trying to find ways out of the country. With the airport made inoperative by the shelling, huge sums were being offered and spent for any kind of transportation capable of reaching international waters. Besides Saigon officials and army officers, tens of thousands of private employees of foreign enterprises also feared for their lives and joined the mass exodus. The Saigonese who were not afraid to lose their shirts and skins just stayed home, not much interested in or aware of what "Big" Minh and his "Third Force" were up to. They just waited for the communists to come. That's what my family and I did.

People were filled with a mixture of apprehension and curiosity. There was certainly fear as well since all sorts of wild tales and rumors had been circulating all over South Vietnam about what the communist troops would do when they got to town. Some people thought single women would be forced to provide sexual relief to the soldiers. Ladies with painted fingers and toes would have their nails removed by pincers. Men with long, hippie coiffures would be treated to compulsory crew cuts. Infants with protruding navels would get them cut short. The most terrifying specter was that of the expected "blood bath" reserved for ranking officials, army officers, civil servants, war profiteers and cruel capitalists who had been living off the "bones and blood" (Vietnamese saying) of the poor. Those particularly who had incurred "blood debts" from the Vietnamese people and all other wicked individuals would be taken to the wall and executed on the spot.

No one could say what would really become of Saigon and its inhabitants in the following few days. Not only were some citizens of Saigon expecting the worst but many in Paris, Washington and elsewhere were also very concerned about the fate of the South Vietnamese population, for many could still remember the horrible acts of barbarity committed against the big landowners and collaborators with the French colonists in the 1940s at a number of localities in both the North and South when the Viet Minh forces took power for a few months before the French forces returned to Indochina after World War II.

At the Postdam Conference in July 1945, President Truman had accepted the decision to divide Viet-Nam at the sixteenth parallel for the purposes of military operations. By September of that year, the first British and French units arrived in Saigon and the Chinese troops of General Lu Han arrived in Hanoi. The London Agreement of October 1945 between France and the UK gave full rights to France for the governance of Indochina south of the

185-CART

sixteenth parallel. Ho Chi Minh and the Viet Minh forces waged an all out fight against the return of the French troops. It was a period of utter violence in both the north and south of Viet-Nam with untold atrocities. It was also a time when many Vietnamese were traumatized and became deathly afraid of anything from the Viet Minh and Viet Cong, as I remembered it from my own childhood.

So, tension, anguish, fear and all sorts of feelings invaded the Saigonese in those last days of April 1975. The news media and reports supplied by suburban dwellers who were still able to circulate in and out of town quite freely made it increasingly clear that communist troops would be in Saigon by the early hours of Wednesday, April 30. Escape activities reached their climax throughout Tuesday night, with Graham Martin stubbornly remaining in his embassy office and desperately trying to arrange all the helicopter flights possible for his ultimate evacuation efforts for the few remaining Americans and many eagerly awaiting Vietnamese. As dawn was about to break, Martin finally acquiesced. At about five o'clock in the morning, the first North Vietnamese troops crossed the Saigon bridge near the American military "New Port," just a ten-minute automobile drive from the U.S. Embassy. With Graham Martin out of Saigon, Secretary of State Henry Kissinger was relieved to announce at his press conference in Washington that all the Americans had left Viet-Nam. Kissinger was really disturbed when he was informed later that many U.S. marines guards were still at the embassy in Saigon until 7 o'clock in the morning doing their last minute housecleaning chores, including the disposal of sensitive equipment and confidential materials. Luckily, the first North Vietnamese tanks lost their way, as foreign tourists do, in the capital city of South Vietnam and had to ask for directions from ordinary citizens on the street. The first tanks with North Vietnamese superior officers did not enter the presidential palace until 11 o'clock. They found "Big" Minh there waiting.

After more than three decades of bloody conflict, Wednesday, April 30, 1975, marked the dawn of a new and completely different day for the Vietnamese people on both sides of the fighting. The day started bright and sunny. It became more and more evident to the invading forces that the ARVN troops had not taken positions anywhere in the city to resist them. There was no indication that any significant shooting would take place inside the city. The prospect of a bloody "Battle of Saigon" vanished quickly. It became obvious that there was no longer any point for the Vietnamese to go on killing one another, and the Saigonese grew increasingly curious to catch a glimpse of Uncle Ho's "bo doi" in their hometown for the first time in history. So that was how it was when the North Vietnamese troops arrived on that historic morning. They could easily have felt a bit like foreign tourists having a ride in the streets of the city often called the "Pearl of the Orient." In their sophisticated T52 Soviet tanks, they had a much better view than any American stretch limousine would provide. In terms of quality/price ratio, it was even better than a package deal for a tour of Las Vegas.

Everything seemed quiet that April 30, 1975. But to avoid posing a deadly danger to my family by my compromising presence at home, I quietly sneaked out of my parents' house after the family lunch and wandered the streets alone. Saigon was still filled with cars, motorcycles, pedicabs and all kinds of people going about as the enemy took up positions at many important downtown crossroads. I came across some of them near the Notre Dame Cathedral and the post office. They were standing around their tanks looking a bit bewildered, not knowing really what to do with themselves. Most of them seemed underfed, pale and skinny, in their late teens, obviously thirsty and hungry after two months on the road at full speed, on their historic march from the central part of Viet-Nam down to Saigon.

So, these were our brother-enemies who had been in the field, not at all like those at the Paris peace talks in their nice suits and ties, nor anything remotely akin to my familiar communist relatives.

I couldn't bring myself to accept these youngsters as my brother-enemies. They weren't much older than most of the kids running and playing in the streets of Saigon. Looking at Hanoi's occupying force—those North Vietnamese teenagers—and thinking of our own young warriors in the ARVN, I went numb for a long stretch of minutes. I was at a complete loss to understand or justify how we, their elders on both sides, had been capable of demanding that such kids kill one another over so many long years. In those minutes there was nothing in my mind in the name of right and wrong, freedom, independence, democracy, economic progress, social justice, self-defense or even God Almighty that could justify the killing by and between these Vietnamese kids.

As I was struggling with these conflicting thoughts, the whole world and sky seemed to crash down around me. I experienced some sort of blackout with blinding colors in front of my eyes. I became dizzy and tried to keep my balance, thinking that there were lots of people around and I shouldn't pass out on the ground there. I felt that life was continuing to go on but there was suddenly a complete void in me. Notions of morality, civilization and humanity incoherently invaded my mind, and I tried to sort out the logic of things but grasped only the feeling that my life had been a farce, a meaningless dream that could not possibly have been reality. Words, concepts, ideas didn't fit where they used to. At that moment nothing made sense any more and I told myself that the best thing that could happen to me would be to receive right away a judgement from God for my part in such horror and insanity among men.

Eventually, regaining a sense of events around me, I looked intensely at those kids once more, trying to convince myself again that they were my enemies, would readily shoot and kill me, but such thoughts didn't have any effect on me one way or another. A few of them glanced my way but they made no move to approach me. Watching those youths, now in our midst in Saigon, concepts of defeat or victory became sheer nonsense to me. Even in self-defense, I would never be able to fire back at them now. I was the vanquished but, if fate and destiny had decided otherwise, I would not have been able to find any sense of victory over these kids. Why hadn't I been able to see and feel this before?

That was how and when I came to realize that the war ended in neither victory nor defeat for the Vietnamese brother-enemies. The blood shed on our soil was the same color, whether communist or not, in the eyes of our ancestors and humanity as a whole. I realized then that no human being could rejoice over the death of another, even that of his enemy. In my heart and mind, as in the minds and hearts of many Vietnamese on that Wednesday, I felt deep relief that the war was over. It didn't matter much to me anymore which side had won or lost. I felt no shame for being on the losing side but was filled with a profound sadness thinking of the grief and sorrow suffered by both victors and vanquished alike in the long and bloody fratricidal conflict.

I then went to the nearby Central Post Office to make a phone call to assure my family I was all right. I was taking a stroll downtown, I told them, to have a look at the situation. When I reached home about an hour later, the dreadful mental shock of the new realities had almost vanished and drowned in the old realities with all the anguish and deep concern for the safety of my parents and other relatives, the uncertainty of the future and also the clear possibility of retaliation of some sort by the communist authorities in the coming days. In spite of everything, life would have to go on one way or another.

* * *

History was made when the North Vietnamese tanks entered the South Vietnamese "Independence Palace" that Wednesday morning. There were exciting and powerful hopes in the minds and hearts of the North Vietnamese officers who emerged from the tanks. They didn't bother to take the elevators but used the stairs to get to the upper floors. They found "President" Duong Van "Big" Minh and all his cabinet ministers solemnly standing in the imposing reception hall as if gathered there for a family snapshot to serve as a memento of the historic event. “Big” Minh and his “Third Force” were still filled with hopes for an amicable and productive encounter with the brother-enemies. “Big” Minh officially greeted the North Vietnamese officers by saying that he and his government had been waiting for their arrival to hand over power.

In the next few moments, however, it finally became clear to them the last long-held hopes of Saigon’s politicians had ended forever. “Big” Minh was quite taken aback by the North Vietnamese officers’ response. They told him that he and his so-called government had no power of any kind to hand over and that the only thing he was able and required to do at once was declare official and unconditional surrender. He was to order the ARVN troops to lay down their arms immediately. He was instructed to make a cassette recording of his declaration of surrender, which would be broadcast over the national radio and television networks to inform the nation of Saigon’s unconditional surrender. That was it, short and simple. There was no surrender signing ceremony, no surrender document of any kind.

It had been, of course, totally irrelevant for “Big” Minh and his associates to formally greet the North Vietnamese officers and proclaim the Saigon government’s unconditional surrender less than forty-eight hours after “Big” Minh had assumed “power.” “Big” Minh was in no way empowered constitutionally or legally to represent the Republic of Vietnam. While it had been a state recognized by and having diplomatic relations with almost all the non-communist governments in the world, the Republic of Vietnam’s “Independence Palace,” seat and symbol of its government, was already a desert island. It had been deserted by its most powerful ally. Was it really necessary then for “Big” Minh and his cabinet ministers to attend and proclaim unconditional surrender in the name of a Saigon regime whose existence had lasted less than forty-eight hours? If “Big” Minh had decided to stay home that day, it would have made not a particle of difference in the course of the communist occupation of Sàigon. It was time for the Vietnamese people, communist or not, to turn an important and very painful page of their history.

In the days immediately following the fall of Saigon, we gathered twice a day for formal family meals which generated much less conversation than they had in the past. There was an overriding question that everyone waited for someone to raise. We, the children, knew what it was and let it lie there unsaid and unresolved because it wasn't our place to do so. We waited several days but never was there a hint or single mention by my parents of doing anything special or fleeing the country. The rest of us accepted and respected the parents' unspoken decision. We were together and we stayed together. No debate needed. No pros and cons discussed. No reason given. Just be together in our home where we all belonged. If we needed a reason, we had to invent one to suit ourselves. That was probably what each of us did, and we settled on the choice to be together there in our home in the days and weeks after April 30, 1975, a date to be known henceforth as "Liberation Day of the South of Viet-Nam," and made a school holiday. Togetherness was really a good reason for me to be home that day.

* * *

The fall of Saigon didn't cause much upheaval in the life of the population. For most people, there were no violent changes or disruptions in daily activities. At first, there were some crowds in the streets, out to watch and greet the invading tanks. But most Saigonese were more circumspect and preferred remaining in their homes to wait and see how things would turn out. There were reports of certain actions and isolated cases of summary executions in some remote provinces due to uncontrollable passions and personal revenge. In Saigon, ranking civilian officials of the former government were left alone but ARVN superior officers were quickly rounded up and detained at various locations. I was able to circulate freely. No one came to look for me or ask questions. I was with my dear ones in our home. Most people felt more or less reassured since the much discussed, feared and expected "blood bath" had not come to pass. The overwhelming number of communist officials treated the public courteously. The communist troops were shy and reticent, hesitant to enjoy Saigon's opulent remnants of LBJ's "guns and butter" policy. Life quickly resumed its normalcy. Water and electricity worked without even the slightest disruption.

In such conditions, I felt neither despair nor much fear but my state of mind was very clearly characterized by a profound sense of helplessness and hopelessness. There was, nevertheless, an underlying hope to remain alive, be with my family and retain the right to participate in the life of the Vietnamese nation and people. It was strange, almost unreal. Things didn't quite jibe with what I had heard and learned about wars. A very bloody, long and cruel war had just ended but life seemed to continue as if nothing really exceptional had happened.

It was nothing like the fall of Phnom Penh two weeks earlier on April 17. Shortly before that dramatic event, I had lunched in Paris with a long-time good friend, the younger brother—nicknamed "Little Lon Non"—of Cambodia's President Lon Nol. There were just the two of us and he said to me: "Phong, I am not a communist but have never been anti-communist. I always hope that all the Cambodians can live peacefully together. The situation is really bad now at home. The Americans have sent me into exile in France but I must go home now. I will wait for the Khmer Rouges to come in." He went home and waited. His brother, the President, had left the country. I was still in Paris when I was told of what had happened to him. "Little Lon Non" was at the presidential palace in Phnom Penh when the Khmer Rouges arrived. Later in the day, people saw him hanging by the feet in front of the Palace with his bowels dripping out from his open belly. That was only the beginning of a human catastrophe and tragedy, the insane ideological cleansing and genocidal killing of millions of innocent people in Cambodia.

In the days following the arrival of the North Vietnamese troops in the city, the overwhelming majority of Saigonese went on with business as usual. Nobody asked anybody whether they were a victor or a vanquished. I couldn't recall anything in the history books that described such an end to a terrible war. Why were there no scenes of defeated soldiers throwing down their weapons, raising hands over heads in traditional gestures of surrender, being rounded or lined up in captivity? Why were there no scenes of mass arrests, of people being dragged before the firing squads or hanged from trees? Instead, there was something of a celebratory atmosphere, like a family reunion being experienced by everyone, with no distinction between former brother-enemies. From such a state are illusions and disillusions, and myths and realities, constructed and established.

My hopelessness and helplessness evolved as the days went by. The hopelessness retreated gradually in the face of realities but the helplessness remained. However, there were at least three possible hopes emerging that began to acquire some momentum. The foremost was for the survival of my family and myself. This had seemed to be realized for the time being, as it had for most of the population of Saigon. There was practically no fighting in town, no strong military action in evidence, no harsh reprisals expected against members of the former regime. That was my impression at that time.

The hope for my family's togetherness seemed distinctly plausible since no coercion of any kind had been exercised so far against the former ranking officials and no demands on the general public had been decreed by the new authorities. And the hope for my family to be permitted to remain in our home and remain a part of the Vietnamese nation appeared to be possible as well. These three hopes concerned the well-being of my family as a whole. But my parents and other members of the family were clearly worried about my particular personal safety. It was obvious that eventually, sooner or later, I would have to account to the new authorities for my past involvement with the Saigon regime.

Hope must have purpose and be meaningful to the person concerned, and hope must not be irrational and unrealistic. But hope is also a world itself filled with illusions and disillusions, a mixture of the true and the false, a constant quest for the good and the right, and an endless challenge of the self.

CODA

Reflections on Hope and Reality

Hope,
latent and inert,
is inherent in life
but requires a meaningful,
reasonable and realistic purpose
to prevail.
Hope—
rejects unacceptable reality
and seeks another reality
to avoid the worst
and obtain the better.

><

Hope,
by nature,
projects into the future.
Hope's degree
of realism and feasibility
situates it
on the spectrum of viability
ranging from mathematical certainty
(scientific reality)

to belief and faith
(mystical, speculative knowledge).
Therefore,
to become operational,
each hope must search for its place
within the wide and varied range
between scientific certainty
and the remote reality
of speculative knowledge.
Thus,
hope cannot provide certainty.
But it can operate
in the realm of realities,
first, seeking survival,
then giving reason,
meaning and purpose to life's function
in the pertinent environment.

><

Hope—
is able to entertain
all kinds of reasons and purposes.
The fundamental act of being
instinctively seeks survival,
then requires reason and reality
for the better.
Life thrives
on reason and reality,
and nurtures the viability of hope
with purpose and meaning.

><

Hope—
is intrinsically incapable of certainty,
but it must comply with reality
or a semblance of reality.
Our ability to recognize reality
is determined by knowledge.
Hope—
is related to reality and knowledge.
Hope—
supersedes knowledge
when reality supersedes knowledge.
Hope—
is inversely proportional
to reality and knowledge
in its intensity.
The less knowledge there is,
the less reality there is.
The less reality there is
the more hope is needed.

><

The more intense hope becomes,
the more abstract or mystical
it tends to be become,
reaching toward belief and faith.
Practical hope
is nearer to reality
than to belief or faith.

><

Hope—
requires a rational or realistic basis
to prevail.

Hope—
has its own *Raison d'être*
for each particular instance
and is capable of generating
its own momentum.
Hope—
is different from knowledge
by the fact
that it cannot provide certainty
but aspires to bear
an acceptable semblance of reality.

><

Unlike knowledge,
Hope does not explain
the how of its operational modes,
but does manifest the why
of cause/effect relationships.
Hope—
cannot be sustained
if it defies reason
and runs counter
to the universally established
order of things.

><

Hope—
may try to defy logic
but cannot survive long
against the prevailing laws of nature.
Many humans hope for
and believe in
resurrection after death,

accepting that it will not be
in current physical life forms
of existence.
Here hope and faith connect.

><

Hope—
requires at least an infinitesimal element
of reality
to ignite, to gain momentum,
to create its forces,
to generate its evolution,
to search for its own realities
and avoid ending in fanciful speculation
and self deceit.

CHAPTER SIX
CIVILIZATIONS: ILLUSIONS AND DISILLUSIONS OF HOPE

Le bonheur des uns fait le malheur des autres.
The happiness of some is the misfortune of others.
French saying

My mental affliction at the fall of Saigon was put to rest, as many of my young life's torments had been, by my beloved mother. It was shortly after the family dinner, two days after the communist troops had taken over South Vietnam. I wanted to be near my mother, so I took a tiny stool and sat on the veranda at the kitchen door, where I could see and hear her as she was washing the dishes and tidying up after the meal. I sat in silence for about an hour while she completed her customary tasks. Finally, she approached me from behind and said, "Why are you sitting there by yourself? Go and play with the others."

I had heard that incantation many times in my youth and could only reply, "I really don't have the heart for it, Mother."

"So you're brooding again," she said.

"I can't help it, Mother."

She then came around to look me in the eyes and asked, "All the Americans have gone, haven't they?" Almost before I could answer in the affirmative, she had a follow-up question: "The war is over for good now, is it not? What are you brooding about then?"

I tried in vain to find a meaningful reply. And then, reflexively, I said, "I love you so, Mother."

She stroked my hair, the way she used to when I had lost a toy or scraped a knee.

"Me too," she said simply and quickly.

Then she went to lay the table for the family breakfast.

I sat there on the veranda until very late. My family was careful not to disturb me, although a few kids did pop their heads in furtively one or twice to have a peep at me. That evening, thanks to my mother, I stopped the useless and endless brooding and ruminating, and was able to achieve some degree of closure concerning past events. As my mother had already prepared for the family breakfast, I had to be able to prepare in advance for what lay ahead for me and my family rather than continue to be tormented by the epic issues of humanity, ideology, liberty, freedom, democracy, sovereignty, and the good and just cause.

I realized that in the ten years from 1965 to 1975, I had not spent a whole week by my mother's side or remembered to tell her I loved her, not even on the phone. The brief conversation prompted me to realize that I had been attending the family meals without actually sharing them, nor had I contributed very much to a sense of togetherness. It then became clear to me that I had to sort things out quickly for myself and be able to turn the page completely, once and for all. I had to find peace with myself very rapidly, but not by ignoring facts, denying illusions and disillusions, or choosing to spend the rest of my life in self-deception, bitterness, and rancor. I knew I must end the useless "what ifs." There on the veranda of my mother's kitchen, I descended into the inferno of my consciousness to come up with answers fair and objective enough for me to accept and live with. I felt both excitement and anguish over what I was about to do, wasn't sure how to begin, and almost abandoned the whole idea when I realized the magnitude and complexity of the task before me.

My mother reappeared and urged me to go to the living room. I told her I was all right and preferred to remain there for a while. Always thrifty, she switched off the light in the kitchen but kept one on in the dining room to provide a soft luminosity where I was sitting. There I was, by myself, staring into the nocturnal aspect of a bare, gray wall. I saw nothing with my eyes, but my mind was a kaleidoscope. Slowly I was able to pluck some ideas from among the distressing ones. It felt like my head was in *un panier de crabes* (a basket of crabs), and I wasn't quite sure what it was doing there. Yet I wasn't discouraged, nor did I feel despair. It was going to be a terrible ordeal, but I had the notion something good could come of it, something necessary. One might say I felt a glimmer of hope. It was the expectation of an end to my turmoil and indecision. I no longer had the impression of being crushed or a sense of depression, and I was prepared to do whatever was required to permit myself to find inner peace.

First, I had to calm down. Yes, the fall of Saigon had shocked and traumatized me, partially paralyzing my thought processes. I had taken it all very personally. I now had to ignore emotions and distill the passions of the war years. Forget recriminations and self-justifications and reduce the realities to simple equations that would permit me to understand, accept, and confront the facts, adverse or otherwise. Since my student days, I had felt that history had always consisted of myths and realities, particularly over the last seven thousand years in great human civilizations from the Nile to the Yangtze. Myths had sometimes become realities over the millennia and would continue to do so for many thousands of years to come. Saigon's fall had come just forty-eight hours before.

My mother's words resounded in my brain: "The war is over for good now, is it not?"

After nearly one hundred and fifty years, the House of Viet-Nam was reunited.

Sitting on that veranda, I began the long journey into that dark night with only *le moi méprisable* (the despicable me).

185-CART

An ironic thought occurred to me. I realized that being vanquished afforded a better opportunity for objective and meaningful retrospection than being victorious did. ("There must be a masochistic thread in me," I thought.) It wasn't often—or was it?—that a person could both be part of losing a big war and experience a transfiguring moment within the space of forty-eight hours. So it wasn't with a completely heavy heart that I started to sort things out that evening. There had been an unconditional surrender, but no one seemed to have a clear idea of who the vanquished were or care about such fine distinctions. Yes, the Republic of Vietnam had suffered defeat, but I doubted then that many in our country bothered to think of it as a defeat for the United States of America. It could easily have been interpreted as a victory for all the Vietnamese people if only because what my mother said was true. With apologies to Sir Winston Churchill, "Never before in the history of mankind had so many suffered so much for so long." For at least that night, I was able to turn the pages from a thick Vietnamese "book of war" and release myself from its tales of horror.

Victory had manifested itself and it would turn out to be for the entire Vietnamese nation. Everybody had reason to be happy that the war had come to an end for good. It was a very difficult reality to accept, but a necessary one. Many people in the world, particularly the United States of America, and the Vietnamese in both North and South Vietnam, would always remember the fall of Saigon, with the images of the North Vietnamese tanks crushing the main gate of the Saigon presidential palace. The matter of who had been the presidents of the Republic of Vietnam was totally immaterial and immediately forgotten. The names of Ngo Dinh Diem and Nguyen Van Thieu might faintly be remembered in the years to come, but those of Tran Van Huong and Duong Van "Big" Minh would be just *illustres inconnus* (illustrious unknowns), as the French would usually say.

Actually, a surrender by one Vietnamese to another on April 30, 1975, was totally unnecessary. As for the United States,

Ambassador Graham Martin might as well have remained in his embassy office to welcome the North Vietnamese officers in Saigon, without any need to acknowledge in any way any kind of defeat or victory by anybody. That would have saved a lot of time for a quick resumption of Viet-Nam-U.S.A. cooperation and good relations later on.

Still sitting on my mother's kitchen porch, I ruminated upon whatever happened to enter my mind, and it soon became clear to me that my mental activities were utterly nonsensical, a succession of faces and places, incoherent events devoid of any meaning, usefulness or value, reason clashing against reason, reasons falling apart against realities, and realities smashing ideas, ideals, and ideologies. There were efforts on my part to cling to the few remnants of my intellect that continued to claim the validity of their existence and truthfulness but were scattered and more or less buried in the big heap of distorted scraps and broken glass called the facts of life.

Submerged in distressing and painful thoughts, I tried to grasp at life buoys for the sake of thinking straight. There was a desperate urge and need in me to sustain or salvage my ability to believe again in myself, to find something I could continue to trust and look forward to. Ethical values and ideals? Human dignity and self respect? Family, friends, country, and a meaningful existence? I had an undeniable need to convince myself that everything was not completely lost; that there must still be things that were undamaged and valid. Was this a sense of hope? It was not hope with any specific aim, but a kind of wish or aspiration that life would go on, that it was not the total end of my existence, that tomorrow would surely come, that things would turn out better.

It was what my mother had said to me that in the end helped me acquire a sense of peace of mind and come to terms with myself. My combat and dilemma that evening on my mother's kitchen veranda was not the fight between the lie and the truth, but had to do with the collapse of ideas against realities. It was a fight between conflicting truths and irreconcilable realities. I could not repress a silly smile to myself, remembering an odd thought from my student days that "some men are more equal than others." Yes, and some truths are truer than others. Standing up and going to switch off the light in the dining room, I felt much better and really relaxed for the first time in many days, or weeks, or months, or even years of personal mental strife.

* * *

After the fall of Saigon, the city was put under the military administration of Lt. General Tran Van Tra, the commanding officer of the NLF forces. He decreed that all officials of the former Saigon regime above the level of service chief (just under a department director), and all armed forces officers above second lieutenant had to report for a thirty-day reeducation period from May to June 1975. All other civilian and military members of the Saigon administration would be required to undergo only seven days of reeducation at their local places of residence.

At last we knew what was in store for us. There would be some degree of reprisal and punishment. Thirty days was a small price to pay, whether it was called reeducation, rehabilitation, incarceration, or even imprisonment. Many ranking Saigon officials and officers would have gladly accepted even three hundred days. I was prepared to suffer much harsher treatment, short of life imprisonment, or a death sentence. I had thought that between five and ten years in prison would be bearable, but twenty years was not to be unexpected. My greatest concern was not for myself, but for the safety and well being of my parents and family members.

Most of the former officials and officers approached the reeducation period with high hopes and in good spirits. Many felt the way I did, relieved of torments and apprehension. Thousands of us began reporting to designated points, mostly primary and secondary schools, in loud and lively crowds, being seen off by dozens of family members. Many came equipped with food and drink, as if for an outing to Coney Island or Battersea Fun Fair.

There were even comic moments. I had trouble getting accepted for the honor of learning the error of my ways. My official title was translated as "Minister of State." The Vietnamese honorific did not include the word for "minister," but employed an archaic phrase from the Imperial Courts of Viet-Nam, "Mandarin for State Affairs." The poor man checking the rolls was at a loss of what to do because my title didn't appear on his list of positions qualifying for admittance. He became really perturbed when I insisted that my position amply qualified me. He remained unconvinced.

People impatiently queuing behind me joined the discussion. "Mr. Phong fully qualifies to get in," they said. The poor man looked around in confusion, seeking confirmation, "You are sure, aren't you?" he asked nervously.

"Sure, sure," they all shouted.

He was still skeptical. He asked me, "So, you are superior to a Chief of Service, aren't you? Otherwise I will be reprimanded."

"Sure, sure," I replied. "I am superior to a Chief of Service."

Finally I was granted the privilege of admission and sent to what had been a girl's school dormitory located near the Saigon zoo.

It might be said I had some sort of hope at this time, inspired by the victors' clemency in allowing me to pay such a light price and still be able to share with my family and country a common lot.

The following day, army trucks arrived to take my group at the girl's school to the orphanage of Long Thanh, about thirty kilometers outside Saigon. There were similar internment locations all over South Vietnam, accommodating more than two hundred thousand former civilian officials and military officers. The orphanage occupied a large, flat, treeless piece of land dotted by a dozen simple brick edifices with aluminum-sheeted roofs and tiled floors. I estimated there were more than three thousand of us secluded there. Men and women were separated, but in daylight hours we were free to mingle in the compound. Life organized itself quickly. Two daily meals were provided, but there was also a

185-CART

canteen for those who wished to buy extra food, drinks, and other articles of daily use.

I was housed in a large, empty building with a group of about two hundred men. I recognized a few former cabinet ministers, among them a childhood friend who had been Minister of Public Works, along with the Minister of Finance whom I had known earlier during my school days in France, the Welfare Minister, the Minister of Education, the Vice-Minister of Culture and the Vice-Minister of Information. The rest were lower-ranking officials of the Saigon administration.

We were to sleep on the tiled floor. I was able to find a relatively quiet corner for my small bag and myself. I discovered that my immediate neighbors were the Vice-Ministers of Commerce and of Information, a national assembly deputy, and an elderly supreme court judge. It was the first time I had made their acquaintance. Of the three thousand inmates, I was able to identify fewer than twenty people that I had met before, although everybody seemed to know who I was and all were very friendly to me. It was a lively atmosphere, almost festive, with very little sadness. People were busy from early morning until late at night, visiting one another, gathering in small groups, chatting endlessly. I didn't feel like talking much and sat apart by myself most of the time. People soon came to realize that I wanted to be alone and were careful not to disturb me, except to say hello or smile at me when passing by.

At first, life went on uneventfully and the families soon discovered our whereabouts. Relatives began to flock at the gates in an attempt to see and communicate with inmates—without much success—but they were able to pass food and drinks, clothing and money into the camp. None of my relatives came because, before reporting for reeducation, I had asked them not to. Simply wait for me to return, I had urged. I was, however, able to receive a couple of letters and some money and to send verbal messages home, acknowledging the money and reassuring my parents that I was all right.

The camp was full of people who had successfully passed the entrance exam for reeducation. Besides civil servants and the military, there were also many civilians, as well as private individuals from the so-called political parties. One such party member indirectly created quite a stir one day, a noisy incident that occurred in the women's quarters. I didn't witness the excitement but heard a lot about it. News spread throughout the camp that a hysterical woman in her early twenties had been crying, screaming, and rolling on the floor, begging Buddha and all the gods of the earth to help her go home! It turned out that the poor, almost illiterate girl was the maid of a wealthy lady, who—just for fame and the hell of it—had served as a member of the central committee of one of the microscopic Saigonese political parties. The lady had dutifully reported and easily qualified for reeducation, having had such an exalted party title. To ensure that she wouldn't want for too much in the way of creature comforts, the lady politician had brought her maid along to see to her laundry and meals. To her misfortune, the maid had been declared by the mistress to be a "secretary" so she could qualify to accompany her mistress. It was not made clear that the girl was supposed to be the lady's private secretary. She was admitted under the title, "bi thu," rather than "thu ky," the term for private secretary. In common political parlance, the term "bi thu" described the important post of "secretary of the party." The mistress had managed to get herself out on bail after a few days of internment, but she was apparently reluctant to push her luck by asking that her maid be released with her. She quickly left the camp without bothering to say a word to her maid, who simply couldn't believe her mistress had gone home without her.

In addition to being beside herself with hysteria, the girl didn't know how to occupy herself without clothes to wash or meals to prepare. Everyone tried to calm and comfort her, telling her that her mistress would soon come to the rescue. Before that happened, the girl's doldrums were partially relieved when she was admitted to the kitchen to help cook the inmates' meals. She was only too happy to find work to do, to be useful without having to dote on a mistress. I never learned what happened to her later.

Shortly after that incident, I went out by myself one night to sit on the edge of the long veranda at the far end of the building where I was housed. Looking out into the dark night of the Long Thanh countryside, I pictured myself sitting on the veranda of my mother's kitchen. I remembered that I had promised myself not to dwell on the past, but the maid's story inspired in me another round of painstaking introspection. How had I come to be there in the Long Thanh orphanage? While my story was more complicated than that pitiful girl's, we both needed answers to the same questions. Most of us inmates were thinking along similar lines. We all shared a common lot and had to answer to the new authorities for our past activities. While we had come from different walks of life, we still found ourselves at the same rendezvous with destiny. But I imagined each of us felt we were different from the rest. We were ready to share the same adverse fortune but couldn't find a common purpose, except perhaps to go home after thirty days and be reunited with our families.

Except for those who had committed crimes or atrocities, the large majority of the inmates, myself included, had concluded we weren't to be taken to the wall and executed. That gave us hope for survival but not much for anything else. I did, however, nurture a strong hope for the well-being of my old parents and other family members. It was an active hope, mainly because we all had been able to learn that life remained fairly normal in Saigon. The maid's story prompted renewed ruminations on my part. My mind began racing again, and I tried to calm down by reminding myself that everything would boil down to the eternal questions of "where did I come from, what am I doing here, and where do I go from here?"

That was the evening the stars began to be my perennial prison-life companions. Watching them flash in the heavens, I felt humble, as we are wont to do when impressed by the immensity of the universe. I was equally bewildered by humanity's boundless capacity for grief and suffering. The smallest and the largest of us have many things in common and are exactly the same in many ways, as Lao-tzu (born circa 604 B.C.) had taught. Thus, I could cling to the whimsical hope that my loved ones at home might be looking at the same stars at that very moment. It was a comforting and helpful thought.

Things seemed to return to their proper perspective. "Render unto Caesar that which is Caesar's . . . ." That was what more than three thousand people from all walks of life were rendezvoused for that night and many other nights at the Long Thanh orphanage.

* * *

I had sprung from modest origins on both sides of the family. On my maternal side, we knew very little of our ancestors. My mother knew nothing at all about her great-grandparents. Her father had only a younger brother, who died unmarried and childless. Her grandfather had fought against the French, was captured and imprisoned for life at the dreadful Poulo Condor penitentiary on Con Dao Island, and died there. (In 1966, at the request of my mother, I went there to find out what had happened to his remains and was told by the prison director that, according to the old records, my ancestor had simply been thrown into one of the common mass graves by the beach.)

It was a sad story, this tale of the only-accounted-for ancestor, an unknown soldier of the early Vietnamese resistance against French colonialism in the 1880s. This martyred freedom fighter of Viet-Nam could not possibly have imagined, and was destined to never know, that his son, my mother's father, would grow up and became a village chief under French rule. My maternal grandfather had no direct contact with any officials and had no idea that in his everyday activities and duties of administrating his native village, he was in the service of mother country France, not his fellow Vietnamese. The French colonials were really clever in maintaining intact the council of notables at the grassroots village and hamlet levels . . . . myths and realities with illusions and disillusions.

On the paternal side, as far as we could determine, the only known ancestors were my father's great grandparents. There were only five known generations down to me. My great great grandparents were buried in my father's native village of Giong Trom about one hundred fifty years ago, and the inscriptions on the tombstones of their graves are now so eroded by time and water that no one can decipher their names anymore. The very old folks in the village talked of having heard about them and told us that our ancestors had been dirt-poor farmhands working in the paddy fields for a small landowner. They were known to have had exceptional physical strength.

The relationship between masters and servants, including farmhands, at that time was not much different from views and practices of slavery elsewhere in the world. Our ancestors were good workers and received good treatment from their master. Unlike large and wealthy landowners, most of the small ones fully shared the difficult life of their farmhands. That characteristic of Vietnamese society had persisted for centuries and continued after the arrival of the French colonials in the mid-1880s. Our ancestors had been given to each other as husband and wife by their master, and by the end of their life were rewarded a tiny piece of land of their own to live on with their three sons. The youngest one died when he was only fifteen. The eldest sired only one girl, so his branch of the family was absorbed elsewhere through the marriage of his daughter, according to Vietnamese traditions and customs. Their second son, my father's great-grandfather had nine children, my father's grandfather being the eldest son and main branch of the extended family. This familial position was transmitted to my father and included the sacred duty of safekeeping the ancestors' altar and cult and maintaining the family's burial grounds. That was also the reason my father remained in the south when all my uncles went north in the 1940s to join the Viet-Minh forces fighting against French rule.

My father remained with his old parents in their peasant family, working on the small plot of rice fields that had grown a bit bigger than the original one from the ancestors. He proved himself to be a good student at the village and district schools, so he went on to the provincial school and was good enough to win a scholarship to complete his junior high school at the renowned college of My Tho in the neighboring province. The tenth grade was usually the maximum education permitted Vietnamese under French colonial rule but, again, my father was good enough to earn the exceptional opportunity to attend the exclusive French Lycée Chasseloup Laubat in Saigon and complete his secondary education among the French boys.

That was how he was able to go to Hanoi for further education and pass the examinations for the position of *agent technique* (technical agent). Although tuition and board were paid for by the French administration, my father's miscellaneous expenses during these long years of study regularly depleted about half the annual income brought by the rice crops his family harvested in his native village. His old parents were proudly willing to bear whatever sacrifices necessary for their son to have an education, the likes of which no one else in the family or even the whole village could have dreamed of. It was quite an accomplishment for a poor little peasant boy.

Thus was my father trained by the French colonial system to become a civil servant performing public service in the field of public works. He remained a public servant for forty-seven continuous years, disregarding rulers and political regimes. In the last few years of his professional career, he reached the top positions in the public works administration. He took retirement at the end of 1962 when he was about sixty-five years old, a few months before the overthrow and assassination of President Diem. With his experience in construction, he could have gone private and become wealthy. But he did not. He remained for most of his professional life a mid-level civil servant drawing a relatively low government salary. Our family was not rich, but we were able to live a comfortable middle-class way of life, not socializing very much, keeping mostly to ourselves.

It was clear that education was a high priority. My father took after his own parents in that regard and was eager to do whatever possible for my brother and me to have an education. That was probably the reason why, soon after the end of World War II, he sent my brother and me to France in 1948 for our schooling. I was in my early teens when I arrived at the Lycée Michelet, near the Porte de Versailles in Paris, for my secondary education. Then, for reasons never known to me, my father sent us to London in 1952, when I was just over sixteen with a very poor knowledge of the English language, except for the "Anglais Vivant" dispensed in those days in the French schools.

My father had a much harder time than his parents in educating his children. Our studies abroad consumed not just half of the family's annual income, but almost all my father's resources. My sister's marriage to a prominent physician made it possible for them to take care of the house and the family needs. I wondered a few times in London whether I was just wasting time and my family's money, because I didn't really know what to do with myself. My brother went home after a three-year stay in England to join Saigon's national carrier, Air Vietnam, at the end of 1955. By 1956, I had improved my English at the French Institute in the South Kensington area of London and completed my last year in the study of commerce. I was barely twenty years old, and I decided I wanted to go to Oxford, which I had visited many times with friends. I was totally infatuated with the ancient city and thought it a wonderful place to live.

I went up to Oxford for the Michaelmas Term in 1956. The only way I could gain admission and obtain the necessary stay-permit from the Home Office was to enroll immediately in a two-year course in economics and political science (having passed the examinations in 1958). The reading involved in these studies was to occupy most of my time, but I was also very much attracted by the multitude of other activities there. Those wonderful Oxford years were full of great excitement and joy. I was eager to discover and learn, fascinated by the presence of people from so many different nationalities. Those wonderful Oxford years were a time in which I established enduring friendships. I was, however, always conscious that the luxuries of these years was a great financial burden to my family at home.

* * *

Sitting on that veranda at the Long Thanh orphanage looking at the stars, I reminisced about seeing the same celestial bodies twenty years before in the skies over Oxford. Names and faces came back to me. Many of them, after returning to their native lands, became very effective leaders in various fields. Only a few weeks before I returned to Saigon from Paris, I'd had the opportunity to reunite with two very close English classmates with whom I had shared rooms and the tribulations of examination-time in 1958. There was Tom Pendry, who had a habit of waking us up doing Frank Sinatra imitations. He served as a Labor member of Parliament for twenty years. Then there was John Mansley, who joined the OECD (Organization for Economic Cooperation and Development) in Paris after Oxford and was still there after twenty years, occupied with preparations of the annual G7 summit meetings.

Vivid memories of my Oxford days kept on flashing back into my mind, and I thought to myself that news of Saigon's fall would have caused concern for my welfare among those friends and other classmates scattered over Europe, the Americas, Africa, Japan, India, the Philippines, Hong Kong, Singapore, Thailand, Australia, and other far-flung locales. It was this cosmopolitan and multicultural flavor that had so fascinated me at Oxford, and had instilled in me a great interest in meeting people of different cultures and civilizations. It was one of the reasons I spent four years in that wonderful old seat of learning. Thanks to my very old tutor, Mr. J. R. Kirwan, M.A. (Oxon), I had pursued a very special program of exciting research and study in the field of international economics and relations.

185-CART

During those years, the great debate was raging between opponents of the European Common Market and of the Free Trade Area. I was deeply drawn into that emerging trend of regional regrouping of nations, believing it to be the obvious and most logical future for the European continent and others. I was convinced that people all over the world would find ways to coexist in harmony and enjoy economic progress and peace, not by arguing the rights and wrongs of things, not by violence and endless debates, but by joining forces and making the best use of the available resources of each and every nation. It was, of course, a bit of naive idealism of a twenty-two-year-old, convinced that, in the final analysis, the key to combating hunger, disease, and poverty would be found in the free market economy and in the prudent management of economic development.

How filled I was with hopes for humanity's peace and well-being. How could I have known the enormous difference between simple ideals and life's sad realities? But I was very fortunate, thanks again to my old tutor, to have had an interesting program of studies during those four years, learning many exciting things from exceptional teachers. I was greatly impressed, influenced, and particularly marked by the thoughts and guidance of George D. H. Cole, Roy F. Harrod, J. E. Meade, E. A. G. Robinson, J. R. Hicks, H. J. Habakkuk, and many others. By traditions and customs, one must never forget one's teachers. They were very good men and taught me to try to be a good man as well, and helped me become conscious and respectful of human life, and the values of freedom, democracy, justice, and progress. These were values upheld and shared by friends and faculty in France and England, values that I considered universal goals and guidelines in the conduct of a way of life. I wasn't aware then that things weren't so simple, that fate would chart another course for civilization in a few short years.

Sitting there with the starlit memories of my student days, I couldn't help thinking that I'd had many good reasons as well as opportunity to remain in England or Europe instead of returning to Viet-Nam. At the end of 1959, I received a Christmas parcel from my mother, who had added a short sentence to her greeting card saying she missed me a lot, reminding me that she had not seen me in the past ten years, that she very much hoped I was in good health and would soon be back home. My father had also inserted a few lines telling me of promises he had obtained that I could get a good post at the Saigon Foreign Ministry, should I decide to return at the beginning of the year 1960.

The hour of fate had arrived for me. I did not know it at that time, but my 1959 Christmas party with friends and the New Year's Eve festivities I enjoyed at the Chelsea Art Ball in the Royal Albert Hall would be the last London merriment for me.

Ah, 1959 . . . . I was also convinced that I was in love. She was a kind and wonderful Estonian girl, Merika, a classmate at the French Institute, who could tell an astonishing story of survival from World War II and resettlement as a refugee in England. We were deeply in love and had known each other for nearly eight years. We had all sorts of plans and hopes. She had a very good job and I could easily have found one in London, allowing us to be together forever. I was doubly excited because, a few days before Christmas, I had received a letter from Brussels offering a job possibility with the European Common Market administration.

But the most fateful event came in January 1960, when I was invited to lunch with George P. Case, of Esso, one of the world's largest oil companies. He was the General Manager of Stanvac, a joint venture between Esso and Mobil, responsible for the South Vietnam and Cambodia Division. A very nice and jovial man, he inquired about my stay and studies in England and told me he had learned about me in conversations with people in Saigon who also knew my father. He was looking for an executive trainee and would be happy to have me with him in Saigon. The terms and conditions of work he proposed were more than excellent by Saigon standards, but I told him that I would send him a formal reply in a few days. I emerged from lunch with Mr. Case with my mind in turmoil.

I wandered the streets of London for hours, besieged by all kinds of incoherent ideas. There were clearly violent clashes between aims and purposes, meaning and reason, aspirations and realities. With no recollection of how I got there, I became aware that I was at Piccadilly Circus. I continued to wander like a zombie in Regent Street, then Oxford Street, and to Marble Arch, sat for a while in Hyde Park, then headed for Knightsbridge and South Kensington, towards Queen's Gate where I was staying. I walked in the streets for more than five hours. I was then twenty-four years old and was profoundly shaken at the thought of having to decide between prolonging my stay in England or going home, finally, after such a long absence.

Sorting things out, I began to be aware that I was hit very badly by a confusion of purposes, meanings, rationalizations, and realities. I was caught up in painful clashes between emotion and reason, facts and hopes, responsibilities and desires, myself and others, joy and sorrow. The acute mental stress and ordeal were actually caused by a natural *ability to hope,* countered by an inability to end at once the conflict of many hopes within me. To stay or go? It was a struggle having to do with purpose and meaning, which turned out to be much more emotional than rational. It was a complex challenge, and I took the time to assess the pros and cons of every possible side. It was a heartbreaking exercise but, in the end, I was able to come to a definite decision as I passed by Harrod's department store. I had been away so long from my parents, and that seemed to be the determining factor in my decision. But I had completely lost track of the reasoning process that had led me to that decision. Once the decision was made, however, I was filled with a strong hope, and the sense that everything would go well for all who were dear to me. Arriving in Queen's Gate, I was absolutely determined to return to Saigon and take the job with Esso.

I went back to Oxford to pick up with the new term, which would end in March. I then spent about a month in London with Merika. We told ourselves that it would be a relatively short separation. Depending on how things turned out for me in Saigon, she would join me there or I would simply return to London.

I returned home to Viet-Nam, welcomed by my parents' great joy and happiness and several days of family reunions. I reported to Mr. Case at Esso on April 16, 1960. I was one of two executive trainees. Mr. Case was the first of three general managers I would work with during my employment with Esso from April 1960 to June 1965. Samuel Strasburger succeeded George Case, who was followed by Frederic Penn. Fred Penn and I got on very well, partly because we were both still single at the time and crazy about sophisticated hi-fi systems. The company also went through a re-organization, a separation of interests between Standard Oil Company, New Jersey, Inc. (known both as SONJ and Esso) and Mobil. By the luck of the draw, I was told, it was decided that the Vietnam-Cambodia Division (previously of Stanvac) would go to SONJ as part of a newly-formed affiliate, Esso Standard Eastern, Inc. It was my first contact with anything American—and it was the largest U.S. petroleum corporation in the world. I had a very happy time at Esso and learned a lot about modern organizational leadership and effective management. The executive training program was really comprehensive. For nearly two years, I rotated through various departments as diverse as the technical phases of receiving and storage of petroleum products at the oil depots, to deliveries and servicing (including airplane refueling), to sales activities, finance and accounting, planning, legal affairs, and economic coordination.

The work was extremely interesting and absorbed me entirely. I was convinced that the private business sector, not public service, was to be my cup of tea. I didn't know anything about the Saigon political regime, nor did I pay any attention to it. But as the months went by, through my professional activities I began to be confronted with some of the sad realities in South Vietnam. I soon found out that law and order and citizen's rights were very different from what I had known and grown accustomed to in Paris or London. Saigon was very much a police state, with witch hunts conducted on anybody suspected of having the faintest connection with communism. I had no knowledge of or interest in President Ngo Dinh Diem and soon discovered that, like the ancient Roman tyrant Caligula, he was supposed to be venerated as a god, with South Vietnam under the iron rule of his sacred family. It was a sickening state of affairs but these appalling realities didn't affect me much personally. I was working for a very powerful American company with the clear-cut ambition and hope of becoming a good business executive.

Eventually, I was assigned to the human resources department in Esso and became deeply immersed in the recruitment, training and administration of a workforce numbering fifteen hundred. The personnel weren't accustomed to being informed squarely of their rights and duties or having job-description sheets that clearly defined the terms and conditions of employment. My work in the employee-relations arena led me into tough negotiations with the Federation of the Petroleum Workers Unions, an activity that occupied most of my fourth and fifth years at Esso. I managed to get on fairly well with the union leaders. Two years of heated horse-trading resulted in the first collective-bargaining pact in South Vietnamese history, an agreement that immediately became the industry-wide model for labor contracts in the rubber plantation and banking businesses. I was proud and delighted to have been able to improve industrial relations and generate new expectations for stability and efficiency for both management and labor.

In my third year at Esso, I had to deal with other realities as well. The armed conflict with the Viet Cong had begun to escalate seriously, with much fiercer fighting, and an increasing U.S. military presence. I was so absorbed in my job at Esso that I didn't pay much attention to these matters until the day I received a draft notice. I was ordered to report for admission to the Thu Duc Reserve Officers Training Military Academy. I didn't worry too much about it. Many young men had been deferring military service, abetted by corrupt contacts in the Saigon administration. My family and I didn't have enough money to go that route, but I believed that my position at powerful Esso and my father's good friends in the government would make it easy for me to obtain successive deferments. It was a period of great upheavals, with the overthrow and assassination of President Diem to be followed by many *coups d'état*.

I also had to face another sad reality. My London love story couldn't stand the test of time. Both of us gradually came to accept the fact that circumstances made it impossible for us to survive our prolonged separation. Letters, which had come weekly in the beginning during the first year of separation, began coming monthly in the second year, and then at longer and longer intervals, until one day they just stopped. I learned from friends that she had left England and started a new life in Spain after more than three years of waiting. I was disconsolate, but other distressing events impended. In the month of June 1965, my destiny's path took another turn.

From the beginning of 1965, the military had been seizing more and more power. Now the Army Council was literally ruling South Vietnam. One afternoon at closing time, I was locking up at my office at Esso when a middle-aged gentleman in suit and tie knocked on my door and asked to have a talk with me. At first I thought he was looking for a job. But he soon explained that he had come on behalf of the Army Council—the supreme authority of the land at that time—with a mission for me. He could have come from outer space as far as I was concerned. The only connection I had with politics or the army was that little piece of paper I had recently received summoning me to report for military service. He started the conversation by mentioning straight off that my military obligations had been deferred several times already. In the next few minutes I learned that his purpose was not to escort me to boot camp. With an air of formal solemnity, he asked me on behalf of the Army Council to accept the post of Labor Minister in the government being formed by the generals. He hastened to add politely that it would be a great waste of my abilities if I had to enter the military academy in a few days, should I decide to reject the Army Council's offer. He expressed the utmost regret for the speed with which events were transpiring and told me the address of a villa on Cong Ly (Justice) Street where I would be expected at eight o'clock that evening.

"We realize you have barely three hours to think about this," he was good enough to say on his way out, "and, of course, you are free to come or not to come to this evening's rendezvous." My meeting with him had lasted about fifteen minutes.

I sat there in my office, stunned, unable to think straight, and kept on asking myself how was it possible for anyone in the political or military circles to have any knowledge of my existence on earth. It seemed it would be nearly impossible for me to reject such an incredible offer, which was, in fact, much more in the nature of an order. I was not the kind of hero or idealist who was ready to fight the generals. I was just a very ordinary guy trying to become a good and successful businessman, utterly allergic to anything political and uninterested in public service. I called home to let my mother know that I would not be there for dinner because of urgent work at the office and made myself a large cup of strong black coffee.

Sitting alone in my office at Esso, I did not at all think about what the work of a ministerial position would entail. Instead, I indulged in two hours of profound sadness, with all kinds of images and thoughts coming into my mind, bringing back enjoyable memories from my days in England and the last five years with Esso since my return to Saigon. A whole world inside me seemed to be collapsing that evening, and I had a presentiment that what lay ahead would not be a good thing at all. I was facing a complete unknown, much too big for me to try to understand or cope with. The realization came finally upon me that one sometimes has to take life as it comes.

When it came time to go to the meeting, I switched off the lights, locked my office, said goodnight to the watchman in the Esso building courtyard (for the last time), got into my car robot-like, started the engine, and began to drive to the address I had been given. I could not have imagined on that June evening in 1965 that I was beginning a ten-year journey that would culminate with my being in the Long Thanh orphanage, where I now sat with my reverie over.

I think that many of my fellow inmates at Long Thanh thought of me as a privileged person, with my French and British education and my ten years as a cabinet minister. But privileged or not, we all shared a common fate. Common fate was the equalizer, I thought, as I sat stargazing and recollecting on the illusions and disillusions of my youth. I returned to the common room and tried with difficulty to get some sleep on the tiled floor.

* * *

At the end of what we had been led to believe would be the thirty-day reeducation period, we were made to understand that we were not going home as previously decreed by General Tran Van Tra, the Military Governor of Ho Chi Minh City. There were rumors that high-ranking officials had arrived from Hanoi to organize and take on administration in the south of Viet-Nam. No explanation or reason was given for not allowing us to go home as we had expected. As with most of my fellow inmates, my hopes were completely shattered. We entered into a new phase, that of again not knowing what would become of us. It was an uncertainty we had experienced in the days immediately after Saigon's fall, but this time we were incarcerated in a detention camp and not at home with our families with the ability to move freely around town.

In discussions with the guards who were willing to talk to us, we were made to understand that we were at fault for having committed offenses and crimes against the fatherland. The phrase "traitors to the fatherland" was not used, but we were made to understand clearly that we were guilty for lending a hand to the American neo-imperialist aggressor, which had resulted in death and destruction to the Vietnamese people and nation. We weren't told whether we would be tried in a court, or on what other basis we might be judged, or what the nature or duration of the penalty would be, or how the period of our detention would be assessed, individually or collectively.

That was why I became more aware of hopes, but hopes that were able to reach into my consciousness by ways of illusions and disillusions. I had meaningful purposes to pursue all kinds of hopes, but reality was not there for the hopes to be sustained. It was clear that I had a hope because I had believed General Tran Van Tra's order about the thirty-day reeducation period. Unfortunately, for us, higher authorities had changed the order, as I was to learn years later, against the will of General Tra. He did not stay long in his job after that.

CODA

Illusions and Disillusions of Hope

The natural gift of hope
is the essence of imagination
in the face of the unknown—
the source and starter
of humankind's abilities
to will and to think.
Hope—
is our endless and unavoidable quest
for the better,
but also the bridge
between our inside world
and the universe surrounding us,
between the imaginary and the real,
the unseen and the visible,

the difference
between one individual and another.

><

Hope—
is the God-given pendulum
for humankind to measure
the illusions and disillusions
of its past, present, and future.
Until the day
when all human clocks
are set to the same hour,
each of us will continue to seek
our own time and destiny,
sometimes missing our appointments
with others,
but always meeting our unpredictable fate
in the midst
of our own illusions and illusions.
Illusions and disillusions—
are natural phenomena
to be expected and accepted.
Illusions and disillusions
are given to us
to help put our clock right
and find the purpose and meaning of time
and our human condition.

><

The process of hope
requires the recognition
of illusions and disillusions,
the challenge

between the true and the false,
the good and the better,
the right and the wrong,
the self and the other,
the now and forever.
Illusions and disillusions—
are intimately related
to myths and realities;
therefore hope
is associated with myths and realities,
which all constitute
the facts of life.
The illusions and disillusions
of hope
are also concrete facts of life.

><

The primordial test of hope
is the ability to eliminate
illusions and disillusions,
which concern purpose and meaning,
the initial parameters and starters of hope.
Illusions and disillusions—
constitute inherent parts
of the process and evolution of hope,
and must be suppressed
in the reconciliation
of the self with the non-self,
and of purpose, meaning,
reason, and reality,
the ability to think.
Illusions and disillusions
constitute inherent parts
of the process and evolution of hope

and must be dealt with
systematically and effectively
in the reconciliation
of the self with the non-self,
and in the confrontation between
Purpose, Meaning, Reason, and ***Reality***.

CHAPTER SEVEN

A LONG-DELAYED TRIP TO THE NORTH: MYTHS AND REALITIES

Lift the rocks to mend the skies.
Vietnamese saying

For me and other inmates, the journey from the Long Thanh orphanage into the unknown that began in June 1975, became clearer and more specific at Thu Duc prison in the suburbs of Saigon. I was a distinguished member of a select group of detainees that included South Vietnamese cabinet ministers, police officials, intelligence commanders, and political party leaders—the *crème de la crème*, it might be said, of *personae non gratae*. My archaic title of Mandarin for State Affairs identified me as the senior cabinet minister who had to answer more than the others for the sins of Saigon's past. For the first time in my life, I was locked in a cell. It was totally different from the orphanage experience. Gone was the prospect of a quick thirty days and then back to the bosom of my family. The festive atmosphere and humorous anecdotes were things of the past. There were bars on the windows and barbed wire atop the fences. Prison.

There were about one hundred of us at this particular reeducation location, all males but one. The woman's name was

Thuy, and she had been head of the Swan Squad of the Saigon Special Police. She was secluded from the rest of us in a far corner of the back of the prison. I was surprised to see her one day in the prison yard. I had expected a sinister-looking femme fatale, but she turned out to be a woman of ordinary bearing, actually, in her early thirties, with a slight limp. She was somewhat short in height, and a bit plump. She was friendly and smiled a lot, as if she were having a swell time. I was told she had been responsible for recruiting, training and supervising hundreds of female agents for intelligence and counter-intelligence. She was walking proof that looks could be deceiving.

The large cell I shared with some twenty others was completely bare, with a big iron door and narrow openings high up near the ceiling to let in light and air. We were allowed to keep our bags and parcels and given straw mats to sleep on. The floor was concrete. Space and freedom of movement considerations aside, hygienic conditions were better than at the orphanage. And the meals were *much* better. My cell-mates, mostly strangers, included high-ranking police and intelligence officials and political party leaders. I was struck by the thought that we might very well be considered a bunch of dangerous war criminals slated for some Nuremberg-type tribunal. We weren't told anything. The iron door was open from five o'clock in the morning to five in the evening, and we were free to roam the courtyard and visit to the washroom.

My first two weeks at Thu Duc prison was a period of unimaginable mental distress. I felt crushed. My sense of despair came not from catastrophic events but from uncertainty. Was something truly terrible about to happen? I was powerless to prevent a future that included the possibility of a horrible death. I felt a compelling need to survive mingled with a feeling of frustration borne of that powerlessness. Yet with nothing but the clouds of despair surrounding me, I still held on to a silver lining of hope. A way out was not entirely impossible, was it?

I didn't talk much to my cell-mates. As dark thoughts of death retreated to some degree with the passing days, other painful struggles afflicted my soul, a combat between truth and falsehood, the real and the imaginary, the good and the bad. Above all, I had to learn and know about myself, where and how I had gone wrong—if I had gone wrong. It was not for public consumption but between me and my conscience. Had I willingly, intentionally, and consciously committed crimes through my involvement with the Saigon government?

In time, life at Thu Duc proceeded not all that unpleasantly. The inmates seemed to behave as if nothing very special had happened. The guards were extremely courteous, even friendly. There were no noisy scenes or disputes, nor grumblings of dissatisfaction. There was nothing to do but wander around and chat about anything and everything. Except politics of the past. No one cared to talk about those things.

My eldest cell-mate was a tall and robust man in his seventies with a shock of snow-white hair and a long, scraggly white beard, Uncle Ho-style. He was Vu Hong Khanh, and he had been the honorary chairman of Vietnam's Kuomintang Party. He had held several top ministerial posts in Ho Chi Minh's governments in the mid-1940s at the birth in Hanoi of the Democratic Republic of Vietnam. Later, his party, an offspring of the Chinese Kuomintang, had followed Chiang kai-shek's anti-communist path. I wasn't sure whether I should consider the presence of this venerable politician—a veteran of at least half a century of activities, including bloody fights against the Hanoi communists, compared to my ten years with the Saigon regime—a consolation or further cause for despair.

In my cell at Thu Duc prison, I continually asked myself how I had managed to get on the tiger's back for ten long years. It was not my habit to regret. I didn't regret having returned to Saigon five days before the fall. I didn't regret having returned from England to South Vietnam in 1960. And I wasn't cursing myself yet for having gone to that June 1965 rendezvous that had sealed my fate as a government minister. I now had plenty of time to reflect on the consequences of that rendezvous.

* * *

As I drove away from the Esso building that night, I hadn't been conflicted about what I was facing. I was certain that boot camp and soldiering was abhorrent to me, and not in the cards if I could help it. If I hadn't been asked to become Labor Minister, I might have become a draft-dodger and deserter. That would have brought a different fate. Anyway, *les dés sont jetés* (the die was cast).

It was only a five-minute drive to the address I had been given, a large villa with a garden in front. Civilian guards manned the gate, which was opened to my car as soon as I gave my name. I considered myself correctly dressed in a long-sleeved white shirt and tie. I was shown into a spacious living room where some twenty persons, all strangers to me, were already sitting. I gave a general nod to those present and found the nearest empty armchair, trying not to stare impolitely at anyone. Most were much older than I, and while I felt a bit uneasy, I was not afraid or apprehensive. After about five minutes, an old, emaciated gentleman entered, whom I was really happy to recognize: Dr. Tran Van Do, a long-time acquaintance of my parents. He seemed happy to see me, too, and we greeted each other warmly before he went on to the others. Dr. Do had represented Saigon at the 1954 Geneva Conference and since then had continued to be foreign minister on and off while practicing medicine. Dr. Do went down in history books for having cried like a bereaved widower at the decision to cut Viet-Nam in two at the seventeenth parallel in the 1954 Geneva Accords on Indochina—which gave birth *de facto,* if not *de jure*, to the so-called Communist North Vietnam (DRV) and Nationalist South Vietnam (RVN).

Soon there was a flurry of activity and the sound of automobiles pulling up through the gate. A young man with a moustache, wearing black air-force coveralls with a two-star general's insignia on them, bustled into the room, issuing a collective greeting and inviting everyone to move to the dining room. I immediately recognized him as General Nguyen Cao Ky. I had seen his picture

85-CART

in the newspapers. The Army Council had recently named him prime minister-designate. We were asked to sit around a very long dining table, and Ky began the meeting by thanking all of us for agreeing to help him form a government that would have to be up and running in just a few days. He explained that over the past two years since the overthrow of Diem, a succession of civilian governments had failed to bring stability to the nation. For that reason, he insisted, repeating the word "stability," the Army Council had stepped up to take power.

From a sheet of paper, Ky read out our names according to the corresponding ministries to which we would be assigned, and attempted to introduce us to one another. Each of us stood briefly when our names were called and nodded to the left and right. I couldn't remember who was who except for Dr. Do and General Ky. At one point, Ky made an observation contrasting the eldest among us, Luu Van Vi, a lawyer in his seventies who was to be the justice minister—with the youngest—me, a businessman, barely twenty-nine, who was to be labor minister. He then went round the table to shake hands with each of us. I assumed he tried to show friendliness with a quick smile but it was hard to tell beneath his moustache.

After the assassination of President Diem in November 1963, the military junta had tried to please Washington by letting the Saigon politicians set up "civilian" governments, one after another, which simply resulted in two years of chaos. President Johnson had had to accept the distasteful rule by the military establishment in South Vietnam as the way to maintain some sort of stability. That was how the Army Council (Hoi Dong Quan Luc) was created in June 1965—for the defense of freedom and democracy, of course.

Ky, then about thirty-five, remained prime minister until he became Thieu's vice-president in September 1967. I don't imagine he had dreamed of becoming a prime minister so young. We had at least one thing in common: we were both too young for the jobs. It seemed quite clear to me that Ky didn't have the knowledge or experience to lead the South Vietnamese government. No one had had it after Diem's demise. Chaos ruled Saigon. Who would be insane enough to take the job? All the other generals were much older than Ky and preferred to remain behind the scenes.

People can say what they want about Ky, but I soon learned that he was even-tempered, calm, and well-mannered. He was also very much a man of action—a complex mixture of impulsiveness, intuition, and decisiveness in times of crisis and emergency. Whether his quick-thinking performance made for good or bad decisions is another argument, but his attitude, together with his natural talent for public speaking and engaging with the public, were strong points. He also had a blind fidelity to associates and aides, good and bad ones alike—but he didn't gather many good ones around him. That was his Achilles heel. He ran his government like the ace jet-fighter pilot that he was, alone in his cockpit. He was very busy with the generals and the war, and the ministries were pretty much left to fend for themselves.

I didn't know what the other people sitting around that table were thinking that fateful evening, what circumstances had brought them there, what their aims or motivations were. I came to see later that Ky, or the Army Council, had concocted a crafty mixture in that gathering: a balance of northerners and southerners, old and young, technicians and politicians, civilians and military. I fit the category of a very young, apolitical, South Vietnamese technician. What precious hopes and purposes the others might have entertained, I knew not. For me there was a void. So it was that I climbed on the tiger's back.

* * *

During my few weeks' stay at Thu Duc prison, worries about my loved ones at home plagued me constantly. We were in the immediate vicinity of Saigon, and I was able to hear the powerful wail of the siren at the Saigon Central Post Office three times a day, at seven o'clock in the morning, noon, and five o'clock in the afternoon. I imagined my parents and other relatives listening to it, too. We were locked inside every evening at five o'clock and were no longer able to gaze at the stars. I'd lie on my straw mat on the hard concrete floor and seek in vain a peaceful sleep. I couldn't help thinking about my years in the Saigon government, probably because I hoped and needed to convince myself that I hadn't done anything terrible, immoral, or criminal, or anything that violated the conscience of an ordinary citizen of Saigon, Paris, or London. So I would slip back into a mood of wistful reminiscence.

The Ministry of Labor that I was slated to oversee had been smaller in size and personnel than the Immigration Office, and its annual budget less than that of the Saigon Public Transport Service. I also discovered that government pay was really lousy. Not being a civil servant or army officer with a classification and seniority rating, I was considered a "notable," entitled only to a cabinet minister's monthly salary. That less-than-tidy sum, thanks to Ky's professed public austerity policy, was only slightly more than the wages I was paying out of my own pocket to my private steno-typist, a person I could trust and work with. There was a so-called "black fund," equivalent to two month's salary for a minister, which could be used without having to submit receipts. It served as a petty cash box, used by my secretary to buy cigarettes, tea, coffee, soft drinks, and occasional sandwiches, since such luxuries could not be absorbed by any accounts in the ministry's budget. As a bachelor, I declined the government's offer of an official residence with cook, butlers, drivers, and cars, and continued to stay with my parents in the more trusted family facilities.

It was not an attractive deal for the prosperous young businessman I had set out to become. There was no insurance, no cost-of-living allowance, no pension plan, or other such benefits. Even later, when I was sent "on mission" to the Paris peace talks, all I got was a lump sum per diem of US$50. The small savings I had accumulated after five years of employment with Esso melted like snow in a furnace. My family wasn't wealthy, just able to make ends meet. It was, therefore, a great surprise for my high-ranking communist uncles to learn after Saigon's fall that I had never owned a house or car of my own, had no money in the bank and easily qualified for the sub-proletariat class by Marxist definitions.

In joining the Saigon government, I had no specific personal aim or purpose. I was concerned only with the job I was assigned to do at the Ministry of Labor. It didn't require much contact with the other ministries. From my negotiating experience with the petroleum workers at Esso, I was familiar with union leaders and labor ministry officials. I was lucky enough to run into another of my father's old friends who had taken advantage of the excellent French colonial training to become the top civil servant at the Ministry of Labor: Nguyen Le Giang. He had twice been Labor Minister in previous civilian governments and continued there in the capacity of Labor General Inspector. He was as glad to see me there as I was to see him, and considered my presence "a breath of fresh air" compared to the Saigonese politicians who usually got the job.

The job didn't excite me much, but I tried to do it to the best of my abilities. I was left alone, and that was what really mattered to me. All in all, my stay at the Ministry of Labor was pleasant with all the people working there, but my first contacts with Saigonese politics and the American intervention in South Vietnam were sheer mental torments. The Ministry had *grosso modo* three goals: improve relations with the unions, create the impression of labor peace, and enforce a labor code that only a handful of Vietnamese companies needed concern themselves about because of the small size of their work force. Foreign corporations mostly ignored the Ministry of Labor. Mr. Giang was like a father—even a grandfather—to me. We enjoyed working together and found a lot to laugh over at our meetings. For example, we worked very diligently to achieve labor safety for workers, but if someone stepped on a booby trap mine on their way to work, well, that was simply bad luck. It was also bad luck again if a rocket happened to hit someone's workshop. And bad luck as well if chemical defoliant stuff (Agent Orange) fell on the plantation workers. There was no such thing as safety in war, labor safety included. It was a swell time for the insurance companies, of course. Did no one ever think to make this point to LBJ? Probably not—it was such a small detail.

By all internationally recognized standards, Mr. Giang was a democrat, and liberal in his vocation for and devotion to the welfare of the Vietnamese workers. We shared the same views about policies, dreams, and utopias advanced at that time by Saigon and Washington. It was an impossible task for us to put LBJ's "guns and butter" policy to work. How could one hope to establish or restore a state of normalcy in South Vietnam under conditions of fierce warfare? Or pretend that everything was going swell for the population with economic prosperity, while millions of troops kept on fighting on the battlefields year in and year out?

Due credit must, however, be given to President Johnson because he was, from among the five U.S. presidents faced with the American War in Viet-Nam, the one who had to deal with the Vietnamese conflict and dilemma at its highest peak, in terms of determination and passion, by both Hanoi and Washington. Later on, President Nixon was faced with less painful choices, because the North Vietnamese leaders, by 1968-1969, had begun to lower their antes for a negotiated (even temporary) way out. LBJ put all his mind and heart into dealing with the War in Viet-Nam. It was not particularly his war, but it became dramatically and dreadfully the longest war in the two-hundred-year history of the American people. The name Lyndon Baines Johnson will be remembered and linked forever with the conflict in Viet-Nam. Such are the whims of Fate and Destiny.

President Johnson was sincere in the formation of his "guns and butter" initiative. It was consistent with the most cherished American ideals handed down by the Founding Fathers. LBJ's mind produced the "guns," but his heart added the "butter," with all the tremendous might and wealth of his Great Society. He made the goals clear at the Honolulu Conference in February 1966, with Saigon Generals Thieu and Ky. The conference was a highly emotional Vietnam-U.S. summit in the middle of the Pacific Ocean, half way between Washington and Saigon, and the initiative was backed up by the presence of powerful Pentagon brass, as well as the resourceful American secretaries for agriculture, health, education and welfare.

It did not take much effort for President Johnson to convince his South Vietnamese allies that his "guns and butter" policy was the very best thing on earth that they could ever dream of. To President Johnson's great delight, the Saigon leaders revealed themselves to be even more Johnsonian than LBJ himself, when they solemnly pledged to personally carry out to the letter LBJ's grandiose program. President Johnson was also eager to show detracting Senators Fulbright, Morse, and others, whose committee hearings were going on at the time, that his American crusade for freedom and democracy in South Vietnam had highly laudable and respectable aims (purpose), was for the defense of the most civilized values of decency and morality (meaning), and that his "guns and butter" policy was the most logical and rational thing to pursue (reason). What was left for LBJ to do was to create *realities* to fuel his hopes.

President Johnson's policy simply aimed to deter North Vietnam from committing armed aggression against South Vietnam. Within the frame of this world view, he very probably thought in all good conscience that he was morally justified in formulating the policy. He certainly believed that he was more than materially capable of releasing the American fires of hell on Viet-Nam. At the same time, he was driven to want to share the American way of life, progress, and prosperity with the destitute Vietnamese in South Vietnam. No doubt, he was sincere. His hope was clearly expressed in the Honolulu Conference's joint communiqué, which forcefully proclaimed the "defense against aggression, the work of social revolution, the goal of free government, the attack on hunger, ignorance and disease, and the unending quest for peace."

In spite of all the good will and the best of intentions, in the end, the policy produced more "guns" than "butter," as things would sadly and rapidly show later. Was it at all possible that President Johnson could have put a little more weight on his "butter" features than on the "guns?" As a Vietnamese saying goes, "Resolve it with your heart and mind," instead of with your mind and heart. It was, of course, a grandiose hope for prosperity and progress, freedom and democracy—the eternal and universal ideals of all times everywhere for everybody. There is no doubt whatsoever that President Johnson instructed his diplomats and generals to give the Saigon government all possible U.S. help to make these things come true. By the spring of 1966, Prime Minister Nguyen Cao Ky repeatedly reminded everybody, very eloquently as usual with his inborn oratory talents, that the vital issue in the war against the bloody North Vietnamese armed aggression was not a matter to best be dealt with by a civilian or military South Vietnamese government, but by a "democratically elected" one. The pronunciation and spelling of these two words in Vietnamese are almost identical: "dan su" means civilian, and "dan cu" means popularly elected. My mother and aunts in our native village of Ba Tri would not have been much wiser, because from then until 1975, all the village chiefs were army lieutenants, the district chiefs were army captains, the provincial chiefs (governors) were army colonels, and the prime minister and president of the Republic of Vietnam also happened to be generals. They were all good democrats, civil servants, and army officers at the same time. Why not? Nothing in the books of political theory had said anything to the contrary. Lots of generals had become presidents all over the world, among the most famous ones being America's Washington, Grant, and Eisenhower, and, of course, President de Gaulle in France.

One could put forth all the arguments in the world in defense of these ideals, but to set up "general elections" was purely a Washington ploy to convince people in America and other parts of the world that it was moving its Outpost of the Free World to a democratic, freely-elected government—never mind who the candidates were. The facts were that at the time there was a military dictatorship in South Vietnam. Everybody was aware that the Saigon generals and military rule provided the only possible "stability" for the South Vietnamese regime to survive. But President Johnson made it crystal clear to the Saigon generals that they must rapidly produce a constitution and organize general elections, free ones of course, at all costs. American dollars and constitutional lawyers would be provided to the extent necessary. The U.S. presence and intervention in Viet-Nam could not be justified and continued without a constitutionally and freely elected government in Saigon. That was how General Nguyen Van Thieu and General Nguyen Cao Ky got elected president and vice-president of the Republic of Vietnam in September 1967.

After three centuries of internal dispute over a throne, more than a century of French colonial rule, a decade of the Indochinese War, and another decade of the American War by 1967—a total of over three hundred fifty years of continuous death and devastation at an intensity never seen before in human history—Vietnamese in both North and South Vietnam were anything except concerned with freely elected and democratic governments. Both sides were very simply driven to winning and ending the war in Viet-Nam, the sooner the better. The foremost and highest priority of either Hanoi or Saigon at that time was, first of all, the defeat and collapse of the brother-enemy. Victory was, of course, either for the Outpost of the Free World or the Viet-Nam Communist Party. That was how democracy was equated to The War in Viet-Nam. And the show went on that way, waiting for the judgment of God by the sword. Mr. Giang and I did not have many illusions in doing our work at the Saigon Ministry of Labor in those years of 1965 and 1966.

Giang joined me in an endeavor that I had strong convictions about. It was the first and most explosive matter on my agenda, and it was much more a political rather than a labor issue, namely, how to handle the Confederation of the Workers' Unions of Viet-Nam (CWUV as it was known in English, and TLDLCVN otherwise). It was presided over by its powerful founder and chairman, Tran Quoc Buu. During nearly a decade, the CWUV had demonstrated itself to be a tool for President Diem and his brother Nhu to carry out their Saigon government's anti-communist crusade. The activities of the CWUV, in partnership with the Saigon secret police, included much witch-hunting since the workers' unions were, by their nature, heavily infiltrated by Viet Cong agents.

Against such a background, I decided to try to institute a more meaningful kind of unionism in South Vietnam despite a military dictatorship and a raging war. It would have been totally futile for me to explain this goal to the Saigon generals, or to Tran Quoc Buu or even to the U.S. Embassy. They all propagated the ideas and policies that the CWUV was a strong and genuine workers' movement in support of the anti-communist government in South Vietnam.

Very quickly I publicly and sufficiently provoked Tran Quoc Buu to sever his long-established, well-known ties and deals with the Saigon authorities. Shortly, violent strikes began to snowball during a whole month, from the dockworkers at the ports to the nurses at the hospitals, culminating in a general strike which was a first in the history of the Republic of Vietnam. In endless meetings with the unions, I did not try to do much to resolve their demands and left it to Tran Quoc Buu to go and seek a settlement directly with the Saigon generals who were horrified by the general shutdown and at a complete loss to understand why their 29-year old Labor Minister wanted to pick a bone with old hand Tran Quoc Buu.

The general strike lasted three days and resulted in an "outstanding victory" for the workers' unions. That was a change for union members because during the previous ten years their activities had consisted mostly of parading and shouting "Tong Thong Diem Muon Nam, Muon Nam" (Viva, Viva President Diem) and "Da Dao Cong San Vo Than" (Down with the Godless Communists).

Months later, when things had settled down a bit, I was able to help Buu understand what had really happened. I was able to generate understandings of the issues and outcomes from the dramatic events with not only Tran Quoc Buu but also with John Condon, the Labor Attaché at the U.S. Embassy, who had been trying hard to be of assistance to Buu so as to enhance the position of the CWUV as a vehicle to promote the democratic label of the Saigon political regime. (Condon and I were to meet again in Paris in 1969 when I was involved in the peace talks and he was Labor Attaché at the U.S. Embassy there. Our friendship has prevailed.)

At the beginning of 1966, I supported, to some extent, the "butter" part of President Johnson's "guns and butter" policy, proclaimed at the Honolulu Conference. LBJ's "guns and butter" policy was too "logical and rational" to deal with our Vietnamese problems, especially the ones I was facing at the Saigon Labor Ministry. Concerned with the task of trying to protect and promote the welfare of the Vietnamese working classes, it appeared to me that the issue was not in projecting a public image of an anti-communist Saigon government supported militarily and economically by the tremendous power of the United States of America in the names of freedom and democracy. Freedom and democracy have never been major tenets in Far Eastern civilizations and their thinking in the 5,000 years of their history. The conduct of peoples' lives and the affairs of state in the East has always been the search for virtuous and just rulers rather than political principles and ideologies. None of the people in the Far East have had anything near the English Magna Carta, the American Declaration of Independence and Bill of Rights, or the French Declaration des Droits de l'Homme.

I was convinced that the viability and validity of the Saigon government were not in the demonstration of the might of the United States of America to go to war against North Vietnam but in the vital necessity for the Vietnamese to have the sentiment of defending their own Vietnamese ways of life which meant, first of all, their livelihood and homes, the dignity of their work and ability to feed their families, to care for their ancestors' cult, and to respect the ethical values handed down to them by their traditions and customs. They were prepared to fight and die for their own ways of life and national identity-not for a Republic of Vietnam, and even less for a so-called "Outpost of the Free World" with all the nice and expensive things given to them by the opulent Americans in the names of freedom and democracy, nor in return for waging war against North Vietnam's communism, or international communism whether it be the Soviet Union's, the People's Republic of China's, Cuba's, or Yugoslavia's. President Johnson's "butter" was supposed to win the "minds and hearts" of the South Vietnamese but, sadly, it was simply directed instead to the "stomachs" in a profusion of consumer goods that gave an illusion of instant prosperity, an antidote propaganda against the misery and poverty of the communist regimes in the world.

Unionism was, in fact, a notion imported from the West. It was as abstract a notion as the notions of freedom and democracy in Vietnamese history and ways of thinking. Even if the notions were valid, the workers' unions in South Vietnam were supposed to be peoples' organizations, not vehicles to be used as tools to fight communism (which, for the poor Vietnamese in South Vietnam, was as obscure as a war for freedom and democracy). I did believe, however, that with proper aid from the U.S., the Saigon government could carry out meaningful economic and social programs to enable the people in South Vietnam to build their own workshops and factories, own their means of subsistence, and possess and defend their own homes. Given such programs with their consequences, "guerrilla warfare" could never prevail if its objectives were directed against the civilian population instead of foreign troops. That aspect was the most painful and challenging issue of the War in Viet-Nam because the whole bloody war was not for "security" and "territorial occupation" but for human dignity and feelings, for the common people to judge who was truly defending their interests, national identity and sense of nationalism. Very unfortunately, President Johnson was much more guided by his mind than his heart, and the realities and hopes he desperately tried to create were rather on the battlefields when they should have been in the paddyfields.

I tried to present such views to whomever was prepared to listen, arguing that-with a crash economic development program for South Vietnam, even if in the order of $5 billion-such an alternative would be far less than the $20 billion swallowed each year by the military option. As the youthful Labor Minister, of course, I didn't stand much of a chance to interest or convince any American officials of such fanciful ideas but beginning in 1965 my efforts did produce lasting friendships with Robert Miller and Philip Habib, both of whom were political counselors at the U.S. Embassy in Saigon. (I was to work with them again in 1968 at the Paris peace talks. Bob Miller went on to become head of the U.S. delegation in Vienna for the Disarmament Talks with the Soviet Union and Philip Habib became the U.S. ambassador to the Republic of Korea, then assistant secretary of state, and later presidential special envoy during the Republican administrations of Ronald Reagan and George Bush in the 1980s.)

In 1965, the Saigon Ministry of Labor's one claim to fame involved its vocational training programs, which really meant helping people find jobs. I soon found out that the Ministry was doing an outstanding job at this with an extremely meager budget. I was able to report that thirty thousand youngsters were taught professional skills. Although ninety-five percent of them became barbers, hairdressers, tailors, dressmakers, and the like. It was better than nothing.

The really unexpected thing that I managed to do that somewhat helped very low income families was a crash program for the promotion of a small, private business of motorized three-wheelers for the transport of goods and people. The initial launching of the program in November 1965 was a big, popular event in Saigon with a parade of 2,000 vehicles by their new owners. This program was able to go on for about three years before reaching a saturation point of three-wheeler "entrepreneurs" in the city.

I lasted about a year in the post. From the very start, I was a lone wolf in government. I asked for no favors, dispensed none, and no one bothered to ask me for any, most likely being aware that the Ministry of Labor was no a fat cow. I was, for the most part, ignored by the Saigonese politicians as well, because I did not mind declaring in cabinet meetings and anywhere else that I did not think much of the multitude of so-called political parties in South Vietnam, which were made up of illustrious unknowns to the vast majority of the population. How could you expect to have free general elections without any meaningful political systems and parties? How could you really expect to create democratic rule—like instant coffee? It had taken two centuries for the American people to create democratic rule, not to mention the British or the French who had spent longer times to achieve it.

I also gave undiplomatic pieces of my mind to the U.S. officials in Saigon about the matters of having a constitution and general elections in time of a fierce war. It was sheer humbug, as the British liked to express themselves in similar situations. Among my suggestions was that instead of the highbrow stuff about constitution and general elections, the Vietnamese in South Vietnam would understand much easier and better a simple referendum, provided it stated clearly and concretely the main things that should be achieved within a strict time frame of three to five years and by whom. We should stop playing open-ended guessing games with the people.

If you think you can claim the right to govern and conduct the war, you should also have the guts to assume the responsibility for that right and not simply resign and retire in case of failure, as corporate CEOs have done. In ancient Vietnamese and Chinese traditions, generals used to make a solemn written pledge before going into battles, and sent back their heads by express mail messengers to their kings in case of defeat. In medieval Europe, the honorable knights used to make the same pledge by "coming home on their swords" instead of on their horses. Such customs and traditions are nowadays considered barbarian and uncivilized practices. In modern times, wars and politics are covered by social security, and defeats are borne only by the victims: the dead and taxpayers.

It was only after being kicked upstairs to become minister at the prime minister's office in 1966, that I began to gain a more complete picture of what was going on in the Saigon government. I was lucky again to find at the prime minister's office another French-trained civil servant, Tran Ngoc Giao, another old friend of my father who also considered me like a son or grandson. My new job was rather simple: I was responsible for the prime minister's in-and out-mail boxes, for coordination among the ministries, and for preparing working files for the prime minister's desk with summaries and comments. I was also charged with keeping the appointment book, organizing inter-ministerial get-togethers, meeting foreign guests no one else was willing to meet, and attending useless social events.

I was busy doing nothing and able to speculate a bit more about the war's evolution and what was transpiring between Washington and Saigon. It was also a time when I began to explore the comparative worlds of myths and realities, the subjective and objective notions that were supposed to constitute the hard facts of existence, but were mostly just products of the human imagination. I began thinking of the tide of history surrounding me as a tale of two cities, that is, of Saigon and Washington.

The only notable thing that I was involved in during that time in my capacity as minister in the prime minister's office was the mission to Manila at the end of October, 1966. I was part of the advance team charged with finalizing preparations for the seven-nation summit about Viet-Nam, which guest-starred President Lyndon Baines Johnson and was hosted by Philippines president Ferdinand Marcos. It was an epic gathering of hopes if there ever was one. It was the time of military escalation, but also the beginning of the U.S. disengagement policy from the War in Viet-Nam. President Johnson fine-tuned his carrot-and-stick speech to sound something like, "Aggression must not succeed, but let's stop the fighting and create a grandiose reconstruction program for both North and South Vietnam funded by U.S. aid." As early as 1965, LBJ had already put out a carrot by his declaration in Baltimore on April 7 of $1 billion of aid to the Southeast Asian countries, including North Vietnam. He did not forget to mention that he was willing to negotiate unconditionally with Hanoi to end the Vietnam War. He was specific at the Manila Summit, proposing the total withdrawal of U.S. troops from South Vietnam within six months, as soon as Hanoi ended its armed aggression against the Saigon government. It was, of course, totally impossible for Uncle Ho to explain such a deal to his people and the world. It was difficult for Uncle Ho to accept LBJ's simple logic of getting rid of the GIs without having to fight them. That exercise in logic *in contrario* would have to wait for President Nixon to begin returning the boys home in 1969 without Uncle Ho stopping the war. President Johnson could see no other choice but to pursue his "guns and butter" policy, which he did until the end of his term in January 1969. He was consoled by the hope that he was doing a good deed for everybody—the Vietnamese, the American people—and promoting civilization and progress for the whole world.

Even in the early 1960s, as Vice-President Lyndon Baines Johnson, he was excited by his idea of having an impressive development program in South Vietnam's Mekong River Delta area. Unfortunately, his great excitement and big carrot had no follow-up. If LBJ had been able to make his program work, the fate and destiny of both Viet-Nam and the United States might have been quite different.

The task of writing President Thieu's speech for the Manila meeting was ultimately dropped into my lap. It was a last-minute job sprung on me just a few hours before the summit's opening ceremony. At about two o'clock in the morning, I found Thieu still working on the speech in his suite at the Manila hotel, where all the delegations were staying. I reported to Thieu about the work of the advanced party for the summit meeting. He then asked me to have a look at the text of his speech, which I hadn't yet seen.

It had been prepared by his aides and set out as a resounding discourse proclaiming Saigon's undying determination to fight on. It was completely off-key for a peace summit and I told him so. Thieu was quite annoyed by my judgment. He then threw the draft to me in anger and told me, then, to fix it. I quickly wrote a speech that would last about ten minutes instead of the original's thirty. By five o'clock in the morning, the Saigon Ambassador in Manila, Pham Dang Lam, was dragged out of his bed and given the tough job of having the redrafted speech printed in time. Philip Habib got wind of the new draft and was very eager to have a copy. It was utterly unacceptable for the Americans not to know in advance what the head of state of the Republic of Viet-Nam was going to say publicly at the summit meeting. Thieu and everybody else, including Philip Habib, only had their first look at the new draft at eight o'clock in the morning, an hour before President Marcos declared the summit open and gave the podium to Thieu. His speech began with three words:

"We want Peace."

These three words immediately earned Thieu a long, standing ovation by the entire international gathering. It's doubtful if anybody knew exactly what Thieu was saying by those three words, but everybody was happy. LBJ appeared to be rejoicing more than anybody else over the three words' wishfullness. But I sincerely meant it when I wrote it, and certainly hoped for an end to the war.

While Thieu was insisting on demonstrating the viability of the Saigon regime both militarily and politically, there was no doubt that the U.S. was beginning to lose patience and had decided at last to seek a way to end the war quickly. LBJ's strategy was to opt for a massive intervention by U.S. ground troops in South Vietnam. But he still didn't understand the type of war he was dealing with. Hundreds of thousands of GIs had already been sent to South Vietnam, but the situation had become even worse. Nearly universal weariness with the fighting had refocused hopes from the battlefield to the negotiating table. It was hope with a common purpose of a peaceful solution, but without meaning and reason acceptable to all parties concerned. Everyone hoped for peace, but no one knew how to attain it. LBJ admonished us that the Manila Summit must not sound like a war pow-wow, and insisted that he should be treated at this seven-nation summit meeting as the smallest of the participants, the last of the "seven samurai" one might say.

Clearly, LBJ's means of hope was to send a message to the world—and again to Hanoi—that he wanted a negotiated solution to the dreadful conflict. President Johnson had already tried in 1965 to convince Hanoi to have talks, but did not really think that Ho Chi Minh would sincerely be interested in anything less than an American defeat in Viet-Nam. Ho Chi Minh and his politburo were prepared to open their own channels in their own mysterious ways for talks with Washington, but were also dead sure that LBJ would never settle for anything less than a Saigon political regime fully backed by American presence and military intervention. It was a dialogue of the deaf.

At the Manila Summit Conference, Thieu and Ky strongly hoped to strengthen their personal positions and convince the allies that South Vietnam was still viable as a Far East Outpost of the Free World, and was still worth the United States' fighting and paying for it in order to preserve U.S. prestige and credibility. Was it not a cornerstone of U.S. foreign policy that the fate of all Southeast Asia depended on the survival of an anti-communist South Vietnam? The feeling among the so-called allies continued to be the vague hope that the U.S. could end its massive military intervention and that the Saigon regime would somehow prevail. Was there, then, really any hope for a negotiated solution?

I led the Vietnamese delegation in the drafting of the joint communiqué with the Americans. William Bundy headed the American delegation, staffed by many old hands of Vietnam service. The drafting committee was also composed of delegations from countries with troops in South Vietnam, including Australia, New Zealand, South Korea and Thailand. The Philippines Deputy Foreign Minister Ingles chaired the session, which was held at the presidential palace, Malacanal. We got down to work at around six o'clock in the evening, and by eleven, we had lost half an hour through a heated argument between the Americans and South Koreans. It was very embarrassing to have those who were our friends fighting over Vietnamese interests.

The dispute started when the drafting committee came to the question of negotiating with the other side. The Koreans insisted that they and other allies of the Saigon government must be present at any peace talks. The Americans argued that it should be an affair between Vietnamese and Vietnamese (we all had the impression that while Bundy's expression was very serious when he said this, his tongue was planted very firmly in his cheek).

As it became quite clear that neither the Americans nor the Koreans would budge an inch from their positions, I proposed a short break to let off some steam. During the break, a Korean aide promptly asked me to see the head of his delegation, who immediately expressed his regret for arguing with our American counterpart. He said he'd received strict instructions from his president on the point at issue, since they had gone through a similar experience with the U.S. in the 1950s. If peace talks ever came, he warned, Saigon would find itself with the Americans negotiating directly with the other side, and Saigon would not have much to say in the matter except to accept and comply. Of course, I warmly thanked him for his counsel and said everyone was fully aware of our Big Brother's well-known proclivity for handling things his own way. We were grateful to our Korean friends for going to bat for us on this vital element, but it was also our duty to do whatever we could to safeguard our interests, with full awareness that the U.S. would not hesitate to do whatever it needed to do to protect its own.

When the committee resumed, I suggested a sentence be inserted in the joint communiqué stating explicitly that, should

Hanoi agree to come to the negotiating table, Saigon would be happy to join them after full consultation with our allies. That was enough to instill hope in the readers of the Manila Summit's joint communiqué.

President Johnson seemed to be quite happy with the summit. I had several opportunities to share laughs with him during the Fiesta Barrio that President Marcos hosted at the close of the high level gathering. He was very pleasant and friendly. Later, I was privately informed by members of the American delegation that the next day, October 26, President Johnson would go, unannounced, to Cam Ranh in central Vietnam, just south of Da Nang, to visit U.S. troops. They said he would not need any Saigon leaders to be there to greet him, but that my presence there would be more than sufficient to keep him company. I was astonished by such a development and at once responded to Philip Habib and his colleagues that for me to do that would be absolutely inappropriate, to say nothing of being a sure way to politically send me to the lion's pit.

Any Saigonese politician would consider himself honored by such a presidential invitation. But I declined, with thanks, and made it clear that I preferred to not accept the "poisoned gift" (*cadeau empoisonné*, as the French would say.) I appealed to my American contacts that they invite the Prime Minister of the RVN to greet the President at Cam Ranh. Hearing about the opportunity, several South Vietnamese political factions initiated efforts to be chosen for the welcoming protocol honor. Meanwhile, I ran for cover and refuge with Mrs. Marcos and her coterie of charming and attractive "Blue Ladies," as they were labeled, who were designated as official escorts for Summit participants during our stay in Manila.

By whom and how I never found out, but it was finally decided that the next day in Cam Ranh, I would stand at the foot of the landing stairs of President Johnson's plane with the South Vietnam Prime Minister, Brigadier General Nguyen Cao Ky, who would welcome the U.S. President and Commander-in-Chief at the enormous American military base. But that was still not to be the end of surprises for me. As soon as LBJ had set foot on our Vietnamese soil and shaken our hands, he said to General Ky with his finger pointing at me, "He is the one with the most difficult job in Saigon." Why did he say that? I have never known. It was said that he was impressed by the three words I wrote that started President Thieu's speech, "We want peace." I have assumed it was something of a compliment from him, but I don't know whether or not he was signaling something about how to find an equitable solution for all the parties that would end the horrible Vietnam mess. Whatever it was, it was a poisoned gift to me, for sure. Very soon afterwards, I was reassigned to another ministerial post.

Lyndon Baines Johnson was a tremendously powerful political animal during his visit at Cam Ranh, talking and shaking hands with everybody, obviously enjoying himself much more than if he were kissing babies or patting old folks' backs at home (the things that one has to do as president of the United States of America!). LBJ seemed quite satisfied to see that his GIs had all the necessary comforts of the Great Society: air-conditioned barracks, hot and cold showers, T-bone steaks, ice cream, cigars, chocolates, radios, TVs and cassettes, etc. It was, in many respects, their billionaires' war. President Johnson was clearly moved by the sight of his boys in Cam Ranh and, as their Commander-in-Chief right there in the field, he did not fail to tell them that he would "...never let you down, nor your fighting comrades, nor the fifteen million people of Vietnam, nor the hundreds of millions of Asians who are counting on us to show here, here in Vietnam, that aggression doesn't pay, and that aggression cannot succeed."

LBJ was sincere in his ideals, wishes and hopes that day in Cam Ranh. What he said was also exactly what he needed to say to his troops, but he must have known that there was no light at the end of the military tunnel. The only hope for him was for the Vietnamese in South Vietnam to live in peace without any war anymore. Again, how? If it was true what people said about the Viet Cong (NLF) not being communist and not under the allegiance of Hanoi, Thieu could accept reconciliation with Madame Binh. President Johnson did try hard to reach this aim at that time. The dilemma was total for President Johnson, considering who the brother-enemies were—Hanoi, Saigon, and the NLF—and how they felt about one another. But it was useless and hopeless for LBJ to ask Thieu—or even the Pope—to bring these three Vietnamese groups together. LBJ did make a try with the Pope. From whatever motivation or for whatever reason, the Vatican did actively join forces with Paris and Washington in ousting Thieu with the hope of bringing "Big" Minh and Madame Binh together for "the salvation of the Saigon regime."

The 1966 Manila Summit was my first contacts with world leaders, and I was touched by the warm conversations I had with several of them. President Park Chung Hee of the Republic of Korea later awarded me with a Korean "national order," with impressive cordon and plaque, pinned on me by then Prime Minister Kim Jong Pil. Australian Prime Minister Harold Holt invited me to visit Australia officially in 1967 (just a few weeks before his mysterious disappearance at sea). U.S. President Johnson, for no reason that I could fathom, wanted me to be present during his subsequent visit to Cam Ranh which lasted less than three hours. (The next American president to set foot on Vietnamese soil would be President William Jefferson Clinton in November 2000.)

The years 1966 and 1967 marked the beginning of a series of crises for the Saigon regime. To begin with, there was a violent and sensitive clash between northerners and southerners within the administration. With Ky, a northerner, as prime minister surrounded by trusted aides who were also from the north, the southerners complained of "ethnic regional discrimination and victimization" and resulted in the resignations of the ministers of economics, public health, social welfare, and others. Fate paid me another visit. I became Minister of Welfare.

The Saigon Ministry of Social Welfare was a fat and easy cow to manage. It was accepted practice to alternate between a Catholic and Buddhist as minister, to keep the priests and monks happy taking turns with the celestial manna. There were no laws or regulations governing welfare programs. They were simply arbitrary distributions of charity to the poor, sick and destitute, to the orphans, widows, and such. The Army Council assigned me to the post probably because I was a southerner (the previous and ousted welfare minister had been a "victimized" Buddhist southerner). I was neither Catholic nor Buddhist, was probably labeled a godless atheist, but, as far as I was able to reckon, I had demonstrated the necessary impartiality for that kind of a job. I had also shown myself to be the type not to take even a nickel from the kitty and the sort to dispense the fat cow's largesse equitably.

My time at the Ministry of Social Welfare was the best years of my life in the Saigon government. I was completely absorbed by activities I had never known about before, and felt I was doing something useful at last. My waiting room was truly a *cour des miracles* (court of miracles), full of people from early morning till late afternoon. At first, I saw no one and completely disregarded outside advice. It took me about two weeks to issue regulations defining the categories of people eligible for assistance. For the first time, social services meant not the whimsical governmental dispensation of funds to favored recipients, but instead was a clearly outlined program of assistance to people truly in need. The poor, the sick, the orphaned, the widowed, victims of fire and natural calamities, all were clearly defined with conditions of eligibility and would receive aid—just fill out the forms correctly and, after facts and identities were checked and officially certified, the help would be there.

My waiting room suddenly emptied out. I didn't expect funding from the government, but I was certain I could get all sorts of badly needed goods, services, and human resources. I ran in all directions, contacting every possible organization inside and outside the country. In less than three months, I was able to set up a formal Association of Welfare Agencies, with a core of over forty large international voluntary institutions and hundreds of smaller groups. Help flowed in from the four corners of the globe. My task soon boiled down to the tough job of establishing relations, mobilizing the welfare organizations, and assisting and coordinating the implementation of programs administered by foreign groups.

After the first year, the results were astonishing. More than two billion dollars' worth of welfare goods were distributed directly to the poor and sick in South Vietnam by these foreign groups and organizations. American Ambassador Henry Cabot Lodge and his wife joined me often for social welfare events. I was invited to lunch and dinner at their private residence several times. (They, too, treated me like a son or grandson. I was to meet them again in Paris at the peace talks in January 1969. Mrs. Lodge promoted a match between me and a very nice young American woman who had been doing social work in Saigon during my time at the Welfare Ministry and had joined us in Paris. Alas, I was not fated to live in Boston, the hometown of the young woman, whom I liked very much and appreciated as a good friend).

At the Welfare Ministry, I tried hard to do whatever was possible to help the destitute, needy orphans and widows, and the maimed and wounded. But their numbers kept on increasing by the thousands every day with the endless escalation of the war. With very limited funds, I was able to set up about fifty Old Folks' Homes in provincial towns to give food and shelter to abandoned persons over seventy years of age. Similarly, we set up over one hundred welfare canteens to provide meals for about the equivalent of U.S. twenty-five cents. We established a National Training Center for Social Workers to provide trained staff for orphanages which were running with a mortality rate for infants at thirty to forty percent. I was also able to implement successfully a "Milk Drop" program with UNICEF help to provide a glass of milk each day to every child in elementary schools in the large cities of South Vietnam. My work at the Welfare Ministry was absorbing but profoundly distressing and discouraging.

Both militarily and politically, 1967 and 1968 were unfortunate years for the Saigon government, although so-called general elections did take place. Thieu was elected president, with Ky as his vice-president, in September 1967. After heated and sometimes violent discussions among the Saigon generals, Ky had finally agreed to be Thieu's vice-president, with the condition that he would name the one to replace him as prime minister. That was how Ky's protégé, the southern lawyer Nguyen Van Loc, happened to be the Saigon prime minister at the time of the devastating 1968 Tet Mau Than general offensive by the communist forces against almost all the major cities in South Vietnam. Prime Minister Van Loc promptly lost his job after the Tet offensive. The more elderly and shrewd four-star general Tran Thien Khiem was quickly nominated to prime minister, where he remained until Thieu's and his resignations in April 1975. The military establishment was determined to take things firmly in hand and not be shamed again by the Viet Cong.

Hanoi and the Viet Cong did not have the slightest hope of beating the ARVN with their half-million GI allies in South Vietnam by the 1968 Tet Mau Than general offensive. It actually lasted less than a month, with scattered fighting here and there, but the communist forces suffered the most serious losses in men, equipment, and physical facilities, including many of their precious secret bases and undercover agents. It was their greatest loss for the entire period of the American War in Viet-Nam. It was an enormously painful price to pay, but the Hanoi politburo knew exactly what it was doing: the 1968 Tet general offensive by the communist forces in South Vietnam demonstrated the obvious failure of the colossal American military intervention in terms of U.S. troops, money, and sophisticated armaments on land, sea, and in the air. Short of nuclear weapons to destroy all the "fish and water" of the earth, General Westmoreland's military strategy and tactic was simply "building sand castles on the shores of the South China Sea" (*Da trang xe cat Bien Dong*, in Vietnamese). The 1968 Tet general offensive also had disastrous effects on the diplomatic and political scenes, both internationally and domestically, for the American president.

Justice must be given to President Johnson, who had in many ways done for the American people a lot more than his predecessors in human rights and social welfare, and had achieved rather good economic growth. He had all the reasons to believe firmly in the success of his Great Society, which showed encouraging signs of being on a good track, but still lacked the steam to deliver the bacon to the American people. Faced with the impossible dilemma of The Vietnam War, LBJ had to decide on a difficult issue of morality. He considered himself a true democrat and decent liberal, with the duty of defending the ideals of Western civilization. He could not do violence to his conscience and not live up to his given word, to uphold American honor at home and in the world. He sincerely thought that America could not be the land of the free, the rich, and the brave, and the American people a Great Society if the American president turned out to be a lame duck coward running shamefully away in the face of an enemy, even if it was in far away Viet-Nam. That was the reason why he continued to unleash the fires of hell on Viet-Nam, to maintain American honor for his Great Society.

Within the five short years between 1963 and 1968, President Johnson did try very hard, but in vain, to bring his concepts of freedom and democracy to the Vietnamese in South Vietnam with his "guns and butter" initiative. Yet he had to learn that his policy for Viet-Nam could not mix with or fit the concepts of peace and prosperity for his Great Society and for the American people. He was shunned by his aides, distrusted his experts, let his secretary of defense go, and realized that he had become the loneliest man on earth. Most sickening of all, Johnson was to find out later that during the 1968 presidential elections in the U.S., he and his Democratic Party had been ignominiously betrayed by the Saigon generals, the very ones he had defended against the advice of everybody and at the cost of his Great Society.

As for me, except for the routine at the Ministry of Social Welfare, I was becoming more and more out of tune with the general situation. Doing welfare work while all the killing and destruction were continuing to go on and on put me in a sort of unreal world that reminded me of the British expression describing a somewhat similar situation: "If you keep on hitting your head with a hammer, it feels really good when you stop." The war was raging on and U.S. troops were all over the place, profoundly disrupting Vietnamese society, much more, in fact, than the enemy forces. I found myself thinking more and more about the possibility of the war ending through negotiations. There had to be a way out somehow. The war was utterly stupid for both sides. I had become really dissatisfied with the whole useless and meaningless show and, by mid-1968, had decided to leave the Saigon government and somehow deal with the consequences. I came to the conclusion that having to enter the military academy at age thirty-two was no worse than being a cabinet minister. Besides, I didn't think that the defense minister, Lieutenant-General Nguyen Van Vy and four-star General Cao Van Vien of the Joint Chiefs-of-Staff of the ARVN—both former colleagues of mine during five long years in the Saigon government—would allow the draft office to call me for military service immediately.

I didn't get the chance to find out what kind of cadet I would have become because destiny intervened once again, this time in the person of another long-time friend of my family, Ambassador Pham Dang Lam. He came to see me about the impending diplomatic event that history would come to know as the Paris peace talks. Unlike my other high ranking mentors in the Saigon civil service, Lam and I were approximately of the same generation; he had always considered me something of a blood brother. He was a legendary public servant and pillar of the Saigon regime, well-trained, like my father, under French colonial rule. Intelligent and disciplined, he made his mark in the field of foreign service. Lam was, in fact, the quintessential diplomat, having served in several echelons of the Saigon Ministry of Foreign Affairs, which he had also managed many years as secretary-general. He had also served more than once as foreign minister in the so-called civilian Saigon governments. The last time I had seen him was at the 1966 summit in Manila, where he was posted as the Saigon ambassador to the Philippines.

Talks were already going on between Washington and Hanoi in Paris, as we all knew, but Lam told me that events were unfolding so rapidly that Saigon would have to join them soon. President Thieu had asked him to head the Saigon delegation in the preparation phase and serve as Saigon's consul general in Paris at the same time. My name had emerged from high-level discussions as to the choice of a deputy leader of the delegation. Would I accept the job and lend him a hand?

Belying a severe outer appearance, thin and tall in impeccable Saville Row suits and Italian shoes, Ambassador Lam was always very calm in demeanor but had a wonderful sense of humor. In private among friends, he could relax. He and I often indulged in wild and crazy pranks. We even found a lot to laugh about in discussing the imminent peace talks in Paris, despite the very serious nature of such an historical event.

Lam spoke his fluent French in a refined style and began his discourse by telling me that the job would consist mainly of a *conversation de sourds* (a conversation with the deaf). Thinking of my "tale of two cities" concept, I remarked to him that from now on we would have a "tale of three cities"—Washington, Hanoi, *and Saigon*—with three deaf participants. Lam, precisionist that he was, was quick to interject, "*Four* deaf participants," reminding me that Madame Binh would surely have a place at the unhearing table, whether Thieu liked her or not. The conversation led us into a ludicrous world of myths and realities, of absurd political configurations. There would be three Vietnamese politicians of sometimes conflicting points of view sharing a Parisian conference table with one American, who would be the only one eager for—in fact, would desperately need—an agreement that would enable the U.S. to wash its national hands of the dreary Vietnamese episode, while at the same time allowing the brother-enemies to live happily ever after. A real fairy tale, that.

Lam and I were dead certain that there was nothing for Hanoi to negotiate with, its *sine qua non* being the total end of U.S. intervention in Viet-Nam and total elimination of the anti-communist Saigon regime. Thieu and the military establishment had no choice but to cling to continued U.S. intervention and preservation of the anti-communist government in South Vietnam. That was the Gordian knot of intractability that Henry Kissinger would have to try to untie later on. Lam and I concluded that our task in Paris would not be much of a sweat because the real negotiations—and headaches for Thieu—would come from the dealings with Washington, not Hanoi. All this having been said, Lam and I were happy to find ourselves on the same galley again for the first time since the 1966 Manila Summit.

The Saigon delegation, including Vice-President and Mrs. Nguyen Cao Ky, arrived in Paris on December 8, 1968. The U.S. had been engaged in private talks with Hanoi since the previous March, with official talks starting in May. Both Hanoi and Washington had finally agreed to admit Madame Binh to the formal, more or less public, sessions that paralleled the private negotiations, provided President Thieu was treated similarly to Madame Binh. As soon as Madame Binh was accepted to appear at the high table, Hanoi cared not at all how many buddies from the whole wide Free World the U.S. brought along to the plush Hotel Majestic, renamed Center for International Conferences, in Paris.

More than one thousand reporters from all over the world flocked to Paris to cover the talks, and hopes were high for a negotiated settlement by everybody—except for those who were sent there to negotiate. Lam and I harbored no illusions as we embarked on those infamous sessions between the "two sides with four delegations" seated at a round table carefully calculated to eight meters in diameter. They were negotiations that were to drag on for more than four years.

The size and shape of the conference table for the Paris peace talks on Viet-Nam received wide publicity. Thieu desperately wanted Washington to declare the proceedings "a two-sided conference," a logical position to hold about a war between two opposing forces. His aim was to ignore Madame Binh and her NLF. Hanoi, on the other hand, insisted very strongly that there were obviously four different parties participating in the conference; it thereby achieved the important political recognition of Madame Binh that it wanted. So the heated discussions about the shape of the table dragged on for months. Most observers were appalled by the absurdity of the situation. The Paris peace talks in search of a peaceful solution to a bloody war were unable to commence because the participants couldn't even agree on the shape of the table they were to sit at. I doubt very much that ambassadors Harriman and Vance cared much what the shape was for that ill-humored piece of furniture and would have gladly accepted sitting in the lotus position on the floor if that would have made everyone genuinely interested in seriously negotiating for peace. To Thieu's gratification, President Johnson supported his argument for a two-sided conference in its form (the table). As for content (agreement), that was a completely different story in the end.

The table dispute inspired all sorts of suggestions by well-wishers and neutral observers. In a spirit of peace and cooperation, some urged that there should be only one side to the table, so the participants could huddle together for warmth during the cold Parisian winter. With this arrangement, all could face a large ornate mirror, hung with the compliments of the former Mother France of Indochina, that would reflect all participants symbolically sharing the side of peace, while also being able to converse with each other through the looking-glass. Others suggested providing each delegate with an individual table-and-chair, like a school desk on wheels, so that everyone could zip around the conference room talking to one another. That would really get things moving. The most appealing idea came from those who suggested that the simplest thing would be to organize a gastronomic picnic on green artificial grass in the plush Louis XV style conference room—with *saucissons sec* and *beaujolais nouveau*, the thrift-minded thought, or with canapés, champagne, and white-tie-and-tails, said those of more elegant bent. That would suggest real friendliness and be peace-provoking, putting everybody in the same mood.

After a long deadlock, the delicate issue was ultimately settled, with assists from the French and the Soviets. The four parties would sit at a large round table (to accommodate in a neutral manner the presence of the four delegations), eight meters in diameter (to make sure no one would get hurt should there be any throwing of objects at one another, such as a Vietnamese coconut or an American baseball at that distance), with two tiny rectangular tables diametrically positioned at the side for the secretaries (a rather cheap cadeau for President Thieu's two-sided obsession and completely useless for everybody else). The table was to be covered with a dark green flannel cloth similar to that of billiards tables. No flags or nameplates were allowed, and all participants would drink the same plain mineral water. No coffee was served so no one would be deterred from enjoying a good nap during the reading of the sacred prepared speeches, which, of course, could go on for hours, weeks after weeks, months after months, and years after years.

I had the much-disputed privilege of being the opening speaker at the first session formally attended by all four delegations. I was followed by Cyrus Vance, Madame Binh (NLF), and Ha Van Lau (Hanoi), at the dreadful round table. The first meeting included no prepared speeches and was intended only to finalize the meeting procedures. It turned out to be the sole meaningful dialogue of the Paris peace talks. It was an exciting preview for the international press, and quite helpful for the freshly elected American president, Richard Nixon—who had the urgent task of nominating someone to replace democrat Averell Harriman as head of the U.S. delegation at the talks. The big show, which was to end up lasting four years, had its glittering premiere on January 25, 1969, with the arrival of Ambassador Henry Cabot Lodge, an old Vietnam hand.

Richard Holbrooke (later to be U.S. ambassador at the United Nations) was already in Paris working with ambassadors Averell

Harriman and Cyrus Vance, when Hanoi and Washington had agreed to meet unofficially in March and then officially in May 1968. Holbrooke and I were about the same age, in our early thirties. I thought it was interesting that he remarked about how young I was for the job. Of course, Harriman and Vance, legendary figures in international politics and diplomacy, were about twice our age. A few days after we arrived in Paris, I was with Harriman and others at a reception, when reporters asked the former New York governor about the prospects for a settlement ending the war.

"Mr. Phong is my best bet," Harriman observed. "The thing to do is to lock him in a room with Madame Binh, throw away the key, and don't let them out until they've reached a solution."

I interjected that I was willing to make the sacrifice but the process had better be quick, because I didn't have the firepower to sustain her well-known delaying tactics. Chalmer Roberts of the Washington Post found the exchange very amusing. Saigon's Ambassador Lam at one point was characterized by Harriman as "a poisonous frog," to the joy and satisfaction of President Thieu, who interpreted the comment to mean that his ambassador in Paris for the peace talks was considered a sort of lethal weapon, by American standards, in the face of the enemy.

Richard Nixon's ascendancy to the U.S. presidency in January 1969 would lead to a change in the cast of characters at the Paris peace talks, with legendary figures replacing legendary figures. Henry Cabot Lodge succeeded Harriman in January 1969, but by December of that year, David K. E. Bruce, at the age of seventy-two, took the helm of the American delegation in Paris. The sessions were dutifully attended by all the four delegations, but the most exciting moments came with the excellent lunches provided weekly by the French Ministry of Foreign Affairs. Meanwhile, the real negotiations were transpiring in private between Kissinger and Le Duc Tho, who had their first secret talks in Paris on January 21, 1970. Their endless rounds with ups and downs were to go on until January 23, 1973.

In their first meetings in Paris, Tho was quick to point out to Kissinger one immutable reality: "You have lost, and we have won." Kissinger didn't need Tho to tell him this, having already taught the precept of victory and defeat in guerrilla warfare to his classes at Harvard (the party carrying out guerrilla warfare wins if it does not lose, while the party being the object of guerrilla warfare loses if it does not win). Tho and his colleagues had endured untold suffering for decades in order to be able to speak those words, so speak them he did.

On the one side, the U.S. trusted in its military power to persuade Hanoi to give up the struggle. On the other side, Hanoi had the more challenging task, but one that would ultimately prevail, as had David over Goliath. Hanoi's strategy was three-pronged: political, military, and diplomatic. First, the political component associated communism with the tremendous force of the Vietnamese people's nationalistic feelings against a foreign and military presence on their soil. This component pictured the communist struggle as one against foreign aggression and characterized it as a war of liberation and self-defense, which mobilized popular support for anti-American sentiment. Second, the military component brilliantly combined the so-called "people's warfare" of self-defense and guerrilla tactics with precisely coordinated conventional warfare. Finally, the diplomatic component relied on mobilizing world public opinion, rather than governmental diplomatic action, and brought it to bear primarily on U.S. public opinion. The success of this component was reflected in the anti-war protests and the level of opposition to the war in the U.S. Congress.

The war would be analyzed, studied, dissected, and written about for many years, and history would blend myth with reality. But one overriding fact remained: Kissinger's main objective was to end the U.S. folly in Viet-Nam, but with honor. The Paris Accords did exactly that. So, what went wrong in the spring of 1975, causing such an irremediable disgrace to the denizens of the U.S. capital?

The long and painful road to peace for Viet-Nam in Paris was initiated by President Johnson in March 1968, was pursued for a period of four years, and was concluded in January 1973 by President Nixon. The Franco-Soviet-designed round table produced results—for Hanoi and the NLF. It was neither "two sides" nor "four parties." My "tale of three cities" and three-deaf-participants concept had turned out to be much closer to the truth than Lam's "four cities" version. Le Duc Tho and Madame Binh were indisputably one for all and all for one. Washington and Saigon should have been of similar single-mindedness but, unfortunately, they were painfully distinct. It didn't take Hanoi and the NLF very long after Saigon's fall in April 1975 to demonstrate their unanimity with the reunification of North and South Vietnams in July 1976 under Hanoi's communist regime, and the birth of the Socialist Republic of Viet-Nam (Cong Hoa Xa Hoi Chu Nghia Viet-Nam). At the Paris peace talks in the early 1970s, it didn't take Kissinger long to see that Thieu and he could never get together. It is what happens in a bad love affair. The lovers were unable to fulfill the mandates of a popular and profound Vietnamese proverb: "To love means for the two to be just one, and yet being just one also means two."

Kissinger tried as best he could to keep Thieu informed of developments in his private talks with Le Duc Tho, but he wouldn't have had the slightest chance to succeed with Hanoi if he had let Saigon in on all the gory details. To be one with Thieu was for Thieu to be like Kissinger and not for Kissinger to be like Thieu, of course. Keeping Thieu happy was, after all, Nixon's job and not his. The only time Saigon had any direct involvement related to the drafting of the Paris Accords was in the very last rounds of the negotiations in mid-January 1973. For reasons known only to him, Kissinger brought Lam and me in on certain of the clauses of the negotiations. There were just a few sensitive clauses left to be redrafted, among them Article 8c, concerning the release of civilian political prisoners detained in South Vietnam, and Article 15, concerning the DMZ, eventual reunification, and relations between

North and South Vietnam. Since these were issues concerning Saigon and, conspicuously, not Washington, Lam and I were invited to meet with the U.S. delegation and asked to draft the articles in question, after being briefed on the heated discussions about these articles between Kissinger and Tho.

On the drive back to our office, Lam assigned the chore to me since I had been present at the meeting, was fully conversant with the issues involved, and my English was adequate to fulfill the task without the help of a translator. The task was to be undertaken with the utmost secrecy. It took me a couple of hours to finish the job, in both English and Vietnamese. I quickly showed the drafts to Lam, because Kissinger was waiting with a certain amount of impatience since he was scheduled to meet with Tho again that evening. I suggested to Lam that he fill Saigon in on the points, but he unhesitatingly responded that it would simply create a nuisance and be a waste of time. Lam was happy to use the lack of time as a pretext not to make the contact. Kissinger and Tho accepted my drafts for Articles 8c and 15 without even changing the semi-colon I had put in. Saigon got at least that. Better than nothing again.

The next time our delegation met with Kissinger, he jokingly complained that I had leaked information about the DMZ to my long-time friend Joseph Kingsbury-Smith, vice-president of the Hearst Group. The press was well aware that Kissinger and Tho had reached the homestretch of the negotiations, and that there were only a few sensitive matters left to be settled. An agreement was only hours away, the reporters knew, and all of them wanted a scoop. They became enamored of the story concerning the DMZ. Would it be made "iron-tight" or "porous" in so far as the comings and goings of North Vietnamese forces were concerned? Of little interest to Kissinger and Tho, the issue was theoretically vital to the Saigon government's security. In response to questions by reporters, including Kingsbury-Smith, I did say that no one would like to see a porous DMZ. Of course, the sacred and damned thing had been porous for twenty years and, porous or not, it would take Hanoi's forces less than an hour to deploy a couple of regular North Vietnamese divisions over the demarcation line, as it had been doing repeatedly over the years. Of course, the official line by The North Vietnamese Democratic Republic of Vietnam was that it had never officially sent its army into the south—they were simply Vietnamese patriots traveling there to help their fellow countrymen. As usual, the issue was more complicated than journalists perceived, but this was the story they were interested in hearing at the time.

It was already agreed between Washington and Hanoi, Moscow, and Beijing that the question of the North Vietnamese troops' presence in South Vietnam would remain unspoken by everybody. They would simply remain in South Vietnam; that's all. It would take a long time, if not be silly, to identify and differentiate a North Vietnamese from a South Vietnamese just by their Vietnamese faces. At one of the secret meetings, Hanoi's minister Xuan Thuy suggested to Kissinger that he agree to a private meeting with a true and genuine South Vietnamese, Madame Binh. Minister Xuan Thuy, also a well known North Vietnamese poet, claimed he was sure the good doctor would find the lady most interesting. Kissinger politely declined, adding that he was scared to death of the Madame. When Xuan Thuy assured Kissinger that Madame Binh would be "very gentle" with him, the doctor replied that, in his professional opinion, the lady would be "very tough." If I remember correctly, this attempt at matchmaking occurred in the beautiful Paris spring of 1971.

Once again, Lam and I had a rollicking time discussing the episode. Kissinger's reputation as something of a lothario added to our merriment. But to be fair to the former Harvard professor, it must be said that he had seen many good days in his fascinating life, and Madame Binh was not really his cup-of-tea, politically or otherwise. He had never given any evidence at any time of politically flirting with Madame Binh. Nevertheless, President Thieu was dreadfully tortured by the "green monster" as everyone after

Shakespeare has called it—everybody knows that the best thing about jealousy is to enjoy the doubt and not the conviction.

* * *

Thus did my mind wander in my solitude at Thu Duc prison. It roamed from government life in Saigon, to the mission to Manila, to diplomatic assignments in Paris, then back to this large cell with the solid iron door. I did not know it while I reminisced that night, but I was about to embark on a new chapter of my long adventure into hope.

Our stay at Thu Duc was to become relatively short, just a few weeks. One morning we were gathered in the courtyard chained two-by-two, and taken to the airport in army trucks. Anxious, but with not a clue about our destination, we boarded a C-130 plane and took to the air. We were told nothing. As usual, the guards were very correct, almost friendly. After take-off, many of us guessed that we were headed for the infamous Con Dao penitentiary, a former French prison in South Vietnam. But when the flight exceeded half an hour, we all knew we were going to North Vietnam.

After landing at Gia Lam airport near Hanoi, we noticed that the flight crew, former Saigon air force pilots, joined us on the trucks that wove their way through the city streets before traveling along country roads that led to our reeducation camp. Along the way, some kids hurled insults—and a few rocks—in our direction. Our guards appeared to be annoyed, and the childish incidents disturbed and worried some of my companions, but I wasn't affected much at all. How could anyone blame these boys and girls, no older than ten? For twice their lifetimes, an image had been created of American neo-imperialists, cruel and mortal enemies of their beloved Vietnamese fatherland. "Human life is measured by ideas and actions, not by time," an old English proverb goes. But it seemed to me that much time and many ideas and actions would be needed before the scars would heal on these rock-throwing young souls.

During the two-hour drive through the North Vietnamese countryside, other landscapes passed through my mind, France and England, Italy and Spain, Holland and Switzerland, Athens, Bangkok, Manila, Kuwait, Amman. All of them were populated by scampering, noisy children. These images then dissolved into the terrible thoughts of violent wars between brother-enemies. There in the wilderness of the north of Viet-Nam, it struck me that humankind had traveled to a place much worse than its point of departure, to a locale where the saying was no longer "*Am* I my brother's keeper?" (Genesis 4:9), which was Cain's reply to God when asked where his brother Abel was. Cain had just killed his brother. Cain's rhetoric was a first in the use of a "question" to answer a question in order to get out of a mess. Nowadays, people are much blunter in their replies. Cain's retort to God has now become "I don't know who my brother is anymore." Worse still, "I have no brother" seems to be the common reply in our modern times.

I have often reflected on that very sad italicized word "*Am*" in the King James versions, both old and new. It is not a problem of semantics or syntax that has caused endless debates among linguists and theologians in the past four hundred and more years. Cain was the first brother of humankind, and he knew well that it would be really stupid for him or any human being to ask God questions. Even his father Adam would not have dared talk to God that way. Cain's reply to God was more of an exclamation than a question; it meant, "I am not my brother's keeper," a denial of responsibility. But he surely must have felt that it was equally silly for him to exclaim such a denial to God. Cain did not yet know much about the "to be and become" of the human condition. His apparent question to God was, in fact, both an exclamation of denial to God and a *question to himself*, without knowing that he had started something big, really big, for everybody. Cain's question has become The Question, if not the most important question of the whole of humankind since creation.

"Brother, how can we get out of Cain's mess now?" The word "brother" has, unfortunately, turned out to be a daily but empty exclamation, from the greats and non-greats of this world in their imposing offices in the inner cities of New York, London, Paris, Moscow, Beijing, and elsewhere, to mean anything from "god" to "baloney."

Fratricidal wars are, therefore, as old as Genesis and worse than anything created by the fall of man. Must we all be Cains and Abels? We are the earth's most powerful and intelligent creatures, but also its most murderous. Viet-Nam has had no monopoly on fratricide. My stay at Oxford acquainted me with many who were brother-enemies. There my Arab and Jewish friends had great times together. In 1973, I made a two-week tour of the Middle East and saw with sadness how, back in their homelands, my schoolmate friends had returned to their traditional roles as brother-enemies. Their grief, enmities, helplessness, and hopes for an end to the bleeding were not very different from my own.

I then came to understand better the word "humanity" as something that can and must be shared in both joy and sorrow, right and wrong, love and hate, life and death. The issues in the Middle East were and are much more complex than those in Viet-Nam, but the need to hope for an end to the killing there was the same. I remember being particularly impressed by my Jordanian friends when I spent five exciting days in their country. I was traveling alone, completely at my friends' disposal, and they were able to show me almost everything there was to see in Jordan: factories, schools, hospitals, historical sites, social institutions, military bases, refugee camps, and border zones. It was a beautiful country in its own way, with hospitable, hard-working, optimistic people—and such a fortunate nation to have trust in and love for an exceptional leader, King Hussein. Not every nation can say that.

My five-day stay in Jordan in 1973 benefited me greatly and provided me with a valuable source of hope, trust, and confidence in human nature and in myself. I met with Jordanian Prime Minister Zaid Rifai, was privileged to sit in on a cabinet session and, through the courtesy of some friends, was guest of honor at a grand reception hosted by the mayor of Amman, attended by hundreds. Then I met with King Hussein. It was the last time I would see him. Of course, fratricidal conflicts entered into our conversation. Hussein had been refusing to see other Arab leaders for months. I was the neutral visitor through whom he would be enabled to formally break the ice without upsetting the diplomatic applecart. We enjoyed a relaxed and open discussion, with no formal consequences, about our respective fraternal conflicts. He told me of his great concern for the quick improvement of Jordan's universities and its economic development. It worried me when he said that if one of his Arab brethren took his disagreement so far as to attack Jordan, he would have no choice but to seek U.S. assistance and, if required, even military intervention ("Good grief!"—I thought of Charlie Brown). We also discussed intellectual conviction, loneliness (a byproduct of his long and outstanding leadership), the personal courage and determination required in politics and wars (a trait he possessed in abundance), human aspirations and limitations, and omnipresent hope.

I will always take comfort from a simple but profound remark Hussein made in our meeting: "You live your destiny." King Hussein of Jordan became a constant source of wisdom and hope for me, and remains so today. His great gift was his exceptional ability to persuade through the heart rather than the mind. Life means much more than dogma and argumentation. That was the precious lesson Hussein taught me. We must be constantly open to precious lessons from the great and the humble. Hussein happened to have been one of the greats.

During my long imprisonment, I was also to draw on the precious lessons I learned from a great little Jewish girl, Anne Frank. Thinking of her story also brought me comfort and hope. She made an eternal contribution to the ideal of hope for humanity in the face of horrors, atrocities, and barbarity.

"It's difficult in times like this," she wrote. "Ideals, dreams and cherished hopes rise within us only to be crushed by grim realities . . . . ," and she added, "Yet I cling to them because I still believe, in spite of everything, that people are truly good at heart." That little girl, who died in a Nazi concentration camp, asked us to share her wonderful trust that humankind would some day overcome its own evil. She taught us how to be grateful for the gift of life in happiness and sorrow, with simultaneous glimpses of heaven and hell.

I am deeply grateful for and profoundly value the gift of life, but long ago lost interest in any mystical notions of heaven and hell. I am convinced that we human beings have a spiritual life, which may or may not continue after physical death, which may or may not permit the continuation of individual consciousness or retain the same individual identity in a different cosmic context as humankind understands it in human existence on Earth. I am totally open to accept any and all good advice from any religion or ideology that brings people together in respect and sharing of their individual diversities, and helps us live the one and only common destiny of humankind on this planet—which might be both immense and minute, depending on how big or small one feels one is. Again, fortunately or unfortunately, most people are inclined to think big.

* * *

We arrived at the detention camp just in time for lunch, which was exceptionally good. We remembered that lunch for years afterward, because there was never its equal in that camp again. The guards remained quite friendly, treating us almost as if we weren't convicts at all, but just some travelers who had happened to drop in for an interesting visit. There was no way for me to know which facts of life were myths or realities. I also felt there was a constant need in me to hope, but it was completely drowned in a confusing world of myths and realities that vividly made up the facts of life for me to deal with, one way or another to the best of my abilities.

5-CART

I thought about my father and how he hadn't joined his relatives who had traveled to the North all those many years ago. Now here was I, making the long delayed journey, not knowing whether or not I would be there for the rest of my life.

CODA

Reflections on Myths and Realities

Similar to illusions and disillusions
in hope,
myths and realities in hope
lead to the confrontation
between the imaginary and the real.
Different from
illusions and disillusions,
which result in the breaking-up
of hopes,
myths and realities
are capable
of generating tremendous energies
in the face of
the impossible and the possible.
Myths and realities
are inherent
in the making-up of hopes
and are concrete facts of life
to be reckoned and dealt with
through the interactive process
of the parameters of hope, namely,
Purpose, ***Meaning***, ***Reason***, and ***Reality***.

><

Hopes
may be called ***true hopes*** or ***false hopes,***
depending on their levels
of realization and viability
in function of the four parameters
of hope.
True hopes and false hopes
are equally facts of life
found in myths and realities.
The energies of hope
are interrupted from time to time
by illusions and disillusions
but are never turned off entirely.
They will continue
to be fueled
by endless myths and realities of life.

><

Myths and realities of hope
are sources
of illusions and disillusions in life.
In turn,
hopes in life
are often smashed
by illusions and disillusions,
which are recycled
into other myths and realities.
Myths and realities
are called the facts of life.
><

Life consists of
to be and ***to become***.
The acts of being and becoming

require future projections
and expectations.
They constitute the very essence
of hope.
Hope—
is inalienable
in the act of being and becoming.
Hope—
generates being and becoming.
No act of being and becoming
can prevail without hope.
Hope—
is an inherent aspect of life.
Hope—
can be denied, rejected,
ignored or repressed,
but hope is indestructible.
Life always has hope,
consciously or unconsciously,
whether in
latent*, *passive*,** or ***active states.
Even if any or all of its four parameters
are inoperative,
hope has the undying capability
of prevailing, even if only in its initial state
as latent hope.

PART TWO

CHAPTER EIGHT

STARLIGHT RETURNS: LATENT HOPE

My only hope lies in my despair.
Jean Racine (1639-1699)

Our new home in the north of Viet-Nam had the simple legal mailing address "Camp A15." We called it the "Hanoi Hilton Annex," since it was located only fifty kilometers from its namesake city. It had been the place of residence for American POWs until 1973. A very large compound, it was made up of a dozen premises about fifty meters long and six meters wide and surrounded by an imposingly high wall. There were about twelve hundred of us confined in the buildings, more than a hundred to each structure. Eleven were made of straw and mud with thatched roofs, and one was brick with a tiled roof. I was assigned to the brick one. They were really large cells. There were four, small, above-ground latrines in a small room off in a corner, double-level wooden bunks for our beds and living space, the usual iron door, and small windows with bars. But there were windows—the stars would return at night to be my companions again.

Living conditions were harsh and primitive by Saigon standards, but quite acceptable for the north of Viet-Nam, not just for prisoners, but also for the general population. Except for being locked up, we were in many respects more privileged than the villagers outside. We got quarterly rations of sugar, soap, toothpaste, and other items considered luxuries by the villagers, and which they sometimes asked to buy from us. Our eight daily hours of heavy labor entitled us to fifteen kilograms of cereals per month, compared to the nine kilograms the guards and villagers received. I understood that a ballet dancer would get eighteen and a mineworker, twenty-two.

I wasn't bothered much by the hard work and lack of amenities—I had lived on much less during my student days in Paris, London, and Oxford, working my way through my education as bellboy, doorman, kitchen helper, farm worker, mailman, Christmas-box wrapper, babysitter, carwasher, barman, morgue assistant, and even ladies' hairdresser. Yes, this wasn't so bad. It was the best detention camp money couldn't buy.

Generals and other superior army officers were housed in another corner of the camp, walled off from the rest of us. In our building, my elite Thu Duc companions—the finance minister, vice-minister for information and vice-minister of culture—were still around, but we were joined by new faces, illustrious unknowns from various South Vietnamese provinces. We were divided into groups of ten and, for whatever reason, I was not included with people who had been political party leaders, high government officials, or known reactionaries. I was included with men in their sixties. I was barely thirty-nine. There was Tam Huu, a tiny and lively impoverished illiterate who had spent most of his seventy-two years as a horse-cart driver in his home village somewhere near Go Cong in the Mekong Delta area. He didn't say why he had to be reeducated, and none of us asked. Our odd little group was exempt from heavy labor, but we still had to clean the latrines. Everybody had to clean the latrines.

What about our reeducation? We weren't required to do very much in that regard in the first year, except listen to Hanoi radio over a powerful loudspeaker. The *Nhan Dan* daily newspaper, official organ of the Viet-Nam Communist Party, was read to us for an hour every evening after we were locked in at five o'clock. Occasionally, we were instructed to write self-critical reports. I would dash off about thirty pages, but I understand that some managed to write thousands. Most of our time, however, was filled with mundane matters.

During the day, we were free to circulate in the courtyard in front of our cell and take turns going to the kitchen twice a day for our per capita one-hundred-fifty-gram basket of "steamed dough" and about a pint of a hot, reddish, tea-like beverage. After that, we got nothing but a couple of spoonfuls of salted water. We were awarded rice and meat on important holidays, such as the first of January, the Lunar New Year, National Day, and Labor Day. We lost weight fast. One night, on my way to the latrine, I stumbled upon my old friend from Thu Duc, the supreme court justice, roasting a snail over a burning piece of paper. We both reacted with confusion and embarrassment. A few weeks later, I spied the old horse-cart driver surreptitiously storehousing three of the nine mice we had caught earlier that evening and laid to rest in an out-of-the-way corner. For many of us, food—or the lack of it—had become an obsession.

I did a lot of thinking the first year there, more than ever before. Those little windows let the stars back in, and they gave me the feeling—more a vague, compelling drive than a hope—that something good might come of all this. Those windows presented the same stellar performance I had witnessed so many times in London and Paris, Saigon and Long Thanh, locales now light-years away. Oh well, I rationalized, at least here there were no exhaust fumes, just the peace and serenity of the North Vietnamese countryside to help me organize my thoughts. This, I told myself, was where reason would come into play, not just purpose and reality. Without purpose, there was no hope, but hope could not be properly expressed without reason translated into meaningful, logical, and realistic action. I thought of all this with the help of Alpha Centauri, and many past events kept invading my mind.

I remembered how, when I returned to Paris in December 1968 after so long an absence, I met an old friend, Elisabeth, someone I hadn't seen for nearly ten years. She was a North Vietnamese girl, from Hanoi, with a story about the ordeals of war as remarkable as that of my Estonian girlfriend in London. She had been having family problems when we came into contact again, and was downhearted and deeply discouraged. I wasn't very busy with the peace talks during that period, so we could meet often. Her family had been quite wealthy in Hanoi. Her father had been a landowner who had not survived the dramatic 1954-55 events there. He had been jailed, and then died in the violent purge of the wealthy classes in North Vietnam. His family managed to escape, joining the mass exodus to Saigon in 1955. His wife and daughter eventually migrated to Paris in the early 1960s.

We were married in July 1971, at the Neuilly Town Hall in the neighborhood of the Bois de Boulogne. It seemed that half the diplomatic corps in Paris attended our wedding. Ambassador David K. E. Bruce, then head of the U.S. delegation to the talks, was among them. Although he usually preferred spending weekends in his London home, he took a special plane and stayed for about an hour before flying back to London. His gift to us was a magnificent, ancient, solid-gold box. We were never able to discover if it was supposed to have a particular use. We admired it for its own sake, and Elisabeth still cherishes it dearly.

Four years later when I returned to Saigon, Elisabeth stubbornly insisted on accompanying me. After my incarceration, she was not permitted to return to France—although she had French nationality—until 1978. It was another terrible ordeal for her, compounding the tribulations of her 1955 exodus from Hanoi. Life was hard for her in Saigon from 1975 to 1978, but she was fortunate enough to receive all possible assistance from the French authorities, who finally helped her return to Paris. She got a modest three-room apartment at a low rent, thanks to the Ville de Paris and its mayor, then Monsieur Jacques Chirac (later president of France.) She obtained a civil service position at the social services section of the Ministry of Post and Communication. She has thus been able to take care of herself in France ever since. I was eventually permitted to travel to France to visit her in December 1988. We hadn't seen each other for fourteen years. Four months later, I had to go back to Saigon to take care of my parents, who were then around ninety and completely destitute by themselves. I didn't have the heart to ask her to go to Saigon with me again. We didn't bring up the subject, operating under an unspoken assumption that each of us would do what we had to do concerning our respective responsibilities to our relatives, without thinking of ourselves. What happened to us personally didn't seem to count for much any more, just what happened to our loved ones in Paris and Saigon. Fate had given us those four early years together in Paris, though even then, the hectic nature of our lives didn't allow us much time by ourselves. Many hopes have been dashed by history. I profoundly respected her sacrifices, pain, and suffering. She was the type to hide her wounds. With respect for her privacy, I can say that in many ways, her losses and sacrifices were the greatest of all in our family.

In the calm of the North Vietnamese detention camp, I began to stargaze about past politics and philosophies, particularly about an issue both sides of the bloody conflict seemed to agree upon, and that had haunted me continuously for years—the need for a Vietnamese identity and nationalism. One consensus clearly produced by the Paris Accords, undeniably felt by both North and South, was that Vietnamese were Vietnamese, belonging to one, and only one, nation. We were all descendents of the same ancestors and products of more than four thousand years of shared history. Why had it been so long since we had shared these nationalistic feelings? Had this very issue of nationalism been the profound cause for disagreement, dispute, and fratricidal killing among us Vietnamese?

In conflicting ways, it had. From the very beginning in the South, Diem had attempted to co-opt the "nationalist" label for his regime as opposed to the North Vietnamese communists. But Uncle Ho, too, had always prominently waved the banner of nationalism—"national independence," "national identity," and other nationalistic catch phrases. For twenty years, Saigon and Washington (through its U.S. Information Service and the Voice of America) had tried to demonstrate that international communism was the antithesis of nationalism and would destroy our national identity and culture. In one of history's customary ironies, it turned out that the brand of nationalism professed by Hanoi was more understandable and acceptable to the South Vietnamese than the sort advanced by Saigon and Washington. Truly, heaven and earth had turned upside down.

To be anti-communist or not mattered little to the ordinary South Vietnamese citizen, who cared even less for the much-ballyhooed struggle against international communism. What they wanted most was to put behind them a century of foreign domination, restore their traditions and customs, toil on their ancestors' little lots of land, and feed their families without being gunned down by people with promises of heaven on earth. In part, because of the Saigon government's poor performance, but also because of Washington's sense that the U.S. had to move the people of its Outpost of the Free World forward, economically and socially, at an increased pace, Washington sent Tribune Westmoreland to South Vietnam with his Pax Americana legions, by far the most formidable and sophisticated seen in human history. The people of South Vietnam, although very impressed, were nevertheless rendered motionless, as if transfixed by the deluge of American firepower. They just wanted to be with their brethren, undivided by a conflict they couldn't understand.

I often tried to interest whoever was willing to listen in my ideas about the importance of a national identity to the resolution of the Viet-Nam problem. I mentioned it to Robert Komer in 1967, when he came to Saigon for the pacification program. And

I discussed it with U.S. Deputy Ambassador Whitehouse in 1973, right after the signing of the Paris Accords.

"What should we do now?" he asked.

"In two words, national identity," I replied.

Throughout those years, each time I mentioned those two words, the Washington crowd, and especially the Saigonese officials, reacted as if I were throwing the words out for discussion at an after-dinner debate of the Oxford Union Society. There were more urgent and concrete tasks to attend to, they said. There was a war going on; there was no time for such philosophical debate. Washington's "guns and butter" strategy would show the South Vietnamese who they really were and why they were fighting and dying. Perhaps national identity was too thorny a subject. Perhaps if Averell Harriman had had his way, the military option would have been abandoned. Perhaps . . . any number of things.

So the nightmare continued with increasing ferocity. Westmoreland asked for 35,000 troops, then 175,000, then 200,000, then 275,000, until in the end, there were over 500,000 U.S. troops in South Vietnam by 1968. In response to this, Hanoi's General Giap's biggest headaches included where to find the same number of bicycles to put on the Ho Chi Minh Trail. When Westmoreland launched his search-and-destroy campaign, Giap asked his teenage *bo dois* in sandals to play hide and seek, teasing even more U.S. troops into the fray. Giap was pleased to hear Westmoreland express a hope to finish the job in four or five years. He would have worried if Westmoreland had said four or five days, but if it was a long-term investment Westmoreland was thinking about, that was all right with Giap. Time was the only ordinance he had that was superior to that of the U.S. General Giap, like everyone else, was assured that General Westmoreland's objective was not to destroy him, but to harass him. Great. He had never dreamed of defeating the U.S. troops, but only of tiring them out. With his well-known and colossal backpack stuffed with sophisticated arms and high-tech equipment, Westmoreland would easily run out of breath, get fed up with being an expatriate for so long, and yearn to spend the next Christmas at home.

"Get lost" was all Giap wanted Westy to do, remember? Then the compelling forces of history would get the Saigon regime to "drop dead" by itself.

Meanwhile, South Vietnamese folk saw Americans everywhere, even in their remote villages. They couldn't help wondering why they couldn't just sit down and savor a good meal with all their relatives, communists included. And they puzzled over why they couldn't enjoy a Saigon shopping expedition or a picnic at that world-class seacoast paradise, Ha Long Bay, without having to declare themselves anti-communist. This was supposed to be an outpost of the *free* world, wasn't it?

"Be patient," the Culture Ministry bureaucrat or travel agent would tell them. "There's a war going on. Have some butter to go with the sounds of guns while you wait."

With these thoughts running through my mind, I was reminded of the time, shortly after the Manila Summit, when I ran into Robert William Komer, who had been JFK's special assistant for national security and had been sent to Saigon in 1967 by LBJ for the pacification program as Deputy to the Commander, U.S. Military Assistance Command, responsible for Civil Operations and Rural Development Support, commonly referred to as MACV-CORDS. Bob and I were glad to renew our acquaintance, which had started at the 1966 Manila Summit Conference, and became good friends. But I let him know right off what I thought of his so-called pacification program, which was aimed at winning "the mind and the heart of the people" and thus denying or preventing popular support of the Viet Cong guerrillas. I was invited to attend a formal meeting when Komer and General Edward Landsdale (the U.S. expert in counter-insurgency) came to Saigon to present LBJ's pacification program. I was welfare minister and expressed my surprise at being present at such a sensitive and high-level gathering. The U.S. officials quickly told me that they had been instructed by President Johnson himself to see that I attended. An impartial observer? Another poisoned gift following the one at Cam Ranh?

This important meeting was held, curiously enough, at the residence of the governor of the central bank of South Vietnam, who was not present, but simply lent his place for the evening. The long American presentation was more than scientific. It was tense, since the whole future, fate, and destiny of the Vietnamese in South Vietnam and America's presence there were seen to rest on the success or failure of this pacification program. At the very end of the meeting, when asked to give my views about LBJ's "guns and butter" policy to win the minds and hearts of the people in South Vietnam, I simply said that butter alone could not win the mind and heart of the people, that even with their bellies full of all the good things the U.S. might provide, people could still blow your head off. I concluded by saying that putting butter into the water (people) would not deprive the fish (guerrillas) of the water. My remarks had the effect of an unexpected and really cold shower. Nobody said anything after that. My thirty years' youthfulness may have allowed a sufficient reason for them to forgive my brashness.

The Saigon government assigned the pacification program to the Ministry of Rural Development, and three-star-general Nguyen Bao Tri was slated for the job. I was surprised when he rushed to me and asked me to take it.

"No way," I said, "not even with a ten-foot pole."

Crafty Bao Tri, who had been Minister of Information, managed to pass the buck to another Saigon three-star general, Nguyen Duc Thang, who had been the commanding officer of Army Corps 4 in the Mekong Delta area. No argument there, since the U.S. thought it fit to put pacification under the Military Assistance Command, Vietnam (MACV), of four-star-general Westmoreland. The "not-to-win-not-to-lose" turned out, finally, to be a rather poor substitute for victory, but pacification was considered a more palatable and, somehow, more acceptable synonym for peace in the dreadful Vietnam War. My mother and aunts in their native village of Ba Tri would not be much wiser.

Bob Komer apparently paid attention to my skepticism, because he selected my maternal native village of Ba Tri to showcase the pacification process (especially for the U.S. congressmen and senators who were flown down there to have a look). After the public works were completed, he invited me to inspect the results. I told him I'd be only too happy to visit my relatives in Ba Tri. I did not inform him that these same relatives had been coming regularly to Saigon to visit my parents and had kept me informed of events down there. There were now asphalt roads, the latest shops and markets, a new school, dispensary, and bus stop, freshly installed electricity and modern plumbing. All these glittering modern conveniences, they were told, were courtesy of the U.S. pacification program. What went with them, however, were a lot of American faces and plenty of government soldiers who had moved in with their wives, children, relatives, and friends—sights that so alarmed my kinfolk and other villagers that they high-tailed it to other, unpacified, nearby hamlets or precincts.

Keeping my promise to Bob Komer, the next morning I boarded a helicopter bound for Ba Tri. About ten kilometers outside the village, the chopper attracted VC gunfire, with at least one shot penetrating the gas tank. I suppose any teenager with a carbine might have done it, and there was nothing you could do to prevent it except not show him a helicopter. We managed to reach our destination without further incident and, thankfully, without running out of fuel. My small native village was bustling that day, teeming with dignitaries, officials, foreigners, South Vietnamese troops, and American GIs. But my relatives? And other villagers whose families had been living there for more than two centuries? They were nowhere in sight. When I got back to Saigon, I rang up Komer.

"Thanks for the renovated and pacified version of my native village," I told him. "But the place looked strange without my relatives and other village residents around anymore." I don't think Bob appreciated the humor.

There were no hard feelings, of course. Bob knew that I knew he had an impossible job. The confusion was, presumably, in Washington, where they didn't realize that there was no war to be won or lost in native villages like Ba Tri, just a peace to be won there, if possible. Komer and his colleagues really did try to win the peace—and the minds and hearts of the people—with LBJ's butter. Perhaps nobody bothered to inform President Johnson that his pacification program had turned out to be, in concrete terms, the "Phoenix Program," another bloody witch hunt for the faceless Viet Cong. In no time, it became quite clear to the villagers that so-called "social workers," particularly the anti-malaria teams who continuously visited their homes, came not to spray mosquitoes, but those suspected of being Viet Cong. It became another aspect of Westmoreland's search-and-destroy strategy, which was lauded as an extremely effective technique of fighting. The basic premises of pacification didn't work because filling people's stomachs, important as it was, didn't guarantee winning their hearts and minds. Yes, the butter half of LBJ's policy brought with it pharmaceuticals, food imports, consumer goods, and petroleum products, but much of these went into the hands of the Viet Cong.

The American War in Viet-Nam was, indeed, a terrible, heartbreaking dilemma for Lyndon Baines Johnson, but it also very much reflected his versatile nature, with all the good intentions in the world. LBJ first unleashed the fires of hell on Viet-Nam not to really annihilate Communist North Vietnam but, in the end, to pacify the poor, destitute Vietnamese in South Vietnam, the main and innocent victims of the Vietnam War. Surely, President Johnson must have tried to infuse a little bit of his hope for his Great Society in the United States of America in the South Vietnamese, and in the North Vietnamese as well, if only Uncle Ho could have found a decent way to accept it. It was, of course, impossible. "East is east and west is west, and never the twain shall meet."

Bob Komer went on to other diplomatic adventures, including a hectic ambassadorship in Turkey, and then Under Secretary of Defense in 1979, which I'm sure he considered a hayride compared to his years in South Vietnam. During my short, three-day visit to Washington in October 1973, Bob was able to reach me only by phone from one of his tennis games. We were really happy to talk and laugh again together, if only briefly. I always liked Bob for his good nature and his ever-present flowery bow ties. The problems we faced in South Vietnam were far greater than the solutions tried with LBJ's guns and butter.

National identity can't be imported. It's a vital element in every individual and community, a dynamic process of popular consensus to embrace a particular way of life. It enables people to see why they belong together, what they must share, and what they should fight and die for—that which belongs to them, as it did to their forebears. National identity presumes a human dignity and an ability to be one's self, along with the pride that comes from being part of a whole. It can be a tremendously meaningful feeling to belong to a nation, which is why nationalism has been the most important motivating drive for peoples all over the world in the post-colonial period after World War II.

To the ordinary citizen, living and working conditions, rather than government and laws, dictate nationalism's efficacy. The practical way to deal with nationalism is in the social and economic evolution of the people. I was convinced that the appropriate option should be mainly economic and social rather than military—and above all, predominantly Vietnamese in its implementation if it was to succeed. Why didn't the U.S. concentrate its enormous resources on the economic front? Was it because it had to respond to popular war with high-tech war? As I've said before, popular warfare can't prevail without the justification of foreign aggression. Otherwise, it becomes common insurgency, ranging in degree from hooliganism to terrorism.

I had a wild dream, one that was shared by Averell Harriman and many economic experts, including Wheerley, MacDonald, and

Parker of U.S. AID. It was that the South Vietnamese would be entrusted with the task of administering a five-year, $5 billion development program designed to transform South Vietnam into a haven of free enterprise. The country would be granted assistance to build and defend its own factories, livelihood, and homes. The South Vietnamese would then be proud and happy to throw their doors open to the whole world, including their friends and relatives up north, inviting all to join them for business and pleasure in South Vietnam, the "Outpost of Free Trade" in the Far East. The Soviets and the People's Republic would be more than welcome. Even if they should decline the invitation, however, they should realize that it would clearly be counter-productive to pursue the old game of blowing up things. It would be a much more difficult decision to bomb and destroy factories and peoples' homes than it was to bomb embassy compounds, military convoys, depots and bases. It would have presented a very real dilemma for General Giap, because he had no experience launching a free-enterprise attack. Without Westmoreland and company playing the villain, the North Vietnamese script wouldn't have worked.

LBJ's idea of "guns and butter" did not come to him after he became president in 1963. After an earlier visit as vice-president in May 1961, with President Diem in Saigon, he returned to Washington and convinced President Kennedy to send the first one hundred U.S. "advisors" to South Vietnam in June 1961. A few months later, Vice-President Johnson also got the green light from President Kennedy for the "guns and butter" strategy, officially known as the Staley-Taylor Plan, jointly named after the American economist Eugene Staley and four-star-general Maxwell Taylor. General Taylor was a World War II hero, had been President Kennedy's military adviser in 1961 and 1962, and then chairman of the Joint Chiefs of Staff from 1962 to 1964, and U.S. Ambassador in Saigon in 1964 and 1965, succeeding Henry Cabot Lodge. Lodge would have to go back and replace Taylor, because the general became so fed up with literally having to perpetually lecture the Saigon generals as if they were West Point cadets (an ordeal which he did not bother to conceal from the international press). General Taylor returned to Washington to be a special consultant to President Johnson.

The Staley-Taylor Plan was conceived in October 1961 under the leadership of Vice-President Johnson. The plan aimed at pacifying South Vietnam in eighteen months, giving the necessary aid to Saigon to beef up the ARVN and make South Vietnam economically strong enough to fight North Vietnam. That was really the start of the American War in Viet-Nam. The years 1961 and 1962 were the times for the big jumps to begin. Within about twelve months, the few hundred U.S. advisors climbed to over 11,000 by December 1962, and the American spending spree began its initial escalation from $200 million in 1960 to nearly $300 million in 1961. That was how LBJ's "guns and butter" initiative in the end skyrocketed to the twelve-digit levels of hundreds of billions of dollars and over a half-million GIs in South Vietnam.

There were, of course, U.S. economic programs in South Vietnam in the mid-1960s, but they were, unfortunately, limited to just feeding the urban population in the context of the continuing war. The only formal economic program was a nice study by the American economist Eugene Staley, put in a new form called the Staley-Vu Quoc Thuc Plan, for post-war development of South Vietnam, jointly named after the American economist, but this time with his Vietnamese economist counterpart instead of General Taylor. The blueprint of this post-war plan, to be implemented only at the end of the bloody killing, was of little attraction to anybody. President Johnson should have stuck to his original idea of a grandiose development for the entire Mekong Delta area. With the concretization of this program in 1963 when he took office, LBJ could have convinced Hanoi and the whole world that the U.S. would be happy to seek peaceful ways to resolve the differences and help both North and South Vietnam. Moscow and Beijing might not have gone along with the idea, but Washington could have made a good case for it and possibly gotten off the hook.

Both Presidents Johnson and Nixon, repeatedly, from 1965 to 1973, offered Hanoi the war-ending incentives of post-war economic reconstruction for Viet-Nam, to the tune of $5 billion, with at least $1 billion for North Vietnam, it was said. However palatable these figures might have been, it should have been quite understandable why Hanoi could only insist stubbornly that the U.S. pay war reparations. Dr. Kissinger could only insist stubbornly, in October 1972, that the Hanoi politburo accept U.S. AID "for the healing of the wounds of war and reconstruction of North Vietnam on the order of $3 billion," a proposal confirmed in principle, but without mentioning any specific amount, in a formal letter dated October 20, 1972, by President Nixon to Prime Minister Pham Van Dong.

In their last round of meetings, Le Duc Tho did not forget to remind Dr. Kissinger of this sensitive money matter on January 11, suggesting the figure of $5 billion. In their January 13 meeting, Tho mentioned the figure $4.5 billion. As late as January 23, when the U.S. and North Vietnamese delegations met at the Center for International Conferences to mark the completion and formal initialing of the mutually accepted draft for the Paris Accords, Mr. Tho raised once again the issue, but with a figure down to $4 billion to manifest goodwill. Mr. Tho and Dr. Kissinger finally agreed that same day on the amount of $3.25 billion, to consist of annual grant aids of $650 million and $1.5 billion in soft loans (just pause and think how that would have affected the taxpayers during the electoral campaign). Dr. Kissinger did not forget to stress again that, "In implementation of its traditional policy, the U.S. will contribute to the healing of the wounds of war and to post-war reconstruction of the DRV and Indochina."

What else could have been expected? The doctor did try very hard, but American honor was not for sale. Neither was Hanoi's. It would have taken another round of secret negotiations, that would last about a millennium, for Ambassador William Sullivan and Deputy Foreign Minister Nguyen Co Thach to draft an additional article of accord that would have been agreeable and signed by Hanoi and Washington on this horrible pecuniary question.

But nothing was too difficult for Dr. Kissinger, especially among people of good will. No need for anybody to sign anything together. There would simply be an exchange of letters between President Nixon and Prime Minister Dong, in which anyone could say anything to the other, and each would be free to understand it in anyway he wished. This exchange of letters occurred on February 1, only four days after the official signing of the Paris Accords on January 27, 1973. Between people of good faith and good credit line, these simple letters were considered acceptable IOUs.

On my visit to New York City in October 1973, I did not think it was too late to present my reverie about the economic development of South Vietnam. Without much illusion, for two full days I discussed with anybody I could the possibility of generating business and economic help for South Vietnam to become an "Outpost of Free Trade." I talked to George Woods (former president of World Bank) at his First Boston office, Charles Allen at his investment bank, and to several other prominent U.S. businessmen. We all had a common friend in Joseph Kingsbury-Smith, Pulitzer prize winner and vice-president of the Hearst press group. These men were outstanding professionals in their fields and were as convinced as I that South Vietnam could be the scene of a small economic miracle if Washington was willing to fund the project. It was not "the sea to swallow," (*là mer a boire*, as the French would say), and a lot less expensive than the military option, for sure.

To expect South Vietnam to be an outpost of the free world was to defeat the very *raison d'être* of the Saigon government, which was supposed to espouse genuine Vietnamese nationalism for all Vietnamese, not just those in the South. Washington was disgusted with the poor performances of successive Saigon governments, which poor performances happened to be, in part, consequent to U.S. action in the war. It was sad because, from Diem to Thieu, Saigon's leaders tried hard—too hard, actually—to please Washington, but the more they tried, the worse they performed, no small thanks to American help.

I wasn't able to peddle my economic dream in the U.S. I regretted I wasn't American trained and didn't at the time understand certain American ways of doing things. I was, however, able to pay a private visit to Ambassador Harriman, who again wholeheartedly supported our dream in discussions at his Georgetown home in Washington. That was the last time I was to see him. In New York City, I called on Cyrus Vance at his Manhattan office (an investment law firm.) Ambassador Vance and I had not seen each other for nearly five years, since the time when we headed our respective delegations at the first meeting with the other side in January 1969 in Paris. As for U.S. policies, they continued to be more than a bit whimsical for me to comprehend.

In a very different context, the Vietnamese populace never comprehended Vietnamese nationalism as a factor in South Vietnam being an outpost of the free world. Just as overwhelmingly, the Buddhist population never comprehended Diem's rabidly visceral Catholicism. He was even more Roman than the Pope. (Diem's brother, Archbishop Ngo Dinh Thuc, was eventually excommunicated by the Vatican.) Diem would point a deadly finger of inquisition at the North Vietnamese demon, preaching that atheist-communism equaled anti-nationalism, and that to be anti-Diem equaled communism. Ranking civil servants and military officers had to get baptized to get promotions. Cabinet ministers were obliged to take leave of the president by walking backwards to the door. Doctrines and practices like these made it easier for Hanoi to equate true nationalism with its brand of communism—it was part of North Vietnam's basic strategy. The self-immolation protests by Buddhist activists—the "barbecued monks," as Madame Nhu called them—only added to Hanoi's propaganda victories and detonated the chain reaction outbursts of indignation in the U.S. and many other places. President Johnson began to see that American honor was a very expensive thing, that freedom and democracy, even by American definitions, were not very evident or easy to explain to his fellow countrymen.

On the other hand, Hanoi's case against American intervention was easy for most people in the world to understand, particularly the peasants of South Vietnam. Le Duc Tho's arguments at the Paris peace talks were easier to make before Kissinger and the world. There was no need to remind the Hanoi team that the one non-negotiable item on the table was the final and complete end to U.S. intervention in Viet-Nam—and that was also exactly what Washington badly wanted. But Uncle Ho had not forgotten to remind his disciples time and again of the two most important things: The U.S. must not be shamed in discussions of substance, and its representatives must always be treated courteously in discussions of form. Anyone who has ever dealt with the Vietnamese communists will tell you that they were a tough and stubborn lot, and uncompromising, not at all interested in genuine negotiations. It was especially true when considering their blind determination to achieve national independence from foreign presence and intervention, a cause for which they had endured more than fifty years of tireless combat.

But an entirely different attitude also ultimately came across to U.S. and many other world leaders. Ho Chi Minh and his government were fully aware of the almost insurmountable difficulties facing them. The Hanoi politburo did, in fact, try very hard to overcome the obstacles. But they never for a minute wavered in their hope to reach their final aim, which was total control of Viet-Nam, free of all foreign presence and intervention. One couldn't be expected to sell one's soul but, faced with epic difficulties, one could always forge an agreement—temporarily.

* * *

Thus did my mind stray through the starlit skies of North Vietnam. I thought back to the 1954 Geneva Conference on Indochina, which in a way was Uncle Ho's first diplomatic victory. It provided him and the Vietnamese Communist Party with a way to stake its first claim to the nationalism title, along with creating the Democratic Republic of Vietnam (DRV) above the seventeenth parallel and giving impetus to his long battle for unification, total sovereignty, and the banishment of foreign intervention. (The U.S. never recognized the 1954 accords.) The bill in blood ran to more than twenty years, and Ho was personally six years short of seeing the payoff, but his vision prevailed. He patiently waited until 1960 before giving up the hope for general elections (which he was dead sure to win), and so the long fighting began. The creation of the National Liberation Front in 1960, led by lawyer Nguyen Huu Tho and Madame Binh, provided the final element in the violent mix that history now knows so well.

Before his death in 1969, Uncle Ho doggedly clung to hopes for a peaceful conclusion to the conflict, and perhaps even fancied that Paris, where he started his lonely struggle a half-century before, might play a role in that conclusion. Indeed, in January 1973, the accords that led to the war's end were signed there. The Hanoi team had achieved exactly what Ho had hoped for, Washington got what it wanted out of Dr. Kissinger's talents, and only Thieu's "anti-communist" government was left out in the cold. Hanoi team leaders Le Duc Tho and Xuan Thuy could scarcely conceal their joy, but, following the precepts of Uncle Ho, they held out for an eventual—although temporary—"non-communist" government in South Vietnam. Once again, all the necessary myths and realities came into play.

But the questions back in 1973, for those who had waited a half-century with Ho, were still "how long?" and "when?" Once all U.S. troops were gone from Vietnamese soil by the end of March 1973, how long would it take for an "anti-communist" government to fail, and when would it give way to a "non-communist" regime? Ho's successor, Viet-Nam's Communist Party Secretary-General Le Duan, said he realistically could wait fifteen years. Giap not so patiently considered five years a humane and decent interval. If Saigon stubbornly remained defiantly "anti-communist," Hanoi figured it would be militarily strong enough to crush any Saigon regime daring to persist in its discrimination against Madame Binh. Back in 1972, U.S. Ambassador Ellsworth Bunker had told Thieu that a massive U.S. military presence was becoming untenable, and that the ARVN had to start fighting its own battles. Ambassador Martin subsequently repeated that argument to Thieu, who listened politely without comment, silently charting a course of his own.

Instead of converting the government from "anti-communist" to "non-communist," Thieu became more intensely anti-communist than ever—he had decided that there was no substitute for Commie-hating. Maybe he had no other choice. At least he remained true to himself. At any rate, he decided to go back to the future, reviving a 1950s-style, hard-line approach, refusing to recognize the NLF, refusing all territorial concessions, spurning all power-sharing proposals, and saying "Nuts" to Madame Binh. He amended the constitution to permit himself a very un-American third term, and dug in his heels.

Thieu, an accomplished chess player, had dealt himself in for a game of poker, with no ace up his sleeve. He counted on Kissinger to link Saigon's survival with American honor, but the good doctor had been crafty enough in Paris to disassociate the two. Now all Thieu would hear from Martin were appeals to end his intransigence coupled with warnings of U.S. total withdrawal. But Washington also miscalculated and was somewhat surprised when Thieu didn't fight back in Phuoc Long Province at the beginning of 1975. Had Thieu suddenly turned into a dove? Was he ready to compromise with Madame Binh?

Thieu confused the Americans further by withdrawing his ARVN troops from the Highlands in February, instead of making a stand and letting his Army Corps 1 and 2 collapse completely. Washington still tried to convince Thieu that, by making a deal, the Saigon administration would be left with the populous and oil-rice-rubber-coffee-and-tea-rich portion of South Vietnam. This would be the ideal moment to turn over the reins to "Big" Minh, who was ready to welcome Madame Binh into the fold. It was like having a Baptist minister preach to a Tibetan monk. Thieu clung to the forlorn hope that Kissinger and Ford would act to save American honor. But Hanoi generals Giap and Van Tien Dung already knew that the game was all but over. They would not have to wait fifteen or even five years. Hanoi's general offensive ended within fifty-five days. And that temporary tenure of a "non-communist" government envisioned in Paris and Washington turned out to be "Big" Minh's less-than-forty-eight hours.

It took many stargazing sessions in the dark and quiet nights of the camp to work out those hard facts for myself—a confusing mixture of illusions and disillusion, myths and realities, objective and subjective realities, concrete and virtual realities. I didn't know it for sure at the time, but it all helped me come even more to terms with myself than I had previously. Right and wrong were no longer clear and valid issues. The only thing that seemed to remain in my mind was the ability to experience some sort of hope. What to hope for and how to hope genuinely—about the morrow if not the future, which would be too much to expect—remained unsolved questions. It would be a day-to-day thing. It was a vague feeling waiting for something to happen, to look forward to, something to cling onto. I could not identify the vague feeling to be "hope" but there was clearly an emotion in me which wanted me to accept it to be hope. One night before falling asleep, I finally conceded and called it *Latent Hope*.

Again, God's mercy came from an unexpected quarter. The inmates were informed that they would be divided into labor teams and assigned productive tasks instead of merely vegetating, which we had done for more than a year. For me, this development shed further light on the mechanics of the hoping process. To become operational, hope requires the full interaction of all four parameters of reality, reason, meaning, and purpose. This is the way it works: The ability to comprehend the truth involves reason and reality, and the ability to will for a good involves meaning and purpose. One can see, then, that purpose and meaning provoke the emergence of hope, and the actual driving forces of hope strive on facts and logic—in other words, reason and reality. It was a passive, even static, hope that emerged in me in that second year of detention in the north of Viet-Nam. It still lacked a unity of meaning and purpose, but that would develop in time, once reality could be assessed properly and reason could become coherently operative. I'm not a Christian but, there in prison, I remembered how once at Oxford I had been taken by the few lines from St. Paul at the beginning of Hebrews 11:1, and was curious enough to compare the English and French translations.

"Faith is the essence of things hoped for, the conviction of things unseen," one English translation gave it. The verse in the New King James version reads, "Now faith is the substance of things hoped for, the evidence of things not seen."

Whether it is the "essence" or "substance" of things hoped for, and whether it is a "conviction" or "evidence of things unseen," I think St. Paul offers one of the best notions I've ever read of hope and faith. He did give a definition of faith, but tried to explain and describe in a pragmatic and useful manner what faith can be and do. Likewise hope, as understood in Hebrews 11:13, was about things seen afar, to be assured of, about a homeland to seek, a desire for the better, a country to return to.

While I still wonder about St. Paul's exact meaning and purpose, remembering these lines helped me a lot in that prison time. It not only provoked hope in me, but also helped me to comprehend a little better what hope might be. It helped me to begin a gradual process of hope, which grew little by little, to something far greater than the desperate hope against all hope, and to something beyond a blind hope to hope. It was still difficult to put my finger on—it was a kind of budding hope which, by the way, I was able to communicate to those fellow inmates who were chosen, as I was, to become masons in the prison.

Another quotation came to mind, one written more than two-thousand years ago by the ancient Roman Terence (190-159 B.C.):

"As you cannot do what you wish, you should wish for what you can do."

Those words, too, shaped my incipient career as a mason in prison, which was to bring much activity, as well as a few adventures. Eventually, this career would provide the mechanism that would give meaning and purpose to my hopes. But I didn't know that then. As I embarked on this new stage of my incarceration, I couldn't help wondering where it would all lead.

CODA

Reflections on Latent Hope

Hope—
is the resulting outcome
of the interaction
of four basic parameters:
Purpose, ***Meaning***, ***Reason***, and ***Reality***.
Human beings
have a natural urge and need
to hope.
Hope—
is inherent in the instinct for survival
and is a necessary feature
of human growth.
Hope—
is nurtured through
recognition of realities
and rational assessments—
through reason and understanding—
so that reality
can be conceived meaningfully
through a logical process.

><

Two basic elements—
Purpose and ***Meaning***—
constitute the starting parameters
that enable hope to emerge
into our awareness.
Even in the face
of the most desperate of situations,
we human beings try to search for
alternative outcomes,
and seek hope.
Hope—
which is constantly latent in us—
reaches the realm of our consciousness from
the interaction
between ***Purpose*** and ***Meaning***.
But hope still must be equipped
with the driving forces of
Reason and ***Reality***.

><

Hope—
remains in its latent state
until it has found and secured
a realistic and rational basis
upon which to stand
and become operational.
Hope—
will ignite its own momentum,
as soon as it acquires for itself
a meaningful context in which to operate
and a purpose for which to strive.
Thus,

hope is born by ***Purpose***, its finality,
and sustained in its manifestations
by the interactions
between ***Meaning***, ***Reason***, and ***Reality***.
That is why, and how,
among many other mysterious ways
of its operational modes,
hope requires a meaningful, rational,
and realistic purpose
to attain realization.

><

Hope—
is inherent in the nature of humankind
and is indissoluble
from life and the condition of being.
><
Latent hope—
can emerge
when it is not overcome
by despair
or repressed by some motive
on the part of the individual person.

CHAPTER NINE
JOYOUS ABANDONING: PASSIVE HOPE

There is no useless wisdom as there is no hopeless sorrow.
Dr. Samuel Johnson (1709-1784)

By the time the prison labor teams were set up, most of us twelve hundred or so inmates at the Hanoi Hilton Annex had come terms with our fear of death—maybe not completely, but to a comforting degree. That is not to say that the sights and sounds and tastes and smells of desolation and despair that accompany the incarcerated state were entirely absent. I spent many nights indulging in a guessing-game about when freedom would come, if ever. When I tried to assess the penalty in relation to the depth of my involvement with the Saigon regime, I came up with an estimate of a term of from five to fifteen years. That would be humane, I thought, and acceptable both to me and whoever had to make the decision.

Strangely enough, five, ten, or fifteen years didn't seem to make much difference to me by the time I was in my third year there. My hope for freedom settled into a state of passive hope, the kind of hope that I thought would be similar to Dom Helder Camara's idea of abandon. I think, however, it's often mistakenly identified as resignation, in the sense of a logical and natural reaction to helplessness or powerlessness. My ancestors have a proverb: "Be happy with what you are and have," which would go together very well with one in the West: "Live and let live."

My sense of "abandoning" helped me enormously, because I became able to laugh at myself and my predicament. Abandoning helped me push aside the negative and destructive elements of my situation and made it possible for me to open up, as I have said before, to a simple hope for the morrow—which rendered a today more bearable. I was accepting reality, an essential ingredient in the recipe for hope. This metamorphosis in my attitude greatly affected my personality, my demeanor, and I became an object of curious attraction to my fellow inmates and the guards. How, they wondered, did I manage to remain—in their minds—so cheerful?

"Let's go see Phong," the inmates would say, when one or more of them got depressed. "He'll tell us stories."

And I did. When I ran out of true stories, I'd invent new ones to keep them happy. The tales they enjoyed most—and which they swallowed whole—concerned how people in the West dealt with the everyday problems of dressing, eating, drinking, smoking, hunting, courting, celebrating Christmas and New Year's, and countless other arcane bits of Occidental behavior. I regaled them with stories almost every evening after the cell was locked. We retreated into our own private and secluded universe for a few hours of escape and abandon. Invariably, however, our repose would be shattered by the soft sounds of nocturnal weeping. Sometimes, it was one man, sometimes two or three, a grim reminder to hundreds of others of the solemnity of our plight.

Abandoning may be a negative sentiment, not very far from that of despair, but it may also be a kind of "joyous abandon", with the ability to disregard helplessness or neutralize hopelessness, a passive state of mind but devoid of anguish and the compulsion to vainly search for some sort of hope. So I stubbornly clung to my joyous abandon, which was the most helpful thing I was able to come upon in prison at that time. It greatly reduced my useless mental torments, guessing games, and futile hopes, with their fanciful wishful thinking about unrealistic and impossible aims.

Being moved to the North signified that the prospect of release had become more remote. It was a common assumption that the most serious cases were taken to North Vietnam. Most former Saigon officials remained in the South. Illusion and disillusion had free reign. I learned years later that those kept down south remained incarcerated as long as those held in the north, though it was true that the "serious" or "dangerous" cases were detained in the north.

So who were my fellow convicts at the Hanoi Hilton Annex? There were a few so-called "common criminals," not dangerous at all. I made friends with some of them. There was, for example, a physician and former hospital director, who was in the tenth year of a fifteen-year term for shooting his wife and her lover. There were also a dozen former Saigon commandos who had parachuted into North Vietnam in the late 1950s and early 1960s on sabotage missions, and who had been caught and interned there for over fifteen years. That made me rethink my earlier estimate and calculate that I might be locked up for at least fifteen or even twenty years.

Such thoughts of exclusion and rejection, I began to think, could lead to feelings of helplessness, hopelessness, and despair, leading ultimately to self-destruction. I had to perpetuate my hope for release on the one hand, while easing my torment at the prospect of such a long incarceration on the other. If only I could be told the exact, or even approximate, duration of my imprisonment, I could measure out my hope. It was surely intentional that, by not setting any specific period of detention, our captors orchestrated our hope. At the beginning of the sojourn up north, I was able to hope every day, especially just before going to sleep, to be released "next week." When weeks passed without number, I began to hope for "next month." When I lost track of the months, it became "next year." Eventually, I blindly hoped simply to be released "soon." Would there be a general amnesty? Perhaps the United

Nations would intervene. Maybe my communist relatives would intercede on my behalf. What if my captors decided to deport me instead of keeping me imprisoned? These musings served as painkillers, but they also were an irrational denial of reality and, as such, destructive of true hope.

One thing was sure: I was alive. I didn't know whether execution was still in the cards or not. When would I be free, if ever? But still, I was alive. I wondered: how was my family faring through all this? I learned later that during the first two years of our internment in the north, our families weren't told where we were (the first visits were allowed only in the fourth year). In turn, we didn't really know what had become of those at home. The separation, coupled with ignorance of their fate, created acute anguish in me. "Rather death than separation," goes the Vietnamese proverb. But, I was definitely alive.

Eventually I gave up on the guessing-games. The assignment to the construction gang and to work as a mason helped me get interested in other things. Through this work, something really positive began to grow within me. I was happy for the opportunity to be trained in the noble craft of masonry and the work was extremely satisfying. For the first time in two years, I was no longer useless. I could contribute my share. Why, we masons now could build our own prison, fashion it into the most beautiful and distinguished reeducation camp in the north of Viet-Nam with facilities fairly acceptable for us to live in by our South Vietnamese standards. Proud of our work, as we Hanoi Hilton Annex masons were, life had meaning and purpose again. I was no longer a non-entity, the grass-chewing member of an idle herd. There was human dignity in this work and once more in me.

As I have described earlier, except for the brick edifice in which I and others were housed, all the other buildings in the compound were of straw-mud with thatched roofs. There was a clear and urgent need for more substantial, not to mention more attractive, facilities. I did quite well with my training and ended up one of the five mason leaders in charge of teams of ten. We then set out to reconstruct our prison, a task we took to enthusiastically, even lovingly. The hardest part—the most emotionally poignant, if you will—consisted of the final phase, putting the iron bars into the windows, from the inside, of course. I did try to console myself by saying "Well, God's fresh air can still come in and out freely."

When I say I took the masonry work to heart, I mean that literally. During those two years of honest productive toil, I became much more receptive to the heart than to the mind. Logic and reason guided my sentient being, but emotions were much more influential and consequential to my total self. Marxist-Leninist principles had no more sway over me than they had had in my Oxford days, but I was struck by the good manners, even sensitivity, of the prison guards. One of them, a man in his early twenties, confided in us that he'd been fortunate enough to have been invited to the Cuban diplomats' Saturday night dances in Hanoi, and he was desperate to learn how to dance so he could impress his girl friend. His excitement was infectious, so my team of masons set out to help him. Luckily, a relatively young former police officer was in our number, an accomplished dancer in the Latin American style and proficient at imparting his terpsichorean skills. So, while the rest of us attended to prison construction, these two would retreat to a discreet corner to dance the mambo and other Cuban rhythms. The guard proved an apt pupil and was soon a mambo king, as well as master of the rumba, samba, and cha-cha. Next, he had to dress the part, so we passed the word around and secured loans of a jacket, trousers, shirt, tie, socks, and shoes, as well as an anonymous loan of a Seiko watch. The young guard went to the party in grand style!

Such sentimental moments occurred quite often. As a trusted convict, I was occasionally designated to accompany the prison van on marketing expeditions to the village. On these occasions, the guards would proceed on their errands and often leave us by ourselves to keep an eye on the vehicle. During one instance, I was surprised by the approach of a very old and skinny woman. "You're from the South, aren't you?" she asked in a strong northern accent.

"Yes," I replied simply.

She gave our surroundings a rapid once-over, pulled out an enormous peasant-style cookie, and thrust it into my hand. "Eat it quick," she mumbled, before scurrying off. I made short work of the cookie before the guards returned. Mother Viet-Nam, it seemed, would always be there for her children, in the North or the South, former enemies or not. Months later, I ran into her again at the village market and was able to return the favor. I was wearing my only woolen sweater, a very fine garment from my Oxford days (Scotch House of Knightsbridge, if you please), which I quickly took off and slipped into her hands. "Please go away quick," I urged. She did not at once realize what was happening, but ran away fast. I sensed she was deathly scared of the guards wandering nearby. I have always hoped that the sweater helped shield her from the hard northern winters.

On another occasion, my team of masons traveled with our carts to a warehouse for building materials. Before hauling bricks and cement bags to our cart, we offered our best wishes to the storekeeper, who was pregnant. She was a simple and gaunt peasant woman who lived with her husband, one of the prison guards, in a tiny, straw-mud, thatch-roofed cabin. She had a medium-sized black dog, whose head I stroked, as I did on every trip to the warehouse because I was always extremely fond of dogs. My British upbringing again, I suppose.

Watching me pet the dog prompted the poor pregnant storekeeper to announce that, alas, the animal was destined to be sold and cooked very soon to help defray the expenses of the imminent blessed event. (Northerners had a taste for dog meat, while southerners preferred what we thought of as more civilized delicacies, such as frogs and snails.) We members of the construction team exchanged looks and tacitly decided on a course of action. We stacked four bags of cement onto the cart, piled the bricks on top and handed her a piece of paper to sign indicating we had received what we were supposed to. After checking the shipment, she protested that we appeared to be short one of the five bags ordered. I looked her straight in the eye and insisted we had taken five bags. My fellow masons agreed. "There are five bags in there," they echoed. I took her aside and whispered that we'd make up the difference by buying another bag in a few days and that she should just let us help her out. The poor girl was shedding tears as we pushed our cart out of the warehouse. I do not remember having experienced any feelings of charity from us or of gratitude from that North Vietnamese country girl. She was simply a sister in need, even if a former sister-enemy, and we tried to share a little of her predicament, as much as we could. I was sure the other members of my team also had similar thoughts.

There is an interesting denouement to this story. A few weeks later, after another trip to the warehouse, our team discovered hidden under the bricks in our cart a token of the woman's appreciation. Wrapped in a newspaper was a generous hunk of roasted dog.

As I have mentioned before, our families didn't know where we were for almost four years, although they could guess that we'd been sent to North Vietnam. However, we were permitted to receive gift-parcels forwarded to us from the South, with the Chi Hoa prison in Saigon as a dispatching point. To the people of the North, these parcels represented undreamed-of largesse. They had never seen such wealth. One small package of medicines, foodstuffs, clothing, and other items we received from our families would mean five to ten years' pay to a middle-ranking civil servant in the north of Viet-Nam at that time.

One of the most striking realities I discovered in those years was humankind's seemingly limitless capacity for physical and mental endurance. Accompanying the arduous work that came to us in the second year of detention in the North, when the labor teams were organized, was a tremendous upsurge of hope. Although not told so officially, we were made to understand that "labor camps" were different from "prisons" in that inmates in the former could benefit from an early release. Thus it was with renewed hopes, and even joy, that we began our "golden eight-hour day's work" that was included between five o'clock in the morning and five o'clock in the afternoon. It was an honest eight hours' work, but very soon, it took its toll. We became skinnier and skinnier, and many of us also began to regret the loss of the months of idleness, as we felt the first pangs of muscle soreness. I was among those who pushed themselves to the limits of endurance. We did this not out of fear of the guards or hopes for an early release, but to prove to ourselves that we were still able to use our heads and our hands, that we were not useless. In such circumstances, it also became obvious that the strength of the body couldn't always match the power of the mind.

The monthly food allowance of ten-to-fifteen kilograms (twenty-two to thirty-three pounds) of cereal was only enough for those of us who were less than one-point-six meters (five and a quarter feet) tall and about fifty kilograms (one hundred ten pounds) in weight. I was over one-point-seven meters tall (five foot six), so after about nine months of labor, my weight dropped to forty-three kilograms (ninety-five pounds) compared to the seventy-two (one hundred fifty-nine pounds) I had weighed at the start of my internment. I came to look like a deflated balloon, especially in the buttocks. Many of us also lost our teeth. I managed to keep six, quite a good cosmetic performance. From the aesthetic viewpoint, the regime was a disaster, but it helped me comprehend more fully the essentials of life, and guided me in my continuous quest for the unadorned human being. It was strange to see one's body reduced to its skeletal essentials, but I stubbornly clung to my determination to expand the limits of my endurance, or "push the envelope."

The process didn't degrade me. On the contrary, it helped me acquire a warmer sense of humanity, a deeper feeling of belonging to and sharing with my fellow masons. I didn't know how or why I felt that way. It was catastrophic physically, but mentally I felt much better in prison than I had felt before. As Charles Dickens pointedly asked, "The men who learn endurance, are they who call the world brother?" It was evident that a new sort of hope had begun to operate in me, thanks to the reality and reason in my work as a stonemason. It was more than just the "hope to hope" of the idle period, and, while it didn't resolve my concern for an early release and return to normal life with my family, it had evolved into a hope that could accept a certain reality with a logical basis. At that stage, it was a hope that fell short of acquiring proper meaning and purpose for itself, but it was a start. I felt better at that time in prison, because I detected a feeling of hope from within rather than from outside circumstances.

That was how I felt in the third and fourth years of imprisonment. I was, at last, really at peace with myself, ready to endure any duration of incarceration, ready to accept whatever punishment might come my way. It was a passive stage of hope or some sort of inactive hope, or even hope which was vaguely present but unable to become active. Prison life began to have a certain meaning, although its purpose remained uncertain, and, of course, a very irrational way to fill the remaining years of my existence on earth. To hope for a release continued to be something quite unrealistic. My hope, then, had no other alternative but to remain passive. My passive hope was waiting and trying to become active.

I came to realize that there was a fundamental choice—or state of mind—for each individual prisoner to deal with. First, we had to overcome the automatic compulsion that wanted to reject the reality of imprisonment, along with the counterpart belief that we really didn't belong there. The next important breakthrough in prison life occurred when one became able to share the pain with fellow inmates. That's what happened to me. My purpose for being and hope for release retreated, leaving room for more meaning in prison life—it was, quite simply, the only life we had at the time. I felt better going to work each morning, enjoyed discussing all sorts of things with my fellow masons and watching our constructions progress according to plan. Instead of hoping for the impossible, I thought of John Stuart Mill's observation: "I have learned that my happiness can be found in restraining my aspirations rather than trying to satisfy them."

I came to all of this not through a process of logic and scientific analysis, but through a gradual awakening to awareness of increasingly familiar daily surroundings and activities. It was as if I had awakened to a hitherto unknown or unappreciated world in which hope became more meaningful and no longer a source of mental torment. Wasn't it King Solomon who said some three thousand years ago, "Hope is the dream of people who are awake"?

In the fourth year of my reeducation I really came to peace with myself because of my new notions on hope. One mechanism that might be called hope is basically the conditioned survival instinct, the hope for the morrow. That's also the other side of the fear-of-death coin. There's also what might be called the hope of the helpless and powerless, the rejected, and the oppressed, which is a negative reaction to these negative states. But this natural mechanism, influenced by the human capacity to think and to will, might be just wishful thinking, fanciful or idealistic, and only capable of action if circumstances permit. This hope could be just a self-deceitful painkiller, but it's better than no hope at all. I came to the conclusion that this painkiller could acquire a high quality if one was able to conceive and live it the way Dom Helder Camara had described it. Then it could lead to resignation, acceptance, and joyful abandon.

My hope had become pragmatic. Prison was bearable because my hope was not only sustaining the test of time, but also reflecting my true state of mind and working well in practice. It wasn't joyful abandon, but simply the natural act of being and becoming, an inherent part of life itself, with notions of today and tomorrow, with time and space becoming interchangeable. It wasn't mystical, but practical, concrete, down-to-earth, and woven into day-to-day existence.

No one can truly say, "I live without hope," because with life, there must be purpose, and with purpose, hope. I came to understand that violence might kill life, but could never kill purpose. And it could never kill hope. Somehow, with this understanding about hope, I was much less afraid of death. My ability to accept my prison existence became possible only when I came to realize that my act of being and becoming was not simply individual and personal, but very much collective and communicative. Of course, it wasn't that simple, but I might have reached at this point what my colleague Lamar Carter at the Center for A Science of Hope has called "the more genuine, bedrock human essentials of being and becoming in the practical, down-to-earth reality."

At this time I suffered no mental stress from ideological conflicts, loss of property, social status, luxuries, or material comfort. Nor did I suffer fear of sickness or death. There was an instinctive drive to survive. I had a compelling need to be back with my parents and family, and an urge to remain a citizen of my country, free to live in the land of my ancestors under whatever regime or conditions prevailed.

* * *

In time, my insights into the phenomenon of hope evolved even further. In the summer of 1979, my fourth year of incarceration, I was washing my clothes in the pond under the suffocating forty-degrees-centigrade sun, when I experienced a sort of epiphany. For years, I suddenly realized, I had been obsessed with the "whats" and "hows" of hope, but had never asked myself the "whys." Why was there that compelling drive in me to hope, even in a completely futile way? Why should humans have this natural ability to hope? Why is hope practically indistinguishable from the human act of being? So many whys about hope rushed into my mind. I was no longer interested in what I should hope for or how I should achieve it. Right then and there, I decided to start all over from ground zero on "this thing called hope." It was an exercise that engrossed my thoughts after lights-out, as I lay on my wooden couch in my eight-tenths-by-two meters of living space in the dark and quiet of my prison cell.

To discover the whys, I was compelled to establish premises: Hope is an intrinsic and natural human ability, an inherent part of the human act of being. It's an inborn capability, not taught and learned, a sort of instinct and feeling. But it is somehow different from the other basic instincts, such as survival, feeding, mating, and procreating, and not quite like other human feelings or passions like companionship, lust for power, possessiveness, knowledge, love, hatred, fear, and joy.

* * *

By the end of my third year of incarceration, we had completed the reconstruction of our prison, so my outstanding team of masons received a plum assignment. We were given the task of embellishing the prison gardens, light work compared to that of the other inmates. We created fishponds, planted flowers in pots and beds, planted trees and did other landscaping work. This lasted for a year and was a pleasant occupation, indeed. It was the prelude to even more pleasant events.

In mid-December 1979, many months and years after starting the "thirty days of reeducation" at the Long Thanh orphanage, I was informed that I would soon be released. No explanation was given, just that I was among a dozen or so who would soon be free. Criteria for the releases were indecipherable. We were a mixture of young and old, of high rank and low, military and civilian, and private individuals with no ties to the Saigon regime. All we knew was, they would try to get us home by Christmas.

The first delay was caused by a shortage of guards available to escort us on the train from Hanoi to Saigon. Ultimately, our keepers shrugged their shoulders and decided that, as long as we were on our way to freedom, perhaps they could trust us to guard ourselves. With a twinkle in his eye, the camp commanding officer, Major Dung, appointed me "head of the delegation responsible for the group's Godspeed." Then he clapped me on the back and bade us farewell.

The guard designated to drive the truck that took us to the Hanoi railway station was glad for the day off. Our railway fares had been provided by the administration, so, after recovering our belongings—civilian clothes, watches and wedding rings, and money we'd received from our families—we were off. We arrived at the station an hour before departure, and some of us used the time to buy food and other items from station peddlers to tide us over for the trip. We sat and ate and slept on wooden benches in a reserved section of the carriage of the hundred-year-old French Alsthom train. The antique machine managed up to forty kilometers per hour. After four days and five nights, we pulled into the Saigon railroad station.

It was ten o'clock in the morning on January 10, 1980, when I stood before the old battered iron gate of my Saigon home. I rang the doorbell. I rang it a second time. I pushed on the buzzer for half an hour without exciting a sign of life. Then I peered through the gate's cracks and kept watch. Finally, I saw my old mother's head popping back and forth at the corner of the house, and then intensely peering back at me.

"Mother! Mother! Mother!" I shouted loudly and repeatedly. "It's your son Phong, your son Phong!"

She rushed to the gate as quickly as her eighty-year-old legs would allow and struggled for many long minutes to get it open. Tears ran down her cheeks, and then she sobbed convulsively when I took her tiny body in my arms. Arms encircling each other, we made our way slowly into the house, and I gently laid her down on her favorite wooden cot. My father was at the barbershop, she told me. About ten minutes later, he arrived. Seeing me, he gasped several times, unable to utter any other sound, and almost fell trying to traverse the few meters separating us. He took me in his arms for a very long time, as if he might find rest and peace on my shoulder.

Then, a completely incoherent discussion erupted, with each of us talking over one another, or talking to ourselves, but somehow we managed to convey bits of information about what had transpired in our lives between 1975 and 1980. My mother insisted on cooking a few extra dishes for lunch, so we moved the confused conversation into the kitchen and caught up while we ate. I learned that my sister and her family were still living there. They had gone to the pagoda that morning and would not be back for lunch. My brother, Thu (Nguyen Xuan), Air Vietnam's last executive-director, remained incarcerated in Thanh Hoa prison in North Vietnam (his reeducation was to last over nine years).

My sister and her husband, along with their youngsters, returned that evening, and we all indulged in a big and joyful reunion dinner. All were much thinner than when I had been taken from them, but they seemed in good health, thanks to my physician brother-in-law, who had taken his Hippocratic oath in Paris in the 1930s. He was then in his seventies, not much younger than my mother. My sister was sixteen years older than I was.

Life was spartan in Saigon in 1980, but I was content to be free. Aside from concerns about my weight loss, my parents, of course, were elated to have me home. For me, a new decade was dawning of family reunification in my hometown, which I now had to remember to call Ho Chi Minh City. I looked forward with hope to that decade.

CODA

Reflections on Passive Hope

The ability to accept an unfavorable reality
(through knowing)
and the ability to understand adversity
(through thinking)
results in a logic of reality
that permits hope to emerge,
associable with that reality.

Hope's level may simply rise
to the rejection of despair,
with the appropriate level of ability
to deal with the adverse circumstance.

><

The ability
to properly recognize
and accept an unfavorable reality
does not necessarily produce ***Purpose***,
and, therefore, hope may remain passive,
and in some conditions,
be unable to move
to active or positive stages.

><

Passive hope—
may imply the presence
of only vague purpose.
It is limited to a feeling of hope
for something better
without knowing
clearly or specifically, what.
"To hope for the better"
characterizes this condition
of passive hope,
which is simply
the hope to hope.

><

The hope to hope
is the emergence of ***Latent Hope***

into ***Passive Hope***.
The practical effect
of the hope to hope
is to neutralize despair,
while generating and providing
enough energy
to seek survival.

><

To hope for the better
is a permanent characteristic
of our humankind's
condition of being and becoming.
The hope to hope
is always there and available
in all and each of us.
The hope to hope
may be properly thought of
as the ***passive*** stage of hope.

><

Passive Hope—
is the stage beyond ***Latent Hope***,
a static state with no, or limited,
meaning or purpose.
Passive Hope—
does, nevertheless, provide a context
for ***Purpose*** and ***Meaning***
to be defined.

CHAPTER TEN
HOME SWEET HOME: ACTIVE HOPE

We must rediscover the distinction between hope and expectation.
Ivan Illich, in *Deschooling*, 1971

Sweet was the sunset that faded softly over Saigon the evening of January 10, 1980, the day that marked my return to the family home. After so many years on concrete and wooden bunks, I enjoyed a wonderful night's sleep in a real bed with a soft mattress and clean sheets. It took me at least a week to regain my senses and restore a bit of the strength I had lost during my long stay in the North. Saigon had changed a lot. Very few cars were to be seen in the streets. A bicycle had become a necessity, but was by no means easy to acquire.

Living conditions were arduous. The availability of food had improved somewhat, but clothing was still hard to come by. I soon discovered that very few things were left around the house that could help our domestic economic situation. Whatever wasn't essential to daily life had already gone to the flea market. My sister had been trying to make ends meet by selling one thing after another, but even with all her sacrifices and sales, it was still a bare-minimum subsistence. It was clear to me that she was exhausted from the long challenge of taking care of everyone. She was, after all, sixty years old.

I fully understood when she took me aside one evening and tearfully told me that she couldn't bear it any more. The only way for all of us to survive was for us to go to France, she said, not only for the sake of our old parents and her husband, who was in his late seventies, but also for the half-dozen youngsters in the household, whose futures we must consider. Two of my sister's grown daughters had already had been living in France with their husbands and children since the early 1960s. They had been successful economically—one son-in-law was an accountant and the other, a physician.

The French side of the family had submitted applications for the Saigon side to enter France under the United Nations High Commissioner for Refugees (HCR) program. I discussed the matter a few times with my parents, who said that they would do whatever we children decided was best. We decided the family would make the journey as soon as permitted, even without me, should the Vietnamese authorities refuse to let me go.

In the meantime, my top priority in the weeks after my recuperation was to find paying work to help the family. The only jobs available were those of civil servants. Everything was strictly under government control. There was only one employer, the State. In April 1980, I was able to find a job teaching evening courses in English in the foreign language department of the Center for Research and Translation, an agency of the Department of Culture and Information of Ho Chi Minh City. The foreign language program had just been introduced at the beginning of the year, with a faculty of mostly former members of the Saigon administration. There were about a dozen of us pioneering the program. In less than two years, there would be more than three hundred of us teaching the language of Shakespeare each evening to more than twenty thousand students at fourteen locations scattered all over the city, the most popular being in Cholon, Saigon's Chinatown. We members of the former regime were fortunate to develop this relatively lucrative livelihood in very difficult times.

French and Vietnamese authorities speedily approved my sister's resettlement application. I was then earning an adequate income with my English courses, and was no longer sure it would be a good idea for our octogenarian parents to live the life of refugees in France with my sister's family. I said as much to my parents, who told me they'd agreed to go because it was the will of the family, adding that, otherwise, they would have very much preferred to remain in our own home in Saigon. That was how I came to stay with my parents in Saigon when my sister and her family left for France. Later, a few months after he was released from nine year's reeducation in the north of Viet-Nam, my brother, Thu, also left Viet-Nam and was reunited with his family in France. He has never returned.

Fifteen years after the fall of Saigon, my parents and I were the only members of our household left in the old family home. It showed the wear and tear of difficult times. There wasn't much of anything of value left around us, but we were still together, as we would be until the end. In the 1980s, I was being paid the equivalent of about fifty dollars a month, five times the salary of the average civil servant in Ho Chi Minh City, but I had to teach ten to twelve hours a day to earn it. It was far beyond what I had hoped for when I was released. I did the marketing, laundry, and housework. My mother continued to cook for my father and me—preparing meals was a daily sacrament to her. If she was unable to cook, it meant she was ill, and not being able to cook made her ill. For her, cooking was not only a duty, but also an art. She was widely recognized as an excellent cook by the professional chefs of Saigon.

During this period, my hope consisted of a common and vague feeling that nothing bad would come to our precarious existence, that I'd be able to continue to care for my parents. I did not hope for the future. The three of us carried on uneventfully with this way of life, subsistence, accepting our lot in our cherished hometown during the two years after my release from reeducation, without anyone making any comment whatsoever about our fate or destiny. One evening, however, my mother broached the subject of my being on a dead-end road.

She said to me, "Son, try to think about your future. You still have many years ahead of you. Your father and I are old, but I can still take care of him and of myself. So don't feel that you have to stay by our side. If you must go, you must go. Your father and I do not matter much anymore."

"I know that, Mother," I replied simply. And our life went on in the same way for about eight more years.

On my parents' seventieth wedding anniversary in September 1990, they took a pedicab ride through downtown Saigon and had a last look at the tiny cubicle near the Ben Thanh central market where they had lived just after their wedding, where they had begun their union and built up our family. They had come, penniless, far from their native villages to Saigon, and were penniless again on that day seventy years later, as they made their last pedicab ride in the city they had come to, to make their start in life as adults. Accompanying them on my bicycle, I was able to share their swelling emotions. They exchanged few words—none were needed, for each surely knew well what the other was thinking. I was glad to pay the pedicab driver double the rate he had asked for the tour.

My father passed away less than a month later, in October 1990 at the age of ninety-four, and my mother, a year later at eighty-eight. They had been born during the French colonial period, lived through the second World War (Japanese occupation), the Indochina War (1945-1955), and the American War (1955-75). For the last fifteen years of their lives, they had lived under communist rule, and in the years I lived with them, I was amazed by their powers of endurance and their attitude toward life. They never questioned the State, and strictly respected law and order. It must have been their simple Confucian upbringing again. When permitted, they made suggestions, and when possible, contributions. They didn't have much education or knowledge of social or political affairs. I had the impression that it didn't matter much to them what the State called itself. I didn't absorb much of the Confucian precepts to "respect your King (State), your Teacher, your Father" (and, if you were a woman, "your Husband and Eldest Son" as well).

My parents accepted whatever conditions prevailed—politically, socially, and environmentally—as God-given and God-ordained. They were allotted a certain time on this earth, in a certain set of conditions, to enjoy and endure a clear and simple purpose of life, namely to form a union between husband and wife, procreate, raise children and help them do the same in whatever conditions nature or God allowed to prevail. Despite this attitude of acceptance, they still had all sorts of aspirations, wishes, and hopes. But their responsibilities to themselves and others were, by the end of the day, reduced to that simple purpose of life. They were so busy with responsibilities that they didn't bother with the questions, "Where did I come from?" or "Where shall I go?" They had a very simple answer to the question, "Why am I here?" Clearly, they didn't fulfill life's simple purpose for any gain or reward. They did it simply out of love—first, love for their parents, and then love for their children. There were, of course, other important things in life, but they were secondary. Nothing in their behavior ever gave the impression that my parents hoped to live long or get rich. They hoped simply to be together and be able to care, give, and share.

In spite of all the suffering and hardship of their existence on earth, my parents had the rare opportunity to share the very simple, but precious and fulfilling sentiment of togetherness. Both parents died at home. I was granted the privilege of holding my old father, and a year later my mother, against my chest with my arms around them, when they ceased to breathe forever. They were both so old and weak that they passed away gently, like a lamp running out of oil, or as if they were falling asleep.

It was a holiday, so I happened to be home the morning my father died. He had for no particular reason invited me to visit him in his room. We chatted for an hour or so, and he then asked me to accompany him to the bathroom. After cleaning him up, I took him back to his bed because he was complaining of a backache. I told him to have a nap and the pain would go away. He dozed off very quickly, and I sat there fanning him for about half an hour. Suddenly I noticed that his chest wasn't moving up and down anymore. I tried to wake him, but there was no response. I shook him and called to him. Nothing. I panicked, uncertain what to do. I pulled him up, took him in my arms, rocked him back and forth, and shouted, "Father, Father!" When I saw there was no reaction whatsoever, I cried out for my mother, who came immediately. She rubbed his body with an ointment for about five minutes, called his name, pulled his hair, and then gently stroked his head and face several times. She simply accepted the fact that he had gone.

She had already seen death so many times in her life. She was very calm, said very little, and set about bringing out all the things she had already prepared for him (and herself) for just such an occasion. She organized everything that was to come over the next few days, slept not at all for three consecutive nights, and broke down and cried only when my father's coffin was removed from our house for burial. Their home from then on would no longer be their home, without him. I had the impression she was glad he had departed first, so that she could take care of him in his last moments. We all knew my father wasn't very good at such things.

After my father's death, my mother became weaker and weaker. It was obvious that with such an important part of herself missing, she could not survive him for long. Life began running out of her because its purpose had been achieved. So she simply deteriorated through a natural process rather than from illness. After a while, she no longer had the strength to get up, and was bed-ridden for two months before her death. She was conscious until the very last minute. As the youngest, or the "Benjamin" ("Thang Ut") as it was commonly and affectionately called in the family, I had received the rod from her more than any of her other children ("I beat you hard because I love you hard," goes the Vietnamese proverb) and had always been her favorite. She reached the point where she couldn't take solid food anymore, was fed intravenously and sustained by various drugs. Then she asked her doctor, a nephew, to cease all the treatments. She died two days later.

I had been spending every night by her side. On the early morning of Christmas Eve, 1991, I noticed her having serious difficulty breathing. I took her in my arms and hugged her gently. She was very skinny (thirty-five kilograms). I wasn't able to behave like a fifty-five-year-old man that morning. I felt the need to be a little boy again with my mother at that moment. I talked to her softly, telling her how much I'd enjoyed the sponge cakes she had made for me to take to kindergarten, how much I loved her. I reminded her of how hard she had tried to make new clothes for me at Tet (the lunar New Year) so I could go out and show off with the other kids, who always managed to display their traditional new clothes for that holiday. I told her that she'd given her children everything, and that I hadn't spent nearly as much time with her as I should have over the years. I also reminded her how she had poked fun at me a few months before when a childhood friend of hers, Mrs. Hoa Loi, had come for a visit, and she had introduced me as her youngest "daughter" because I had been doing all the housekeeping. I had responded by telling both of them to be patient, for I'd soon get pregnant and give them a baby boy to play with. When they had first met at the Ben Thanh market, my mother was eighteen and Mrs. Hoa Loi, fifteen. They had shared so many experiences over the years, and I was happy to share a little of myself with them.

Holding my mother in my arms that morning, I knew the time had come for her to leave us. I hoped she would be able to rejoin my father and be happy, as she should if there was any justice at all after these long years of her existence on earth. I wanted to hold her tight, but I feared I was hurting her. So I rocked her gently, as people do with babies, and I was sure she shared these moments with me though her eyes were closed. This lasted an hour. Then she suddenly opened her eyes, looked at me for a long moment, during which I felt sure she was seeing just a very little boy, her little boy, because that was how I felt too. Then a single tear rolled slowly down her hollow, wrinkled, left cheek, and she closed her eyes forever. It was a moment of both intense happiness and profound grief. I knew it was the end, but I had to check. There was no breathing. There was no heartbeat. There was no pulse at her wrists. My mother had gone.

I didn't try to revive her as I had my father. I took her again in my arms and kept hugging her, still feeling the warmth of her body spread all over me, as if she sought to pass on to me the very last departing bits of her energy. I held her tightly against me, fully conscious of the natural and common reality of death. At that very moment, I hoped that, surely, one day I would be with her again. I hoped and wished so intensely at that moment that all of us would be together again sometime, somewhere, somehow. This couldn't be the end. Whoever or Whatever has the power and wisdom to make us live and die cannot possibly amuse Himself, Herself, or Itself by dismissing us so summarily. Human emotions, feelings, love must have more than physical life, and must have come from something more than dust. That moment was the strongest moment of hope in my life. I still don't want or try to understand it, to explain or reason about that feeling or moment of hope, just remember it and be filled with that intense sentiment and moment again.

In death, my mother looked very serene and at peace with herself and the world. Her facial expression was contentment. Looking that moment at the mother who had brought me into this world, I saw the past fifty years of my life flash through my mind, and understood better the meaning of the word "stupidity"—my stupidity. My mother's death reminded me about life with purpose and meaning. An obvious, simple, basic, and natural thing. Only life with meaning and purpose can give life with hope in the pursuit of our ideals and convictions. Purpose and meaning make all the difference in quality of life for rich and poor alike. They are within everyone's reach. Humanity is indivisible in the act of being and becoming, in happiness, sorrow, and common purpose. For the time being, I would settle for my mother's hope of togetherness in the way she had taught me: togetherness for and in each of us, for and in all the members of the family, in an individual and collective sense of belonging and sharing. That was my mother, a very simple woman, like many, many other mothers and women on earth.

I was able to give my parents proper funerals and carried out their last wishes, which was for each of them to be buried by their own mothers' sides, two hundred miles apart. So after seventy years of life together, they had fulfilled their filial duties to the best of their abilities. They had been worthy of the union chosen not by them but for them by their parents, as traditions and customs required. They had lived a simple matter of morality between simple people. A natural union between a man and a woman, to exist, be together, share, procreate, raise offspring as conditions permitted, and hope that their children would do the same. My parents had surely hoped strongly all their lives to return one day to their respective mothers, as good children should after school.

My parents' union gave our immediate family togetherness. At the same time, each of us was also part of another togetherness of our own. These constructs were grounded in each of us, as it was for many other families of our time—go and live your lives together, have a family, pass. At their wedding, my father was twenty-four and my mother, barely eighteen. When they had left their small native villages and arrived in Saigon, all their belongings filled a small wooden trunk. They told me that at the start, they'd had only enough to buy a primitive bed, a tiny table, two wooden chairs, and a few pots and pans.

My parents' life was simple. Their first purpose and hope was for my father to further his training, so my mother worked hard to pay for his studies. She was able to do only the things her mother had taught her: mending and sewing, baking and selling cookies, washing and ironing. They shared every minute of sweat and tears to meet the challenge. My mother also managed to give birth to her first child, my sister, when she was just nineteen. Then another girl came, followed by a boy. Three births in three years. It took my father four years to become a construction technician. Then it was his turn to earn the money, and he gave my mother every penny. He roamed all over southern Viet-Nam with his wife and children, living on junks and in tents for over twenty years, building thousands of kilometers of roads and hundreds of bridges. During that time, he was also able to travel to Hanoi to pass his civil engineer exams. By that time, my mother had given birth to two more sons, with me being the last. But it was also a time of profound sorrow for my parents because of the death of their second and third children, who died within five days of each other, victims of dysentery at the ages of four and three. Such tragedies were common in Vietnamese families in those days of the 1920s, due to poor living conditions. For my mother, who was then only twenty-four, it was a taste of hell on earth. For me, it was a sister and brother I would never know.

For seventy years, my parents gave us, their children, all that they were able to, so that through education and experience, we could have a better life than theirs. They provided and they gave. None of us had ever heard my parents say, "I love you," and very likely they never said it to each other. Their upbringing taught them that people of good education didn't say things like that. The only way they knew how to express their love was to share and give, and they did this intelligently and effectively. They gave their children and grandchildren everything they had in life. Then both decided at the end of their lives to return to their own mothers as their last act of belonging, to return to the very source that had given them life, with love, respect, and gratitude. It made an abstraction of all the pains and sorrows of the human condition.

I think hope was omnipresent in my parents' lives, because they had clear meaning and purpose. No grandiose ideals for them. The natural and simple purpose of life, in its continuous change and evolution, was their motivating force. My mother was a very

5-CART

rational person in dealing with problems, but when it came to her purpose in life, reason didn't seem to matter much. To care, love, and keep the togetherness alive in her family was not a matter of reason, but rather *the* reason for her existence. Accordingly, she displayed more affection to the black sheep instead of bestowing more rewards on the good children. Many considered her way of dealing with children and grandchildren contradictory and illogical. She was very strict with all, but gave more time and care, not tolerance, to the naughty ones, with me probably being the worst.

She explained her theory to me during one of our regular chats, about a month after my father's death, when it was just the two of us left in the old house. "Your father always reminded me of an old Vietnamese proverb, that our hand has long and short fingers, and the short ones need more help," she said. "I always hoped to be my children's best friend. When you get into real troubles, your parents should be the first ones to know, not the last. You have no better friends than your parents to help you on this earth."

I often remember vividly that talk about "long and short fingers." I then understood better her idea of togetherness during all the good and bad things in life. All the fingers can't be stretched to only long ones in the name of virtue, or reduced to only short ones for the sake of equality. There are so many common denominators to be shared in togetherness and so much to gain in diversity. In her own way, my mother had to deal with one of the most difficult aspects of human civilization: the individual and the collective, with all their sub-sets of chaos, coercion, barbarity, absolutism, and totalitarianism. As if those aspects weren't enough, there was also the ideal of togetherness in diversity and not in hegemony. Enormous and complex, this human problem has dragged on for thousands of years in the East and West alike, with the rise and fall of empires. (*Plus çà change, plus c'est la même chose.*) An end to all this is not yet in sight. Egalitarian doctrines will never eliminate humankind's natural diversity.

The *raison d'être* of the international community is above all its humanity, a matter of giving and not demanding. The wonderful magic of life is in this "long and short fingers" metaphor, but why have we human beings tried to reject this precious essence of humanity and to keep on concocting superior races, imposing absolute truths, and even claiming immortality, instead of fostering togetherness and being simple mortals as nature intended?

My mother's "fingers" story emphasized the simple things in life and how she, like many other mothers on earth, dealt with the difficult problem of togetherness in diversity by merely applying one little rule each time she told her kids, "Eat your spinach if you want the sponge cake for dessert"; "Finish your homework, after which you can go out and play ball"; or "Tidy your room first, and then you may go to the movies". I must admit that I thought in my youth that my mother had been unnecessarily strict or unduly uncompromising when it came to those chores. But to her, it was an immutable rule for her children. She would have said it should apply to everyone: commoners, kings, or presidents, governments and states alike, including the United Nations (*le machin*, as De Gaulle called it), if need be.

In other words, you have no rights if you haven't first done your duties. There was no confusion in my mother's mind on this issue. It was elementary arithmetic for her to match the minuses with the pluses on her abacus to determine whether we were cheating or not. The individual's natural gift of choice was respected. Equally shared duties for togetherness were assured, and rights were earned accordingly. The terms "right" and "duty" functioned synonymously in my mother's mind. Her love for us was totally unconditional. Only when we failed in our duties she would beat us hard, because she loved us hard. Fair enough. That should help clear up the prevailing global confusion about who has the duty to do what to whom.

I was drawn to my mother's ideas of togetherness in diversity, with duties clearly defined, understood, and respected. She wouldn't have gone to the UN to claim any rights and would have certainly considered it very bad manners to go there and demand rights. She wouldn't have understood why we've set up a fan club for rights instead of duties. She would consider a fan club of duties to be much more enjoyable, even if it merely consisted of inevitable endless debates competing for defining and agreeing on duties. Something must have gone off the tracks from the very start for us to be quarrelling so endlessly. Except for the *ver solitaire*, my mother certainly would have preferred to say that humans are born with inalienable duties to respect life, promote togetherness, and contribute to the pursuit of happiness for all. "Ask not what your country can do for you; ask what you can do for your country," as John F. Kennedy famously said in his inaugural address. If he had used the word "family" instead of "country," my mother couldn't have agreed more.

What matters is how to use properly this sense of togetherness, which is not man-made but a natural and powerful urge in humans, who need to belong and are quite willing to share with others both the good and bad in life. In other contexts, togetherness is also concerned with national identity, or nationalism, something the Vietnamese had wanted more than anything else since 1955, when their people and nation were divided by the Geneva Accords. We wanted togetherness and a sense of belonging everywhere at all levels.

To take the issue one step further, togetherness involves the hope for a fully accepted international community one day, though we have a long way to go to reach that level. The UN's effectiveness today clearly lies in its humanitarian, social, and development activities—trying to bring very different peoples together, which neither means dispensing charity nor reducing everyone to a single ideology, to this sort of democracy or that kind of freedom—rather than its painful peacekeeping role. Coercion may be necessary in cases of urgent assistance to people in danger but it's evident that the solution does not lie in reducing everyone to the same mold by putting more international policemen on the beat, who often generate further antagonism and unrest. The day will surely come when the motto *e pluribus unum* is accepted and will be a reality for all the peoples in the world—not just exclusively by and for the people of the United States of America—and also when the sad and dreadful dictum, "If you want peace, prepare for war," is banished from all the nations on the planet and from the minds of humans who will no longer have to claim their right to kill in self defense so that they may live.

The United Nations has done important work and is the form for a budding, if faint, hope for world law and order. Isn't it high time for all the governments of the world, particularly the great and powerful ones, to stop the maneuverings and other games of politics, and honestly try to introduce the much-needed reforms through the UN's General Assembly? The Secretary General's role also needs strengthening—at least be decent enough to spare him the currently thankless job of an errant pauper begging left and right to get things done.

The problem with the UN's past fifty-five years is that it has been made to persist on the old paths of so-called civilization and progress, freedom and democracy, peace and rights of all sorts. It has not yet really communicated the message of duties and togetherness, tolerance and diversity, sharing and humanity, which are equally—if not more—difficult and painful tasks and challenges in the face of continued cruelty and barbarity. I don't have the answers to those big problems but, as Anne Frank taught us, I can at least cling to the hope and conviction that, in spite of everything, people are truly good at heart, evil will not last forever, the common destiny of humankind is good, and the clock of hope chimes always for the better.

* * *

The fundamental act of being requires purpose and meaning. Life with purpose and meaning generates hope. Furthermore, life with meaningful purpose can't ignore reason and reality to transform its passive hope into active hope, but active hope also requires giving, sharing, and togetherness to acquire its human context. My old parents helped me see that it's not hope that gives life with purpose, but life with purpose that generates hope.

My years of imprisonment helped me come to an understanding of the mechanics of hope. Its evolution began as processes within me, pushing me to search for purpose and meaning. The other two parameters of hope—reason and reality—activated my ability to know, think, and decide. The effective interplay and interactive operation of all four of these parameters makes it possible to assess and determine the level of viability of hope in any given set of circumstances. Failure of any of these parameters to act in an appropriate manner would prevent hope from arriving at its active state. It would remain static and passive.

At my parents' side, I was able to discover that hope could be found much more in giving, sharing and togetherness, and that it was enhanced by one's ability to communicate, diffuse, and propagate it. Hope was at first very personal, but I also understood that hope needed something concrete, more solid, and broader to prevail. I had lived in our home for years at different stages of my life before, but I had never been much aware of hope related to the family. Was it because of my hardships that I became able to see at last the most obvious starting point for my thoughts and feelings? The undeniable basis for my existence, for anything, related to my being on this earth, was the sense of coming from and belonging to certain common roots and origins, something much bigger than just the safety and well-being of myself.

Individuality and egocentricity were inherent in my act of being, but had operated as stumbling blocks rather than moving forces for hope, until they were made to join and participate in something broader, more meaningful, and fulfilling. After my soul-searching and painstaking efforts to find purpose, meaning, and reason, I realized that I had been drawn into a violent confusion, battling with all sorts of realities and desperately trying to defend, maintain, and save whatever sentiments of hope had emerged in my consciousness. That was my precious experience of hope, gained through the experience of hope with my fellow-mason inmates.

My understanding and ability to hope were much improved and made more workable by that experience, but back home in the bosom of my family and by my parents' side, I found myself in a new set of realities. In me, as in any living creature, hope could not remain static for long, but must evolve with life itself. Hope finds its starting point with each individual's genuine inner sentiments, the most basic and natural elements of his or her act of being and becoming: namely, family, country, and people with common culture, traditions, and customs. Hope is essentially personal, but it also requires universality to transform itself from individual hope into communicative hope.

My parents showed me that hope wasn't only the ability to reconcile my purpose, meaning, reason, and reality, but it required a much broader and deeper context in which to operate. My parents hoped for a whole and fulfilling way of life, the ability to know oneself and others. It wasn't just the act of being and becoming, expecting the good and trusting in the unknown, but of placing unyielding trust in others, with love to give, sacrifices to endure, and joy and sorrow to share. In spite of the utter simplicity of their lives, hope, for my parents, lay foremost in the family they created, an undeniable part of nature, with ugliness to bear, beauty to discover, and light to shine in the home and over the land. That's how I finally learned to feel hope. It is still not quite clear in my mind but much less frightening. It is still hope with confusing logic and mixed-up emotions but much more friendly and comforting. It is hope as an endless source of loving memories from my parents, the hope to be, to give and share with others. In the very last minutes of her existence on earth, my mother taught me that hope was a powerful feeling. Since then, her death has reminded me again and again that hope is a wonderful but strange emotion, a kind of overwhelming sensation like an invading warmth of the flickering sun piercing through the early morning mist of our mysterious life with the poetry and music of the heart inside us and the world around us—for each and all to have together.

We can be reasonably sure that all the clocks of hope, whether individual, family, country, or nation, will one day come to the same hour, not to be adjusted by supermen and gods, but by the peoples of the world themselves. It has become more than evident that whenever people are able to move around, they will get together to share what they have and be together. And whenever ideas are permitted to travel, whenever barriers are brought down, and where cultures and customs meet and merge, tolerance and goodwill gain ground, human civilizations complement themselves and progress together, and peace is enhanced, sought, shared and propagated. This has been an irreversible and accelerating evolutionary process, and Anne Frank was right. No question about that. Why don't we make a sincere effort and give ourselves a good kick to move ourselves toward it?

Barbarity, greed and cruelty, chauvinism and fanaticism, totalitarianism and absolutism, all these negative and unfortunate aspects of humankind will be crushed by the Wheel of Time, which is also the Clock of Hope, with its purpose and meaning of life, its reason and reality in the common destiny of humankind on this planet. The question for us and our offspring in the years to come is when, when, when? How many more myths, illusions, and disillusions must we go through again and again? How much more additional killing and devastation must we endure? In fact, it very much depends on each and all of us to make these things happen.

We can now stand upright, walk, fly and go into space. We can all marvel together at the beautiful things of Mother Nature and the many hopes we share. Human aspirations are plentiful in face of the exciting wonders of life with the gates of hope wide open for all of us to get in together. It is much more worthwhile than the futile and deadly battles of words and swords, which are not worth a nickel. We have the conviction, will, capability, and hope to make the good of humankind prevail. We have the dream of the awakened, the hope to hope, and the hope against all hope. Our minds have certainly evolved to the point that we can know that the human race has a common hope to seek, have, and share, for we will all end up in the same and only destiny of our humankind, in the whole universe of which we are a part.

This, finally, came through to me as a type of hope with implications, particularly in terms of including other people rather than remain something strictly individual—where one is concerned only with one's personal self. I have come to call this feeling in me "communicative hope."

CODA

Reflections on Active Hope

Hope—
is an inherent aspect
of the act of being.
Hope—
cannot be dissociated from life.

><

Hope—
in humanity
is a natural response
to life circumstances,
which express
the conscious inborn aspirations
for survival,
for betterment,
for self-realization.

><

5-CART

Hope—
is the negation of despair,
the natural reaction
to adverse situations,
the denial
of controlled or imposed realities,
and the expectation
of a better or alternative outcome.
The natural urge to hope
does not in itself produce hope.

><

Hope—
requires some rational and realistic basis
to emerge and prevail.
It can be repressed
or permitted to operate;
it can be conceived
and can evolve.

><

Hope—
can release
unsuspected and tremendous energies,
consciously and unconsciously,
individually and collectively,
for good and bad alike.
We all have a natural urge to seek hope
and require hope
to sustain our act of being.

><
Hope—

is its own r*aison d'être*
for each particular instance,
and is capable of generating
its own motivation and momentum.
Hope—
is difficult to comprehend
in its operational modes,
yet it does provide
Meaning and ***Purpose***,
its own logic
in the face of prevailing realities,
with cause and effect relationships
throughout its evolution.

><

Hope—
can take on as many facets
as human nature can,
and is the resulting outcome
of the interaction
between
Purpose, ***Meaning***, ***Reason***, and ***Reality***,
in the specific environmental contexts
in which we find ourselves.
Hope—
is thus basically subject
to at least these four parameters
in its process of conception and operation
to become ***Active Hope.***

><
Hope—

is a natural human aspiration.
In concrete terms,
hope is characterized
by a future-related projection with ***Purpose***,
and is subject
to degrees of ***Reality***, ***Reason***, and ***Mean-***
ing—
with possibilities of realization
ranging from uncertainty at level zero
to absolute scientific determination,
and from uncertainty at level zero
to pure speculative mysticism.
When hope moves
beyond the limits of reality or reason,
it tends to merge
into the concepts of belief or faith.

CHAPTER ELEVEN
THE LONGEST ROAD: COMMUNICATIVE HOPE

To enter the world is to commence the struggle.
Francois Voltaire (1694-1778)

In the years after my incarceration, both before and after my parents died, I came to know how wonderful it could be to walk the streets of one's hometown, rediscover the familiar places of one's childhood, relive the crazy things one did as a child, and hear in one's mind the voices and noises of the distant past. It matters not how life has treated you, your roots always remind you of how, where and how you came into the world and became part of a land and people here.

The familiar houses and streets of Saigon were mostly as they had been, but unkempt and dirty. There were countless bicycles but very few cars. People wore much duller clothes than I had remembered, as they went about their businesses at a somewhat slower pace. I was told that life had been hard in the years between 1975 and 1980, particularly regarding the availability of food. As far as I was able to figure it, the average family income in Saigon in the early 1980s was about fifty *dongs* per month—that would have been the equivalent of about ten dollars in the United States.

Although my English was rusty, I got along quite well in my teaching job, giving me a renewed appreciation and respect for the Oxford dons who had taught me so well. Fortunately, I was paid at an hourly rate, and ten to twelve hours of classes per day brought me an income of about five hundred *dongs* a month, ten times the average civil servant's pay. It was more than enough for me to sustain my parents and myself with not only the necessities, but also some luxuries, like cookies, fresh fruits, condensed milk, tea, and coffee.

My orientation into Ho Chi Minh City's new ways of life—I had to constantly remember not to say Saigon—went smoothly. Immediately upon my return, I had to present myself to the local police for registration and be granted temporary residence at my parents' home. At the time, high-ranking officials of the former regime weren't permitted permanent residence in Ho Chi Minh City. Reeducation returnees were also required to write weekly autocritiques and submit them to the local police. Police officials instructed me to present myself every Saturday with my piece of writing. My first essay, scribbled in a schoolboy's exercise book (my Oxford training again), was acknowledged with satisfaction, dated, and duly signed by the local police cadre.

That was the only one I had to write because, the following week, I was summoned to Ho Chi Minh City's central police headquarters, where I was received by a very friendly officer who inquired about my health and well-being, and warmly offered whatever help he could to stabilize my re-entry into the family fold. I told him that I was, of course, very happy to be home with my parents, that I had reported to the local police, and had already submitted my first weekly autocritique. The man expressed great surprise and emphatically explained that I was obliged neither to write the essays nor report to the police. I manifested an even greater surprise and told him I thought all reeducation returnees were required to do these things and would eventually have to apply to regain their civic rights. Returnees, I had understood, were on a sort of probation and would have to demonstrate good conduct over a period of time before receiving an official certificate attesting to the reinstatement of their civic rights. Again to my great surprise, the police officer told me that I had never lost my civic rights and, therefore, didn't have to apply for any certificate of reinstatement. For a minute, he almost gave me the impression that my five years of reeducation in the north had never happened. I then thanked him warmly for his help, but wasn't much convinced by his good words, and waited anxiously afterwards to see whether what he had said was true or not.

I didn't have to wait long. Local elections were coming and, sure enough, I received a voter card with my name, birth date, and place, with my address being that of my parents. My electoral card didn't mention whether my address was temporary or permanent. It was really a big plus, since I didn't have identification papers of any kind, and there was no way for me to establish my identity, when necessary, by any official document. I quickly had my voter's card laminated and kept it carefully in my wallet.

The matter of temporary or permanent residence was vital for everyone in Ho Chi Minh City, particularly reeducation returnees. It was a tricky catch-22, because if a person didn't have a permanent residence, he or she couldn't get formal employment, and without formal employment, one wasn't allowed to have a permanent residence. I was lucky to have my parents in our family home, which had been my permanent legal address since my return from England in 1960; therefore, I was allowed a temporary residence there after my release. The overwhelming majority of returnees had to go to the so-called "new economic zones." Luckily again for me, I didn't have to endure the catch-22 for very long. After only a few months, I was granted permanent residence status at my parents' address. Although I wasn't on the government payroll as a civil servant, I had a formal job as an English teacher with a governmental organization, which helped a lot.

My life, to use the vocabulary then in vogue, became "stabilized" much sooner than I had hoped. I was told, however, that in the years between 1975 and 1980, it had been very difficult to find work in Ho Chi Minh City. Many, those who became known as boat people, had taken to the sea under very dangerous conditions in an attempt to emigrate to a better life elsewhere. They often ended their journeys at the bottom of the Pacific Ocean. Some were fortunate enough to be rescued by foreign vessels. Some were confined in refugee camps in various countries for years, and many perished at the hands of pirates. Certainly, life in Viet-Nam was uncomfortable and difficult in those years, and hope as well as despair was operating very intensely. I remembered that in extreme circumstances, hope and despair could operate side by side, that any human being could perform desperate deeds and indulge in all kinds of hopes, including hope against all hope. It took great courage for those boat people to throw themselves into the vast and deadly Pacific Ocean for the sake of a precariously uncertain hope for a better life and the opportunity to share bounty elsewhere. It must also be said that the hardships and challenges of those who stayed behind in the land of their ancestors were of another dimension, but no less heartbreaking. They, too, simultaneously hoped and despaired in their daily struggle for survival. Communicative hope requires sharing not only the munificence in life but also, more frequently, the bad moments.

The Vietnamese economy was in a sorry state after more than a hundred years of colonial exploitation, which was followed by the devastations of World War II (Japanese and Chinese), the French Indochina War, and finally the American War. The northern population had long been accustomed to material deprivation. During those war-torn decades, the North Vietnamese had rigorously fulfilled their role as the rear base for the enormous logistics required in the war. They also sacrificed much to provide not only the required production and supply, but also the assistance and manpower for the battles on the southern front. The foreign aid Hanoi received from the Soviet Union, the People's Republic of China, and other communist countries had come mainly in the form of military, not consumer, goods. The Vietnamese in North Vietnam had literally lived on a sort of spinach (*rau muong*) and had very little meat or fish during the twenty years of the American War. In the South, the population had been conditioned to a more plentiful life—thanks to LBJ's "butter"—but felt the pinch when the old stocks ran out. No more steaks and beer, perfumed soaps and scented shampoos, blue jeans and leather shoes. Very soon, an occasional scoop of ice cream or a pocketful of spare change had retreated into the realm of hopes and dreams rather than simple realities.

I recall an episode just a few weeks after the fall of Saigon that illustrates the sharp difference between northern and southern living conditions. Some relatives had returned from the North after having been there since the late 1940s. I gave a few uncles a guided tour of Saigon—Ho Chi Minh City—a city they hadn't seen for nearly three decades. They had left South Vietnam for the North right after Japan's unconditional surrender to the U.S. and the return of the French expeditionary forces to Indochina in September 1945. In those first days of May 1975, my uncles were, of course, much impressed by the living standards, plentiful vehicles, private cars, tall buildings, and profusion of consumer goods. They were dazzled by my invitation that they join me in a restaurant to partake of a popular chicken noodle soup. When the steaming bowls arrived at our table, they all reached for their wallets, and I had to insist that I was their host. They had had no intention of paying, they humorously explained, since they had no money anyway. They had reached into their wallets, they demonstrated, to retrieve small envelopes containing a white powdered substance. No, not cocaine or heroin—simply glutamate seasoning to sweeten the soup. They had been using the stuff for years because their soups had always been just noodles in plain hot water. After being away from Saigon for so long, my revolutionary uncles once again had the pleasure of real soup with genuine chicken broth. After draining their bowls completely, my uncles looked left and right at the other restaurant patrons, and then gave each other a puzzled glance. I asked them what the matter was.

The youngest of my uncles, about fifty-five at the time—Uncle Nine, we called him—then inquired: "Don't we have to produce our food coupons to order our soups?"

"No food coupons of any sort for any kind of food are required," I replied.

"In that case, people can eat as many bowls as they wish?"

"You can eat as many bowls as your wallet can afford," I assured them.

They were delighted to hear it, and we ordered a second round of *real* chicken noodle soup that morning in liberated Ho Chi Minh City.

Nevertheless by 1980, the living conditions of my hometown had deteriorated considerably. My immediate family, my uncles, and all the other relatives were reduced to the common denominator of equal hardship. One was still free to order as many bowls of soup as one's wallet would allow, but wallets were allowing much less. I was fortunate with my well-paying job, but my uncles' government salaries barely paid the bills. It became clear to my revolutionary relatives that the challenges of peace could be even more difficult than fighting the French or the Americans.

In early 1980, I recalled that my greatest concern in the 1960s—Viet-Nam's economic growth and development—had become a dramatic reality by any international standard. I had presumed, even then, that the great minds and leaders of the world would have a profoundly painful ideological and political task ahead in their quest for the well-being and prosperity of their peoples. I remembered having read a short pamphlet, "The Basic Approach," by a good man and exceptional leader, Prime Minister Pandit Nehru (1889-1964) of India, who had been compelled to make a choice for more than a half billion of his countrymen in the 1950s. He was at an historical crossroads and, with all the wisdom of his long and precious experience, he chose the only possible third alternative—a sort of synthesis of capitalism and socialism, hoping to incorporate the positive elements of both systems, and willing to endure their negative aspects as well. There was no way for Mr. Nehru to know at that time that many of his problems would be taken care of by themselves thirty years later by the natural processes of regionalization, globalization and integration—not very new things, really—which may not be beneficial to everybody; but that's how life has been for thousands of years under some form or other. When people, thoughts, languages, and objects are permitted and able to move around, they meet, and clash sometimes, but always get together and generate progress. You can close your door sometimes but not all the time, just as you can fool some of the people some of the time, but not all the time, however clever and powerful you may be.

These ideas began to be formed for me in the 1950s during my Oxford days. I had kept them in my head in the 1960s and 1970s while in private business and public service. I was unable to find any notions to replace them after my release from reeducation and my return back home in Saigon in the 1980s and 1990s. Of course, these thoughts also had been with me at the time of the Paris peace talks, when I became closely acquainted with Nguyen Co Thach. He was a true brother-enemy, but a civilized, intelligent, good, and understanding man. Thach, in his role as Hanoi's counterpart to U.S. Ambassador William Sullivan on the Paris Accords drafting committee, really got under Kissinger's skin. I had a friendly inclination toward Thach right away. Maybe it was because he had the same name as my father's family (Nguyen Van Thach and Nguyen Co Thach).

I didn't have much hope for a negotiated solution from the peace talks. But I derived personal satisfaction from my conversations with Hanoi's politburo Le Duc Tho and Thach, who was then deputy foreign minister. There were amusing moments during those long peace talks. One evening in Paris, at a reception given by the French foreign minister Maurice Schuman, Dr. Kissinger took me by the arm and insisted on introducing me to Le Duc Tho. It was an awkward moment for both Mr. Tho and me, but the behavior was typical of high-ranking American officials at the time, despite their having the best of intentions. Mr. Tho and I had already had opportunities to meet and talk on many other occasions. Neither of us said anything to that effect, but by the prolonged look we gave to each other while shaking hands, we clearly communicated to each other that we should let the U.S. presidential advisor enjoy the satisfaction of having performed his good deed of the day.

As for Thach, he wasn't really ideologically dogmatic with me, nor did he use the *langue de bois* (wooden tongue) in our discussions. We did not agree on positions, but he could understand what I was talking about, especially national identity, and social and economic development, among many other things. Thach defended his views meaningfully and intelligently instead of just reciting the party lines, like so many others did.

I have always asked myself about the differences that divided the Vietnamese for so long and with such lethal consequences. Viet-Nam had become ensnared in a tangle of politics and power plays but, by the end of the day, weren't both sides risking the loss of their Vietnamese souls to outside forces? Was there no other choice, no other way out, a way where North and South could get together to deal with this strictly Vietnamese problem? Had it never been possible, from 1945 on, for communists and non-communists to engage in meaningful and objective discussions in a spirit of mutual comprehension, reciprocal tolerance, brotherly love, and common interests? Was it so hard for brothers to compromise rather than kill? I wasn't around when the whole thing started, but I would surely have found myself facing an impossible dilemma if I'd had to go to my mother and tell her that my brother wanted to cut my throat because I didn't agree with his ideas. Would I have been able to claim self-defense and cut his throat first? It wouldn't have been much different from him and his arguments. I still don't know the answer. And what if it were my father who would not agree with my human rights? Should I throw away Confucius' (551-478 B.C.) "Respect of your parents" or Moses' "Honor your father and mother, that your days may be long upon the land which the Lord your God is giving you" (Exodus 20:12)? Of course not. I would have to just wait and keep on trying to explain.

Thach and I were able to discuss these questions, and I often had the strange feeling that he and I could have easily switched roles and would have gone through the same lines of reasoning to arrive at the same conclusions, regardless of sides or ideologies. Thanks to my four years of studies in political theory with George D. H. Cole at All Souls College, I didn't have much trouble following Thach's reasoning, although my reading at Oxford brought me only up to the so-called "Two-and-a-Half-International," nowadays called "Socialist International," of many present and past world leaders, such as Tony Blair and Harold Wilson (UK), Lionel Jospin and François Mitterrand (France), Olaf Palme (Sweden), Pierre Trudeau (Canada), Golda Meir (Israel), Indira Ghandi (India), and Lee Kwan Yew (Singapore) to cite a few. The Two-and-a-Half International situates itself somewhere between the Second International of the Webbs and Lenin's Third International.

It seems to me that circumstances and environments shape all our destinies, even with our gift of choice and individual freedom. That has been the reason why I've never been affected much by ideologies or motivated in any way by politics. My concerns have always been much more elementary: the preservation of life, survival, subsistence, work, productivity, freedom from hunger, sickness, and poverty, caring for the young, the old, and family. That's been more than enough for me to worry about, without having to debate ideologies and politics. They are very important things for leaders and people who enjoy them, like intellectuals and politicians. But I've noticed that most people don't understand, or care much, or have time for such ephemeral topics.

We keep on shouting at the top of our lungs about freedom and democracy, social justice and human rights, and related concepts. Such abstract notions did not reach the Vietnamese peasants during the American War in Viet-Nam and continue to remain mysterious political slogans to the majority of people in Asia and many other parts of the world. It is, of course, self-evident and easy enough for everybody to accept that life is to be preserved and respected, that liberty must be enjoyed equally by human beings, in terms of rights and responsibilities; but when it comes to the pursuit of happiness, it is not very evident any more. Freedom, democracy, and human rights can mean anything under the sun, and in fact, usually mean completely different things to different peoples within their different cultural values, customs, and traditions. Utmost care and precaution must be exercised on these extremely sensitive matters in the fight and struggle for them. To take to the streets, provoke violence and riots, destabilize governments, or impose economic sanctions often cause more disservice to than promotion of human rights, freedom, and democracy. The solutions are elsewhere. There must be other ways to resolve these problems, and it's too easy to blame or call on the educators for treatment of the social ills of the world.

The ancient Greek philosopher Aristotle (384-322 B.C.) said that "Man is a political animal when his essential needs are satisfied," which means that when his essential needs are not satisfied, he is just an animal. This is an undeniable fact of life, nothing to be argued about. Very likely, four-fifths of humanity is right now concerned with minimum subsistence levels and survival. Freedom, democracy, and human rights are simply luxuries to them. But in the rich and developed countries, it also appears that material well-being and opulence is not enough. Do we know what we are really talking about nowadays when we keep on claiming freedom, democracy, and human rights, not only for the peoples in Asia, Africa, Latin America, and the Middle East.

Centuries ago, the French philosopher Jean Jacques Rousseau (1712-1778) asked a question to which no one has yet found an acceptable answer: "Has the progress of the sciences helped the advancement of our ethical ways of life?" (He was also the one who introduced the popular expression "social contract," to establish the relations between the citizen and his society. Much lip service has been given to the social contract idea, but it is sheer humbug. How can an individual be expected to have any kind of equitable contract with a society or government?) Rousseau also raised the question about the "common good" and its difference from the "good of all." If answers could be found to just these questions, we would be able to stop playing with words. Everyone knows and sees these senseless games of semantics, but nobody wants the good show to end.

Liberty does not only mean the people's right to choose and decide by themselves and for themselves, but very much more their ability to do something with themselves in order to obtain, first of all, their daily bowls of rice and pieces of bread. Any first year undergraduate will tell you the difference between negative and positive liberties. Philosophers like Engels and Green demonstrated long ago that liberty and freedom mean, in fact, opportunity and the ability to act. The fight for freedom is not a fight among ideologies, between capitalism and communism; it is, first of all, the same and common fight against hunger, sickness and ignorance. That is the continuing common denominator for everybody everywhere, for a very long time to come, before we need to get on our high horses over ideological disputes and wars. That is why I have come to consider war not only dreadful, but ghastly boring. There are many other things more enjoyable to talk about and more interesting with which to occupy ourselves.

An individual's life pales in comparison to humanity's destiny—and it must have a destiny. Yet individual persons are also able to aspire to their own infinity in their existence. Logically, infinity should be an eternal two-way street to the infinite macrocosm, as well as the infinite microcosm, a continuum with neither a beginning nor an end. Are we going to end up in the big or the small end? Again, no problem, really, for Lao-tzu has said that big and small are the same thing. The big is small and the small is big. The void is everything and everything is the void. This philosophy guided me in my confrontations with Thach's Marxist-Leninist outlook. In good conscience, I was prepared to accommodate any form of atheism, should Thach bring up such matters. Of course, he didn't, and our discussions were strictly down-to-earth.

By custom and tradition, I come from a peace-loving Buddhist family and have been also strongly influenced by my Christian Western education. I have equally admired Judaism, one of the most exceptional monotheist doctrines to have survived through millennia in the face of barbarity. I have also been deeply impressed by the teachings of the Koran, with its bewildering diversity coupled with intense determinism. I am, nevertheless, somewhat confused by how adherents of particular religions use them as rationales to punish, degrade, and even go to war against others. My mind has lazily come to rest on the notion of the infinite void, without beginning or end. My little mind is comfortable with the notion of a self-sufficient Eternal Big Void Infinity Almighty and/or God. There are physicists who have proposed the Big-Bang theory. Why not several or even billions of big bangs—who knows? Thanks to those thoughts, I'm able to agree with my beloved mother that wars are like natural calamities, just petty quarrels among people of the same family.

I was, therefore, not at all nervous talking to Thach. It was an intellectual exercise of discovery. What kind of person or brother-enemy was he? If Thach wanted to explain to me that our common Vietnamese interests would be best served by his methods, I was totally disposed to hear them. Like my fellow students, I had—according to the "in vogue" trend of the 1950s—been sincerely attracted by socialist dialectics, but have never been convinced that the solution to the equation of economic growth and social justice was to be found in the centralized state and monopolistic management advocated by Marxist-Leninist doctrine. I doubted its viability not because it might be morally, politically, or socially right or wrong, but simply because it wasn't workable in a market-oriented system. My formal training had led me to conclude that, by the end of the day and for many years to come, we would have to live with the market-economy system, learn how to respect it, and use it to engender the most rapid social and economic development possible.

From the time of my student days, I had come to consider the natural market economy the highest form and truest expression of individual liberties and collective freedom. The market isn't merely business, or a commercial and economic tool, but the inevitable and most comprehensive development process inherent in human nature. Impulsion may be given to the market, but if some form of control is imposed to meddle with it, deform it, or even hope to master it, the market will just go berserk, continuously expressing the choices and will of the people, individually and collectively. The market and the basic principles of the market economy are natural manifestations of human existence, the reflection of human nature in its individual and collective meaning. Such things have precedence over and contribute to the common denominators of all ideologies, whether capitalism, socialism, or communism. The essential thing for any ideology is to respect, first of all, the basic and fundamental aspect of humankind, and no cheating in the political games. The people deserve better than that. Thus, insofar as effective economic management is concerned, the problems are identical, whether with private or state capitalism. We have to face squarely the facts of life, for there is only good or bad economic management in strict respect of the natural forces of the market operational processes.

The basic issue of modern society is how to generate the necessary economic growth rate and secure an acceptable level of social justice at the same time. I've never questioned the sincerity of people's ideals of social justice and nationalism (such as Thach's), but I've doubted that their management methodology and ideology could be effective when confronted sooner or later with the inevitable market-economy system. Thach, of course, would not accept that kind of reasoning, and we'd be miles apart. The basic disagreement between Thach's people's democracy and my Western democracy would be his aim of government versus my simple form of government without any preordained aim. Naturally, he wouldn't concede to me my natural gift of choice in this matter, on the premise that I could only choose to agree with his unquestionable good goal, because there couldn't be any better goal for me. Thach knew well that no agreement between us would be possible on that fundamental issue, and that's why it wasn't necessary for us to raise and discuss such esoteric abstractions.

I remember my appreciation of an unexpected gesture from Thach at the signing of the International Act on Viet-Nam in Paris on February 3, 1973. As soon as the conference was declared closed, Thach took the trouble of walking alone across the large meeting chamber to shake hands with me, while I and all the others were still in our seats. Thach and I were the only ones among the brother-enemies to do this. I've always considered Thach's gesture as having a personal rather than political connotation. He also reflected the spirit I'd had with my relatives on the other side. We tried to avoid the issues dividing us and sought whatever might unite us, simply because we belonged to the same nation, country, and people. There were moments when I realized that reason and logic became futile when confronted with the meaning and purpose of life.

At the beginning, Thach and I addressed each other by our formal titles. Then one day he said, "Why don't we use the term *anh* (brother) between us?"

"I very much prefer that, but dared not suggest it because I'm the much younger one," I replied. We've now carried on an unusual friendship, even mutual affection, for over twenty years. We've probably hoped to share an impossible common hope.

After my release from prison, I met occasionally with Thach in Hanoi on a strictly private basis, and he was always very correct, receiving me at the Ministry of Foreign Affairs or government guest house, always with an aide present to take notes, and always walking me to the main entrance to see me off. Thach was a good strategist, with the people's interests in mind. We talked mainly about two things: liberalization of the Vietnamese economy and normalization of Vietnamese-U.S. relations. Each time we met, Thach explained to me measures recently taken by the government to free prices and the movement of goods, to promote services and increase production—and waited for my reaction. Of course, knowing him for twenty years, I would have liked to please him by offering my unqualified approval, but I had to tell him that in my view, the system is still extremely monopolistic, too centralized and quite different from accepted international business practices. He tried very hard to deal with the sensitive matter of Vietnamese-U.S. relations. I think U.S. Secretary of State James Baker found Thach a good interlocutor. Perhaps Thach tried too hard and too soon to promote Vietnamese-U.S. relations, and by doing so, was relieved of his work as deputy prime minister-cum-foreign minister and politburo party member.

Since he left office, we have been freer in our discussions. He has been absorbed with economic problems (no wonder, with Viet-Nam's per capita GDP at about $200) and even joked to me one day that to progress, one must accept being exploited a little. That is an inevitable reality, but an anathema for a Marxist-Leninist to admit. It's worth mentioning here that one of Uncle Ho's last wishes and instructions to his lieutenants was the wise idea of preserving the economic and social autonomy of the South Vietnamese population, on account of their well-known qualities of entrepreneurship and dynamism. He was recognizing the considerable accumulated assets in the south, which could permit positive growth rates and a smooth and gradual North-South integration, aiding the rapid development of the whole country.

In the early 1970s, South Vietnam advanced more, economically, than many countries in the region, such as Thailand and South Korea. Unfortunately, Uncle Ho's foresight (one Viet-Nam, two systems) was not respected like some of his other last wishes were—a clear loss of from thirty to fifty years for the Vietnamese to endure. All other things being equal, there was no reason why Viet-Nam, not a comparatively small or poor country, should not have had its proper place in the international community by the 1990s, with anything between a $5,000 to $15,000 per capita GDP. Viet-Nam is a beautiful country worthy of a booming tourist industry, is conveniently located for trade and services, and has relatively good and plentiful natural resources for processing and manufacturing. Viet-Nam ranks fourteenth in world population with nearly eighty million people, both an asset and liability, especially with over two percent in annual demographic growth and seventy-five percent of its population living in rural areas. It's clearly an enormous consumer goods market, but its per capita GDP will continue to linger at around $350 to $400 dollars (if translated in PPP [Purchasing Power Parity], this per capita would be around $1,400), even with an encouraging annual GDP growth rate of anything between five and nine percent (its lowest was at 2.6 percent in 1986 and it highest was at 9.5 percent in 1995). All things considered, Viet-Nam's Investment Capital Output Rate (ICOR) would be anything between three to five (economic multipliers) per annum (the best performance to date was in 1989 with 1.5, and the worst, 5.6, was projected for the year 2000). Realistically, Viet-Nam will need an average of $4 annually in the next five years to turn out $1 in GDP income per year (with the ICOR at four in economic multipliers). That leaves still a very long way to go.

These were the things that Thach and I discussed very frankly and amicably in our meetings. They involved the basic economic problems facing every nation on earth. With such simple and concrete issues, there are very specific problems of management to be resolved quickly, without any necessity to get into passionate or heated debates about ideologies. Thach and I felt really comfortable and open in our discussions, and one day he said to me that the most fundamental issue was how "to integrate or join all the available synergies of the Vietnamese nation to the common prevailing synergies of the whole world."

That was what I had hoped to hear from him for a long time. Of course, I leaped at the opportunity to tell him honestly and sincerely, "If that's what you're after and you really mean it, I'm one-thousand percent for it and don't need or care about anything else." As far as I'm concerned, Thach's statement will fit any ideology without much difficulty, whether Tory or Laborite, Republican or Democrat, Gaullist or Socialist. It doesn't matter what you call yourself, as long as you demonstrate that you're doing just that.

To me, Thach represented another aspect of our fratricidal conflict. Should the outcome of the war have been the reverse, the personal relations between us would have been no different. Fate and destiny made his side the victor and mine the vanquished, but Thach provided me with the opportunity to work out my own problems in defeat, and to come to terms with myself, my country, and my people. I would have been miserable for the rest of my life had I been compelled to discover what hatred is and have to harbor it for my former brother-enemies. Even now, however, after twenty-five years, there are still some on both sides with much hatred and bitterness in them. Hatred and bitterness have never generated anything really good in the end.

I have come to accept that the rejection or denial of reality cannot generate hope, but the recognition of an unacceptable reality can lead to either despair or hope. An attempt to comprehend the process of hope may indicate the following sequences in terms of the four parameters of: purpose, meaning, reason and reality. Faced with an unacceptable and impossible situation, humans react instinctively for survival, for a status quo, and refuse to recognize the unfavorable reality, and instead search for a more bearable alternative. This instinctive survival reaction also embodies humanity's natural urge to seek a hope to hope, which doesn't yet involve the activation of any of the four parameters. This hope to hope is also a natural emotional reaction resulting from the conflict between an impossible reality and the urge to survive. Without the concourse of reality and reason, this hope to hope appears to be a desperate hope, one devoid of a realistic and rational basis. Hope against all hope may be the ultimate spiritual force or very last driving energy in human bondage. In simpler terms, it is actually hopelessness. The hope to hope makes an abstraction of knowledge (reality) and logic (reason). The state of hopelessness is not a state of despair, but the inability to develop a realistic, rational, and meaningful hope with a consequential purpose. It's a situation in which the four parameters of hope have not yet come into play. The hope to hope doesn't have a specific purpose, but it does have the capability of neutralizing and denying despair.

In all circumstances, life has hope and hope is inalienable. Hope is always waiting to ignite and begin its operational process and evolution from Latent Hope to Passive Hope, from Active Hope to Communicative Hope.

CODA

Reflections on Communicative Hope

Hope—
is life with meaning and purpose.
Life without meaning and purpose
cannot generate hope.
Life is individual,
but also collective.
So, there are individual hopes,
but also collective hopes.
There are
personal hopes,
but also shared hopes,
hopes to share with others,
and hopes of others to share.

><

Hope—
is an inherent feature of human nature.
Hope—
is initiated and sustained
as the resulting outcome
of the interaction between
its four parameters
and the response of the individual
to the environment.

><

Hope—
is always latent in us human beings,
is able to emerge into awareness
with the hope to hope.
A passive hope
can move to active hope
if it can connect with,
and sustain, a rational basis
upon which to operate.

><

Reality and ***Reason***
permit hope to become operational,
but without ***Meaning*** and ***Purpose,***
it will dissolve
into a sense of helplessness
or frustration.

><

For hope to become active and operative,
it is necessary to assess carefully
each of its four parameters—
Purpose, Meaning, Reason, and ***Reality***.
The interaction between them
will provide
a coherent relationship for the person
to comprehend the emerging hope,
through succeeding processes
of coordination and reconciliation
between the two sets
of unique human abilities—

the mind (***Reason*** and ***Reality***)
and the will (***Purpose*** and ***Meaning***).

><

Hope is a wonderful God-given gift
for each person to seek and have.
But hope is also
to share and be shared.
Each human being
is part of a family,
a group,
a community,
a people,
a nation,
a world.

><

Humankind is a social
and cultural entity.
Our personal, individual hopes
need to acquire
their social aspect and bearing
in order to prevail.
The sharing of a common lot
in terms of
Reality (facts),
Reason (logic), and
Meaning (values)
also requires togetherness in
Purpose (aspired-for objective).

><

Thus, hope can be recognized
in its process of evolution
through four main stages:
Latent Hope,
Passive Hope,
Active Hope, and
Communicative Hope.

EPILOGUE

A MODUS VIVENDI: LIFE, HOPE AND DESTINY

Hope springs eternal in the human breast;
Man never is but always the best.
Alexander Pope (1688-1744)

Some readers of the manuscript that became this book have seen it as a personal life history within a time of political, social, cultural, and international turmoil. While those threads run through the story I've tried to tell, I see deeper themes permeating the story having to do with the fundamentals of what it is to be human, individually and collectively. For me, hope is a feature of all the fundamentals. I did not know this in my earlier life, but as I was confronted and challenged to the depths of my being from the 1970s onward, hope emerged as an absolute necessity. Prompted by my friend, Howard Schomer, I at first dallied with the idea of hope, but as time and circumstances went along, I realized how it was a defining condition of my being. If I was going to write anything at all, it would have to be with hope as the North Star—or the Southern Cross.

History has amply shown the tremendous force of faith, even in its extreme expressions. Hope in its great intensity isn't very far behind faith. Hope isn't simply the expression of a desire and a goal, but also includes the determination and effort to realize the goal. What Howard Schomer wrote about hope in 1987 reflects this: "So ***hope*** involves not only a ***wish*** and an ***expectation,*** but also the ***will to strive*** for the object desired. Clearly, hope energizes . . . ."

Hope surely has its connections with faith, can reach a context of faith, and should be able to merge with or transform itself into faith. But hope by nature must deal with things that belong more to Caesar and, thus, requires a higher content of practicality and feasibility than faith does. A line may be drawn between hope and faith, a line where hope will cease to be hope and transform itself into faith. Tolstoy's "faith in the force of life" may be paraphrased here as "hope in the purpose of life," or as in the Irish poet's "when hope rhymes with history." The problem is that there are so many "histories" with different purposes for different people. Remembering again St. Paul (Hebrews 11:1ff), I have the feeling that hope is somehow instrumental and some sort of a vehicle to faith. One may have hope without having faith, but it would not be possible to have faith without hope. So, it seems that hope is in everything, everywhere, at all times. I do not really know what faith is, but I can now say that I have hope as an essential part of my being.

In a strictly practical sense, it should be possible to work out a certain pattern, device, or process somehow to comprehend, manage, and even control hope, since it is one of many of humanity's abilities that are very real and present in everyday life. The ability to hope is not physical, like walking or talking or like the senses, but it is no less valid than the abilities to think, know, will, love, hate, rejoice, and grieve. One can also construct abstractions and adopt the materialistic view that the ability to hope is just one of the faculties of the human brain, which would mean "if no brains, then no hope." I'm inclined to say that even without brains, there's hope in stardust.

Can one also say that to hope is just one of the functions of thinking? Can one say it's tantamount to thinking, analyzing, planning, projecting, calculating, and assessing levels of feasibility? If so, would this be equivalent to computerized hope?

If one should claim that to hope is an act of the will to seek the good and not of the mind to seek the truth, then to hope is an aspect of to will, wish, aspire, desire, expect, trust, believe. Depending on tastes, would this be called "speculative hope"?

Hope can be any of the above, but, surely, it is much more. These, in my opinion, are various aspects of hope that emerge as we try to learn what it really is. The point of view may be taken that, with our limited human capabilities, we are only able to comprehend hope in terms of its pragmatic manifestations—like "love is to sacrifice," "a hole is to dig" or "honor is to respect." But I've come to know hope as a driving force, something like $E=MC^2$ at the "first moving thrust," or the lightning from the Big Bang, or even something from that wonderful "gentle breath" that causes life to begin. It gives the gift of choice, right and wrong, good and bad, happiness and sorrow, love and hate, humanity and bestiality, and many more yet-to-be-discovered wonders from the endless mysteries of creation.

Hope is an undeniable reality in all aspects of everyday life. Hope does concrete things to people all the time and must have a working mechanism of its own that functions in each individual according to his or her own characteristics. Each person must make use of this mechanism differently. This is what I have understood by individual hope. Yet, humans are also very much alike. All will have to come to the same truth, the same good, the same aim. Therefore, whether we like it or not, we'll all one day have the same collective hope. This is what I have understood by communicative hope, my own hope that can be shared with and by others, the hope of others that I can make my own.

It would be a difficult task, indeed, to propound a clear definition of hope. It would be more useful and practical to make the best use of this natural ability, which is, first of all, very personal. A modus vivendi of hope may, then, be worked out by each individual for each to live by. The ability to hope is inborn, a natural reaction to an unacceptable or no-longer-satisfying situation, coupled with a desire for change, an expectation for the future. This very personal ability requires the individual to be aware of hope's latent state, conscious of its manifestation, able to comprehend it as much as possible, and comply with its working mechanism. To paraphrase the French philosopher Rene Descartes (1596-1650), "I hope therefore I become."

The ability to hope, like the ability to walk or talk, can be learned, trained, practiced, and made effective use of. Hope has a considerable role and influence in every person's life and, like humankind's other abilities, can be made into a discipline, a science, as have other fields of human behavior. To begin with, it should be feasible to establish a set of reflexes and responses operating in reaction to environmental stimuli, and interacting with the characteristics of an individual's psyche. The stages of hope, as I have tried to understand it, together with its parameters, should enable us to draw a "Roadmap of Hope," to weigh and measure both qualitatively and quantitatively the effects of hope in various circumstances.

This working mechanism of hope is highly complex and sophisticated, but learning the mechanisms should help make us be more effective in our use of the ability to hope. Nowadays, this type of operation could be easily computerized (and promptly turned into a CD-ROM game of "Hopeopoly"). During my long years of imprisonment, I played a game of hope. It was an utterly unavoidable part of prison life. Prison is one of those places where hope operates most intensely, not quite as pleasant as buying a lottery ticket, but it is certainly much stronger.

Science is the coherent, systematic organization of knowledge, but for many years to come, if not always, science will continue to entail a certain measure of the unknown, a degree of doubt, which scientists may try to deal with through laws of probabilities. That which is unknown by science constitutes an inherent, as well as essential, aspect of life. With their wonderful intelligence, human beings will rapidly find out all about the whats and hows of human

DNA, but they will continue with the endless search for the why and what-if of DNA for a very long time. That constant unknown is and must be filled by hope: the hope *of* life, not the hope *for* life. Each person must find a modus vivendi for his or her hopes, to live with and by. Hope is ever present, waiting, searching for wishes, desires, and expectations to arrive, bonding mind with will, reality with reason, and meaning with purpose. Hope is filled with the tremendous forces of nature, helping us with being, belonging, and becoming, in the endless evolution of the world around us. It is also a precious gift of creation, meant for us to make the best use of every minute for a better tomorrow and throughout this existence, in our constant search for the meaning and purpose of this mysterious life.

Looking back at more than fifty years of my adult life, my schooling days in France and England, my years at Esso, the war in Vietnam, whether the American one or the one of brother-enemies, the defeat and shame, the self and the others, my beloved parents and family, the individual and society, the now and forever, confusion is still there—but even with confusing hopes, I feel much better. I am grateful that I do not have hatred in me and no longer have to deal with despair and hopelessness. Even with hardships galore and in store, I am now able to feel good at the sunrise, eager to welcome its first faint and glittering sunrays piercing through the morning mist down onto me with the wonderful warmth of Mother Nature, reminding me to thank again and again my Creator for the Gift of Life as well as the Gift of Hope, and for helping me continue with the endless struggles of the human condition in both joy and sorrow, myths and realities, illusions and disillusions.

Hope is an undeniable human ability and a constant companion, ever present in each of us for better or worse. The wonderful thing about the Gift of Hope is that it permits at the same time the Gift of Choice, enabling each of us to affirm his or her own self, individuality and responsibility in whatever circumstances that confront us; and still we have a say, however small, every second and minute in our everyday activities, as to our different fates and our common destiny.

It has taken me fifty years to be able to tell a story among six billion others. Stories still occupy a great deal of space in our lives. Human life is also the telling of endless stories. Little children all over the world adore listening to story telling, especially fairy tales. Other types of fiction are for grownups. The aim of my story telling is to share with others my thoughts, feelings, and sentiments about hope, and my hope that it will be of some use to others in their search for hope. I have tried to do this and it has not been an easy thing to do. But the wonder of hope is in its mystery, which is the mystery of the whole of Creation. We are all very fortunate, indeed, as my mother would say, and would again remind me, that by the end of the day, what really counts is the sharing and the togetherness.

Most dictionaries define hope as an "expectation of something desired" and as "desire accompanied by expectation." True, but our youngsters have lots of homework to do and will surely come to understand one day greater depths of what hope really means. It's the whole process of life with purpose.

CODA

Reflections on Life, Hope, and Destiny

Life has hope,
and hope is the essence of Creation itself,
the negation of the meaningless void.

><

The genesis of hope
is the manifestation of change itself,

the endless evolution of all things.
Hope is change with purpose
and evolution with meaning.

><

Hope—
is to be found
in the act of being and becoming itself,
helping us human beings along
on our mysterious journey,
searching for our different destinies,
and seeking for the common destiny
of all.

><

The gift of hope
is the gift of life itself,
both individual and collective.
Life with meaning is hope,
both personal and communicative.

><

The gift of hope
is also the gift of choice,
the ability and opportunity
for each and all of us
to have a say
in our separate destinies,
to be accountable
for our own personal decisions and deeds,
and to assume
the common responsibility

of the one and indivisibility of humanity
in face of the apparent indifference of
Creation—
the tremendous challenge
of the human condition,
individually and collectively.

><

Hope—
such an intangible notion—
cannot be invented.
Hope—
can be made a concrete element, however,
a vital, qualitative, and quantitative factor.
Hope—
can be assessed and measured.

><

Hope—
can be applicable to any purpose,
good or bad.
Hope—
in its poetic form,
can have a far more reaching
impact and consequence
than science
can measure or explain.
The power of hope
equals the force of life itself.
Hope—
can mobilize masses.
Hope—

can drive humans
to salvation . . . or perdition.

><

Hope—
is the search for the self
beyond the self,
the journey from the seen
to the unseen,
the difference between
the true and the false,
the good and the better,
the right and the wrong,
the meaningful and the void.

><

Hope—
is the mystery and challenge of life
for each and all
to be and become.

"Good Morning, My Brother"

I say to myself,
Hope is trust in the unknown, the pain to end and the life to be.
Hope is to fill emptiness and the rescuing hand from despair.
Hope is the wish to come, the love to give, and the morrow to bear.
Hope is the endless quest, the timeless change, both cause and destiny.
Hope is the purpose for each and all to seek, to have and to share.
Hope is there, but search it not in the passing clouds or deep blue sea.
Hope is right in you and in me . . . and also from the first Big Bang.
Hope is that Spark of Creation
For you, me, and all things to be,
For the many in One and the One in Many.

N.X.P.

ROADMAP OF HOPE

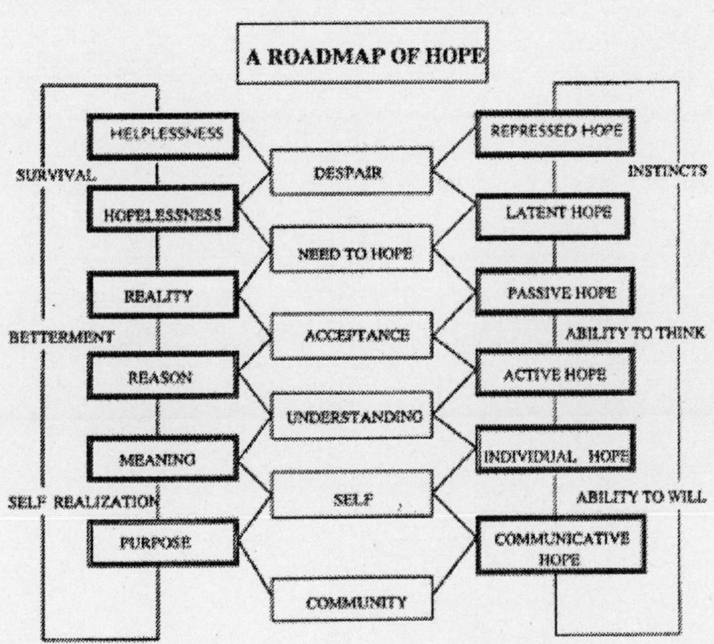

ABBREVIATIONS

AI
Amnesty International (an international private organization for the defense of human rights)

ARVN
Armed Forces of the Republic of Vietnam (1955-1975).

C.O. or **CO**
Commanding Officer

C.O.S. or **COS**
Chief of Staff

DAO
Defense Attaché, Office of the U.S. Embassy in Saigon which assumed the task of providing the Saigon government with military assistance after March 1973 within the framework of the Paris Accords, resulting in the total withdrawal of American troops from South Vietnam and the end of the U.S. Military Assistance Command, Vietnam (MACV.)

DMZ
Demilitarized Zone established at the seventeenth parallel in Viet-Nam by the Geneva Agreements on Viet-Nam, Laos and Cambodia signed on July 20, 1954. The DMZ was defined by the Geneva

Agreements to be a military provisional demarcation line (the river of Ben Hai) for the regrouping of opposing forces, prohibition of the introduction of additional troops, war equipment and supplies, construction of new military bases, and of setting up new military alliances and use of either zone north and south of the DMZ for military purposes.

DRV or **DRVN**

Democratic Republic of Vietnam proclaimed in North Vietnam by Ho Chi Minh's Declaration of Independence on September 2, 1945 and commonly referred to as North Vietnam during the American War in Viet-Nam. The DRV was replaced by the present denomination, Socialist Republic of Vietnam, at the reunification of the country on July 2, 1976.

ICC or **IC** or **ICCS**

International Control Commission, established by the 1954 Geneva Agreements and rendered obsolete by the 1973 Paris Accords with the establishment of ICCS, the International Commission of Control and Supervision composed of representatives from Canada, Hungary, Indonesia and Poland.

ICRC

International Committee of the Red Cross.

MAAG

U.S. Military Assistance Advisory Group set up in South Vietnam in April 1956 to provide training to the South Vietnamese troops after the departure of the French forces, and replaced in 1962 by the U.S. Military Assistance Command, Vietnam.

MACV

The U.S. Military Assistance Command, Vietnam, superseded and replaced the MAAG in South Vietnam in February 1962. MACV phased out on March 31, 1973 when all the U.S. troops were withdrawn from South Vietnam as per the terms of the Paris Accords.

MACV-CORDS or **CORDS**

Military Assistance Command, Vietnam, set up in May 1967 under the responsibility of Ambassador Robert Komer as Deputy to General William C. Westmoreland, Commander of the U.S. forces in South Vietnam.

NLF

National Liberation Front of the south of Viet-Nam (or South Vietnam) founded on December 20, 1960 by prominent personalities in the south of Viet-Nam who had fought and opposed President Ngo Dinh Diem, including Nguyen Huu Tho (lawyer), Trinh Dinh Thao (lawyer,), Mdm. Nguyen Thi Binh (teacher), Mdm. Nguyen Thi Dinh (3-star general deputy commander officer of the Viet Cong forces), Nguyen Van Nghiep (M.D.,), Mdm. Duong Quynh Hoa (M.D.), Mdm. Ngo Ba Thanh (lawyer), among others.

PAVN

People's Army of Vietnam, the armed forces of the (DRV) Democratic Republic of Vietnam, or the North Vietnamese troops during the war in Viet-Nam. The PAVN is also now considered the regular army of the Socialist Republic of Vietnam and claims it was created on December 22, 1944 with the formation of the "Vietnam Propaganda Liberation Troops" by Ho Chi Minh.

PRG RSVN

Provisional Government of the Republic of South Vietnam (an offspring of the NLF) created on June 6, 1969. Thus, the Delegation of the National Liberation Front (NLF) of the south of Viet-Nam, with Tran Buu Kiem as head of the delegation, was replaced at the Paris peace talks by the delegation of the PRG RSVN with Madame Binh as head of delegation in her capacity of Foreign Minister.

RVN

The Republic of Vietnam, proclaimed by Ngo Dinh Diem on October 23, 1955 by way of a referendum in the south of Viet-Nam, which deposed Emperor Bao Dai. The RVN was commonly referred to, between 1955 and 1975, as the country south of the seventeenth parallel in Viet-Nam. The RVN was recognized by over 100 countries in the world and had diplomatic relations with almost all the non-communist countries until 1975.

NOTABLE PERSONS

Vietnamese

Bao Dai. Born Nguyen Vinh Thuy in 1911, succeeded to the throne of the Kingdom of Annam in 1925 at the death in exile of Emperor Ham Nghi, his father. Crowned Emperor Bao Dai of the Nguyen dynasty in 1932. The last of the Vietnamese monarchs, he was deposed by Ngo Dinh Diem by a referendum in South Vietnam on October 23, 1955. During WWII, Bao Dai was forced to declare the "independence" of Vietnam by the Japanese on March 11, 1945 and lend his name in collaboration with the Japanese forces of occupation. After the surrender of Japan, and upon the return of Ho Chi Minh to Hanoi on August 25, 1945, Emperor Bao Dai abdicated and became three days later "Citizen" Prince Vinh Thuy, Supreme Advisor to the communist-dominated provisional government set up in Hanoi on August 28,1945, led by Ho Chi Minh. After the Elysees Agreement which he concluded and signed with France on March 8, 1949, Bao Dai, as Emperor, once again declared the so-called 'independence" of Vietnam and consorted with the French Union (Union Francaise) in the creation of the "State of Vietnam" with himself as "Head of State." Ousted in 1955 by Ngo Dinh Diem, Emperor Bao Dai lived in exile in France where he died in 1997.

Cao Van Vien. Saigon General, Chief of the Joint Chiefs-of-Staff of the Armed Forces of the Republic of Vietnam (ARVN). Only 4-star general in active service during the American intervention in

Vietnam from 1965 to 1975. Moderate and profoundly religious, Vien was highly respected in the armed forces and political circles in Saigon as well as by people in Washington and Paris. Under the rule of President Thieu (who was also a Lieutenant General), Vien was considered a convenient, untroublesome and rather nominal general of the Joint Chiefs-of-Staff of the ARVN. Most of the important decisions about the conduct of the Vietnam War were taken by U.S. Commanding Officer General William C. Westmoreland and other Washington personnel. Following the fall of Saigon in April 1975, Vien has lived in the United States.

Duong Dinh Thao. Official spokesman of the National Liberation Front (NLF) of South Vietnam at the Paris peace talks. A diplomat of high ranking political cadre; a cousin of the author on the paternal side, now lives in Ho Chi Minh City after serving many years as Head of the Cultural and Indoctrination Committee of the Viet-Nam Communist Party for HCM City.

Duong Van Minh aka **"Big" Minh.** Popularly known as "Big" Minh for his tall and robust physical bearing, a 4-star general with the highest seniority and army rank in the ARVN following the time of President Ngo Dinh Diem. French trained, in 1955 helped President Diem defeat the Binh Xuyen underworld armed band in Saigon. On November 2, 1963, led the coup d'état that overthrew and killed President Diem and his brother Ngo Dinh Nhu. Headed the Saigon Military Junta as Chairman of the Revolutionary Military Committee (government) from November 1963 to January 1964. Made Head of State of the Republic of Vietnam from January to October, 1964. Ousted by his Chief of Staff, General Nguyen Khanh, and went into exile in Bangkok, Thailand from 1964 until 1968 when he returned to live in Saigon an uneventful existence except for his well-known passion of growing orchids. Considered the last president of the Republic of Vietnam (Saigon government), he was forced by the North Vietnamese officers invading the Independence Palace in Saigon on April 30, 1975 to declare the total and unconditional surrender of the Saigon government. Was spared reeducation and was later permitted to go to France to live with relatives.

Gia Long. Born Nguyen Phuc Anh, also called Nguyen Anh and referred to as Nguyen The To, a descendant of the powerful Nguyen family of generals (who were in continuous bloody conflicts with the other powerful Trinh family of generals during three hundred years from the mid-sixteenth century in the Trinh-Nguyen dispute). In his late teens, Nguyen Anh suffered successively heavy defeats and was chased out of the south of the country and forced into seeking refuge and help in Siam (Thailand). Eventually, with the help of the French Bishop of d'Adran (Pigneau de Behaine) and French troops (mercenaries), Nguyen Anh was able to defeat the short-lived Tay Son rule (1788-1802). Thus, after three centuries of internal division, Nguyen Anh reunified the northern and southern parts of the country. Proclaimed himself Emperor Gia Long and for the first time gave the country the name Viet-Nam. Reigned for only 17 years until his death in 1819. His son and successor, Emperor Minh Mang, renamed the country Dai-Viet. The descendants of Gia Long, the dynasty, were to be the last monarchs of Viet-Nam, ending with Emperor Bao Dai's on-and-off reign from 1925 to 1955.

Ha Van Lau, Army colonel turned diplomat with the rank of Ambassador in the Hanoi government. Director of the Operations Department of the General Staff of the People's Army of Vietnam (PAVN) in the 1950s. A member of the North Vietnamese (DRV) Delegation at the Geneva Conference on Indochina in 1954 and at the 1961-1962 Geneva Conference on Laos when he and Minister Xuan Thuy, head of the Hanoi delegation, made the acquaintance of Ambassador Averell Harriman whom he was to see again in Paris in his capacity as Deputy Head of the Hanoi delegation at the first U.S.-North Vietnam meeting on March 13,1968. Ha Van Lau was later replaced in Paris by Nguyen Minh Vy in 1969.

Ho Chi Minh. Born Nguyen Tat Thanh on May 19,1890; died on September 2, 1969. Assumed many aliases, the better known being Nguyen Ai Quoc, and Ly Thuy but known best as Ho Chi Minh. Left Viet-Nam from the Nha Rong wharf in Saigon on June 5, 1911 for France on the French s/s La Touche Treville as a cook, then traveled the world, including time in New York. Remained in Paris from 1917 to 1924. Became a member of the French Communist Party in 1920. Went to Moscow in 1924 and then was active as an undercover agent in China for many years. Founded the Communist Party of Indochina in Hong Kong on February 2, 1930 (later dissolved on November 11, 1945 and became the present Vietnam Communist Party). He returned to Viet-Nam at Pac Bo on February 8, 1941 for the Eighth Plenum of the Indochina Communist Party held from May 10-19, which resulted in the founding of the Vietnam Dong Minh Hoi, commonly referred to as the Viet Minh, a unified alliance of all the Vietnamese forces fighting against French colonial rule. At a mass rally held in Ba Dinh Square in Hanoi on September 2, 1945, Ho Chi Minh presented the Declaration of Independence and proclaimed the formation of the provisional revolutionary government of the Democratic Republic of Vietnam which was able to establish itself in Hanoi only after the French defeat at Dien Bien Phu (May 7, 1954) and the partition of Viet-Nam at the seventeenth parallel (the Ben Hai River) by the Geneva Agreements on Vietnam, Laos and Cambodia (July 20,1954). From the creation of the Democratic Republic of Vietnam on September 2, 1945 until his death on September 2,1969 in Hanoi, Ho Chi Minh remained President of the Democratic Republic of Vietnam, commonly called North Vietnam from 1955 to 1975.

Hoa Loi (Mrs.). Long time, 70-year friend of the author's mother. Her children and grandchildren still run the tiny food and bakery shop she started seventy years ago in Ta Thu Thau, now Luu Van Lang street near the Ben Thanh Central Market in Saigon where she and the author's mother met when they were still in their teens. Mrs.

Hoa Loi, in her late 90s, continues to live in her home town now called Ho Chi Minh City.

Le Duan. Early companion of Ho Chi Minh, also a co-founding member of the Indochina Communist Party in 1930 (to become later the Vietnam Communist Party in 1945). One of the top Hanoi leaders in the field directing the subversive war in the south of Viet-Nam. Became secretary-general of the Vietnam Communist Party after the death of Ho Chi Minh in 1969. Born in 1908,died in 1986.

Le Duc Tho. An early companion of Ho Chi Minh as a co-founding member of the Indochina Communist Party (later the Vietnam Communist Party) in 1930 and of the Viet Minh Alliance in 1941. One of the top leaders in the Politburo of the Vietnam Communist Party in charge of the party's organization and human resources. Was also responsible in the Party's leadership for the southern part of Viet-nam and conduct of the war in South Vietnam. Represented Hanoi in the private negotiations with Henry Kissinger in Paris from the first meeting on January 21, 1970 to the last meeting on January 23, 1973, leading to the signing of the Paris Accords on January 27, 1973. Jointly awarded, with Henry Kissinger, the 1973 Nobel Peace Prize which he declined to accept. Born in 1912 and died in 1990.

Le Thi Man. The author's mother, 1902-1991. Native of the village of Ba Tri, province of Ben Tre in the Mekong Delta. Only completed elementary school. Married in 1920 to Nguyen Van Thach, the author's father. They celebrated their seventieth wedding anniversary in 1990.

Ngo Dinh Diem. Born in 1901 into a devout Catholic family in central Vietnam, former Mandarin of the Court of Anam. Served as Minister of the Interior. Refused office in Ho Chi Minh's government and went into exile in the United States from 1945 (associated with Michigan State University) until 1954 when he returned to Saigon to replace Prince Buu Loc on June 18 as Prime Minister of the State of

Vietnam under Emperor Bao Dai. With strong support from U.S. Secretary of State John Foster Dulles, President Dwight D. Eisenhower and New York Cardinal Spellman, Diem deposed Emperor Bao Dai by way of a referendum and created the Republic of Vietnam (South Vietnam). "Elected" the first president in the south of Vietnam, rejecting the general elections prescribed by the 1954 Geneva Agreements. Started the increasing intervention of the United States which grew to become the American War in Viet-Nam. Diem's rule in South Vietnam was dominated by his family. They were arbitrary, dictatorial, repressive and furiously anti-communist, generating wide-spread discontent even among non-communists, which led to violent revolts. To avoid further unrest, Diem was urged by the U.S. Ambassador Henry Cabot Lodge to get rid of his brother, Ngo Dinh Nhu. Diem was overthrown and murdered with his brother Nhu on November 2, 1963 in a coup d'état by his own generals with the presumed concurrence of Washington.

Ngo Dinh Nhu. Younger brother of President Diem; a graduate of the French Ecole des Chartes. Machiavellian and ruthless, an opium addict, practically ruled South Vietnam under the nominal title of Adviser to the President but with a loyal and terrifying secret police. Killed, together with his brother, President Diem, in an M113 armored vehicle after surrendering to the military in the coup d'état on November 2, 1963.

Madame Nhu (Tran Le Xuan). Wife of Ngo Dinh Nhu. Madame Nhu acted as the official "First Lady" for bachelor President Diem during his Saigon regime and was remembered by most people as intelligent but cruel and ambitious. Mdm. Nhu went into exile in Rome after the November 1963 coup d'état. Now lives in Paris. (Madame Nhu's father, Tran Van Chuong, was a well-known and highly respected lawyer and a Saigon ambassador in Washington in the 1960s who resigned from his post in protest against Diem's dictatorial rule and remained in the U.S. He and his wife were later murdered in their Washington home by their son Khiem, younger brother of Mdm. Nhu, simply for not giving him enough money to spend. The author visited Mr. and Mrs. Tran Van Chuong in Washington D.C. in October, 1973. They had been long time friends of his parents going back to the early 1920s. Mr. Tran Van Chuong was the elder brother of Saigon Foreign Minister, Dr. Tran Van Do.)

Ngo Dinh Can. Youngest brother of President Diem, Ngo Dinh Can was a well-known deranged eccentric who remained in Hue and acted as a viceroy in the central area of Viet-Nam, with his own secret police, working in close cooperation with his brother's (Nhu) secret police in Saigon. Was caught in the coup d'état in November, 1963 and executed by firing squad at the Ben Thanh Central Market place in Saigon.

Ngo Dinh Thuc. Eldest brother of President Diem, became a Catholic priest and Archbishop of Vinh Long. Notoriously involved in financial deals, real estate acquisitions and other lucrative business activities. Eventually excommunicated by the Vatican. Died in 1986 in the United States.

Nguyen Ba Can. A high ranking civil servant trained under President Ngo Dinh Diem. Was Speaker of the Saigon National Assembly under President Nguyen Van Thieu. Named prime minister for one week by President Tran Van Huong to replace Prime Minister and 4-star General Tran Thien Khiem who resigned with Thieu on April 21, 1975.

Nguyen Cao Ky. Born in 1930 in the north of Viet-Nam, went south as a refugee in 1955 after the Geneva Accords. Jet fighter pilot with military training in France. Was considered one of the Saigon "young turks." As Brigadier-General, became Commanding Officer of the South Vietnamese Air Force in 1963 and was instrumental in the military coup d'état overthrowing the civilian government of Dr. Phan Huy Quat in 1965. Was designated Prime Minister by the Army Council from June, 1965 to September, 1967 when he was elected

Vice-President on the same ticket with President Thieu. Quite charismatic and appealing to young Vietnamese. Very effective in public speaking, arousing emotions instead of pursuing logic. After the first term with Nguyen Van Thieu, ending in 1971, Ky strongly indulged in political opposition to Thieu. With the rapidly degrading situation in Saigon in April, 1975, he unsuccessfully tried to stage a coup against Thieu. He managed to escape in the early hours of April 30, 1975 in his own helicopter to a U.S. naval vessel at sea when the North Vietnamese tanks launched the final assault against Saigon. Now lives in the United States.

Nguyen Co Thach. Hanoi career diplomat, was Deputy Minister of Foreign Affairs at the time of the Paris peace talks. Was an assistant to Le Duc Tho and counterpart of U.S. Ambassador William Sullivan in the drafting committee for the Paris Accords. After the reunification of Viet-Nam in 1976, he became member of the politburo of the Vietnamese Communist Party, Deputy Prime Minister cum Minister of Foreign Affairs. He held discussions with U.S. Secretary of State James Baker but was not able to reestablish or improve relations with the U.S. Considered to be part of the liberal trend in the Party, he was opposed by the die-hard core and pro-Chinese veteran leaders in Hanoi. He was ousted for his attempts to open cooperation with the United States.

Nguyen Huu Tho. French trained and well known Saigon lawyer in the late 1940s and 1950s, fought against and repeatedly jailed by French colonial rule and President Diem's dictatorial rule. A long-time friend of the author's parents. After the reunification of Viet-Nam in 1976, Nguyen Huu Tho became Vice-President of the country and Chairman of the Viet-Nam Fatherland Front.

Nguyen Minh Vy. Replaced Ha Van Lau as Deputy Head of Hanoi's delegation at the Paris peace talks in 1969. A high ranking official of the Viet-Nam Communist Party, he served as head of the Party's Central Committee for Culture and Indoctrination.

Nguyen Thi Binh (Madame Binh). Widely known and referred to as Madame Binh, long time resistance fighter against French colonial rule and the dictatorial regime of Diem and was jailed many times. After 1960, served as a charismatic representative of the National Liberation Front (NLF) on the international scene, and Minister of Foreign Affairs of the PRG (Provisional Revolutionary Government of the Republic of South Vietnam) at the Paris peace talks from June, 1969 to January, 1973. After the reunification of Viet-Nam in July, 1976, served as Minister of Education and later as Vice-President of the Socialist Republic of Viet-Nam. Now in her mid-seventies and lives in Ho Chi Minh City.

Tran Van Huong. School teacher turned politician, representative figure of South Vietnamese nationalist intellectuals and political groups. Joined the Viet Minh forces and was repeatedly imprisoned for opposing French colonial rule and Ngo Dinh Diem's dictatorial regime. Served as Mayor of Saigon in 1954 under Bao Dai, as Prime Minister in 1964-65 in the short-lived civilian Saigon governments and again briefly under President Thieu in 1968-1969 after the Viet Cong's Tet general offensive. He was Vice-President in Nguyen Van Thieu's second residential term in 1971. He became President when Thieu resigned on April 21, 1975 and one week later on April 28, handed power over to "Big" Minh who acted for less than 48 hours as the last president of the Saigon government.

Nguyen Van Thach. The author's father (1896-1990), originating from the village of Giong Trom, province of Ben Tre in the Mekong River Delta. French trained civil engineer in public works with a 47-year career in the construction of roads and bridges.

Nguyen Van Thieu. Born in 1924, originating from the Binh Thuan province in South Vietnam, was in the Viet Minh forces in his younger years before joining the South Vietnamese army created in the early 1950s. He had military training in both France and the U.S. and was a colonel in the ARVN. He led units of his infantry division to attack the Saigon Independence palace, overthrowing President Diem on November 2, 1963. By 1965, he rose to the rank of Lt. General and was made by the Army Council "Chairman of the National Leadership Committee" and "Head of State" of the RVN, a powerless figure-head compared to Prime Minister Nguyen Cao Ky who was Chairman of the Central Executive Committee. At the general elections in September, 1967, Thieu stubbornly insisted on running for President against Ky and his generals eventually agreed to the Thieu-Ky ticket. In his second term presidential elections in 1971, Thieu had Tran Van Huong as his Vice-President; they were unopposed after Ky and "Big" Minh withdrew from the race claiming unfair elections. President Thieu resigned on April 21, 1975 following repeated and heavy pressure from Washington in view of the dramatic situation in the Saigon government at that time, and reluctantly left the country in the evening of April 25, 1975 for Taipei. He has lived in exile in the United Kingdom since then.

Nguyen Van Vy. ARVN Lt. General; French trained and former officer in the French Army. Considered to be of the "old guard" rather than of Thieu's generation, he was made Defense Minister in 1966 to replace the less trusted and ambitious Lt. General Nguyen Huu Co who was forced into exile. General Vy returned to France after 1975 and died there, receiving full honors by the French army at his funeral.

Tran Thien Khiem. ARVN General, was in the triumvirate "Minh-Khanh-Khiem" ruling South Vietnam after the military coup d'état overthrowing President Diem in November 1963. He helped General Khanh to oust "Big" Minh in 1964 and occupied the posts of Defense Minister and Commander-in-Chief of the ARVN. He was Ambassador to the U.S. from 1964 to 1965 and to Taiwan from 1965 to 1968. He returned to Saigon in 1969 to serve briefly as Deputy Prime Minister, then Prime Minister under President Thieu from 1969 to 1975. He left Saigon with Thieu on April 25, 1975 for Taipei on a plane provided by the U.S. Airforce. He lives in exile in the United States.

Tran Van Don. A three-star General of the Saigon regime under President Diem, born in 1917 and educated in France. Son of a South Vietnamese medical doctor, Dr. Tran Van Don (a schoolmate and long time friend of the author's father and a former Saigon ambassador to England). General Tran Van Don was also called Andre Don to distinguish him from his father and his two younger brothers, former diplomat Robert Tran Van Don now in exile in the U.S. working as a travel, real estate and insurance salesman, and Claude Tran Van Don, an M.D., who has lived in Paris since the early 1960s. Both Robert Don and Claude Don were classmate friends of the author during their secondary schooling. General Tran Van Don was among the leading generals with General "Big" Minh in the November 2, 1963 military coup d'état overthrowing President Ngo Dinh Diem. He was considered pro-French and an advocate of President De Gaulle's policy for a "neutral Indochina." General Don retired from the ARVN in 1965 and became involved in political and diplomatic activities. In April 1975, he was Defense Minister in the last government of President Tran Van Huong. He was able to get out of Saigon before the arrival of the North Vietnamese troops, and taken to the U.S. He later made his home in Paris. At his funeral in 1998 he was buried with full honors for a general officer of the French Army.

Tran Van Tra. Born in 1918, originating from central Vietnam. A 3-star General Commanding Officer of the Viet Cong (NLF) forces. Together with Hanoi's COS General Van Tien Dung and PAVN forces, he carried out the final attacks against Saigon; acted as Military Governor to administer the city of Saigon after April 30, 1975. He wrote a book relating the Viet Cong's campaign and offensive against Saigon which was banned by the Hanoi government and withdrawn from circulation, Retired, he now lives in Ho Chi Minh City.

Van Tien Dung. Born in 1917, one of Hanoi's outstanding generals. Distinguished himself for the logistics support he provided at the Dien Bien Phu victory. Headed the DRV military delegation at the Trung Gia conference with the French which later became the Joint Military Commission. In the spring of 1975, as PAVN Chief of Staff, he directed the final offensive against Saigon. In 1979, he replaced General Vo Nguyen Giap as Defense Minister. He is retired and now lives in Hanoi.

Vo Nguyen Giap. Born in 1912, originating from central Vietnam. He started out as a high school history teacher and a law student in Hanoi. An early companion of Ho Chi Minh at the Pac Bo meetings in May, 1941 during the formal founding of the Vietnam Doc Lap Dong Minh League (commonly referred to as the Viet Minh) and the formation of the Vietnam Propaganda Liberation Troops. He was Minister of Home Affairs in the provisional coalition government formed by Ho Chi Minh, Nguyen Hai Than and Vu Hong Khanh on December 24, 1945. Became President of the Resistance Committee set up in March, 1946, with Vu Hong Khanh as Vice-President, to organize and carry out the armed struggle against the French forces in Indochina. Considered an outstanding thinker and military leader in "people's warfare," he directed the PAVN against the French forces and the American armed intervention in Viet-Nam. Reported to have been against Hanoi's military intervention in Cambodia in 1978-79. Highly respected but without much political power, General Giap retired from active service from both the army and government official responsibilities, and became active in the fields of science and technology. Lives in Hanoi.

Xuan Thuy. High ranking member of the Vietnam Communist Party, politician and poet. Foreign Minister from 1963 to 1965. Hanoi's representative in the U.S.-North Vietnam meetings in Paris with Averell Harriman in March Head of the DRV delegation at the official Paris peace talks from January 1969 onward. Also deputy to Le Duc Tho in private negotiations with Henry Kissinger from

January 21, 1970 to January 23, 1973 which led to the official signing of the Paris Accords on January 27, 1973.

American and European

Creighton W. Abrams. General, Commander, U.S. Military Assistance Command, Vietnam from 1968 to 1972; U.S. Army Chief of Staff from 1972 to 1974.

David K. E. Bruce. Career diplomat. Was with the U.S. OSS intelligence agency during World War II; U.S. ambassador to Germany, United Kingdom and twice to France. Replaced Henry Cabot Lodge as Head of the U.S. Delegation to the Paris peace talks from 1969 to 1972; then Special U.S. Representative to the PRC, preparing for the reestablishing of U.S.-China diplomatic relations.

William Putnam Bundy. U.S. Assistant Secretary of State for East Asian and Pacific Affairs during President Lyndon B. Johnson's tenure in the mid-1960s, during the intensification of the war in Vietnam.

Ellsworth Bunker. U.S. Ambassador to South Vietnam from 1967 to 1973, replacing Henry Cabot Lodge and succeeded by Graham Martin.

Christian Marie de Castries. Comte de la Croix de Castries, a count of the French aristocracy and World War II hero. A Colonel made Brigadier-General while he was commanding officer at the resounding fall of the French garrison overrun by the North Vietnamese forces at Dien Bien Phu on May 7, 1954. He was captured with the survivors of his troops, and made prisoner. He was later released and repatriated to France.

John Foster Dulles. U.S. Secretary of State during the presidency of Dwight Eisenhower, 1953-1959. Brother of Allen W. Dulles,

Director of the CIA. Rejected the 1954 Geneva Agreements on Indochina and supported the creation of the Republic of Vietnam in 1955 by Ngo Dinh Diem.

Gerald R. Ford. U.S. President at the time of the fall of Saigon in April 1975.

William Averell Harriman. Financier, politician and diplomat. U.S. ambassador to the Soviet Union and the United Kingdom, 1947-46; Secretary of State, 1947-48; Governor of the State of New York, 1953-55; Assistant Secretary of State for Far Eastern Affairs, 1961-63, distinguishing himself for the settlement and neutralization of Laos in Geneva in 1962; a well-known diplomat familiar with Russian affairs during the Stalin era, and an influential personality of the Democratic Party; Head of the U.S. delegation in the official meetings in Paris from May 1968 to January 1969 for the peace talks on Viet-Nam and was replaced by Henry Cabot Lodge after the election of U.S. President Richard Nixon.

Lyndon Baines Johnson. U.S. President following the assassination President John F. Kennedy in November 1963. Elected President in 1964. Opted for the escalation of the war in Viet-Nam to its highest intensity from 1964 to 1968. Refused to seek second term of office in the 1968 presidential elections and retired from public affairs.

Robert Jungk. Journalist and futurist, with home bases in Europe. Established the Hope Library in Switzerland.

John F. Kennedy. U.S. President after defeating Richard Nixon in the 1960 U.S. presidential elections. Supported the Republic of Vietnam (South Vietnam), and provided U.S. aid and advisors to President Diem. Assassinated in Dallas, Texas on November 22, 1963 and succeeded by his Vice-President, Lyndon B. Johnson.

Henry A. Kissinger. Harvard University professor, became Presidential Advisor for National Security Affairs after election of President Richard Nixon in 1968. Through French channels, initiated contacts with North Vietnam leading to official meetings in Paris in May 1968 and opening of formal sessions of the Paris conference in January U.S. Secretary of State in 1973. Carried out private negotiations with Hanoi's politburo member Le Duc Tho from January 1970 to January 1973, resulting in the signing of the Paris Accords for which he was jointly awarded the 1973 Nobel Peace Prize with Le Duc Tho, who declined to accept. Dr. Kissinger remained Secretary of State for President Gerald Ford after the resignation of President Nixon in August. 1974.

Robert William Komer. Special Assistant to President Kennedy for National Security Affairs in 1961-63, and to President Johnson in 1966-67. In 1967-68, was Deputy to General William Westmoreland, U.S. Military Assistance Command, Vietnam. Responsible for CORDS (Civil Operations and Rural Development Support), an euphemism for President Johnson's "Pacification Program" in South Vietnam. After a subsequent ambassadorship in Turkey, he became Under Secretary of Defense in 1979.

Edward G. Landsdale. Major-general and U.S. counter-insurgency expert attached to the CIA. Made adviser to South Vietnam's President Diem from 1956 to 1962 and Special Assistant to U.S. Ambassador Henry Cabot Lodge in Saigon from 1965 to 1967.

Henry Cabot Lodge. Republican Congressman from 1933 to 1936; twice U.S. Senator from 1936 to 1944 and from 1947 to 1953; U.S. Ambassador to the United Nations from 1953 to 1960; Vice-presidential candidate with Nixon in 1960; U.S. ambassador in Saigon in 1963-64 and again in 1965-67; head of the U.S. delegation at the Paris peace talks in 1969; Special U.S. Envoy to the Vatican from 1970 to 1977.

Graham A. Martin. Last U.S. ambassador to Saigon from July 7,1973 (replacing Ellsworth Bunker) to April 30, 1975 (the date of the fall of Saigon). Was also U.S. ambassador to Thailand from 1963 to 1967, and Special Assistant to Secretary of State for Refugee and Migration Affairs from 1967 to 1969.

Howard Schomer. Theologian, educator and social policy consultant. Ordained to the ministry to the Congregational Church in 1941. Affiliated with many religious and social organizations from the 1940s to the present, including: American Friends Service, 1941-45; American Board Mission fellow to chapters that included Chambon-sur-Lignon, France, 1945-55; Assistant to rapporteur of the UN Commission on Human Rights, UN Economic and Social Council, 1947-48; Interchurch Aid Secretary for Europe World Council of Churches, Geneva, 1955-58; and others. President and professor of church history, Chicago Theological Seminary, 1959-66. Executive Director, Department of Specialized Ministries, Division of Overseas Ministries, National Council of Churches, New York City, 1967-70. Indochina Liaison Officer, World Council of Churches, Participant in many assemblies throughout the world devoted to advancing human rights, including national advisory board member to New York State Martin Luther King, Jr. Institute for Non-Violence, and Cambodian Foundation for Justice, Peace and Development. Member of Advisory Boards or Boards of Directors of many organizations concerned with contributing to advances in understanding human dynamics and processes. Noted orator and writer.

David R. Schwarz. Chairman, Center for A Science of Hope since late 1980s. Previously engaged in management of industrial firms connected with the life sciences, including Vice-president for the Laboratory Education and Science Group of Becton, Dickinson and Company. Consultant on biological sciences to the Department of Defense, 1959-1968 and private consulting on management of innovation. Active in integrative understanding of the sciences and the humanities.

Cyrus R. Vance. Secretary of the Army in 1962-63; Deputy Secretary of Defense to McNamara up to 1967 and deputy to Averell Harriman at the Paris peace talks in 1968-69. Secretary of State in 1977 in the Carter administration. Returned to investment law practice in New York City. In the 1980s and 1990s, acted as United Nations peace mediator in several armed conflicts.

William C. Westmoreland. Born in 1914, U.S. General, with a distinguished military career during WWII. Was CO of the 9th Infantry Division in 1944-45; CO of the 82nd Airborne Division during the war in Korea; Commander of the 187th Airborne RCT from 1951 to 1953; Superintendent of the U.S. Military Academy from 1953 to 1963; Commanding General of the XVIII Airborne Corps in 1963-64; and Commander of the U.S. Military Assistance Command, Vietnam (MACV) from 1964 to 1968 during the highest intensification of the Vietnam War by President Johnson. Was U.S. Army Chief of Staff from 1968 to 1972 after which he retired from active service.

Frederick C. Weyand. Born in 1916, U.S. General. Commander of the 25th Infantry Division from 1966 to 1968 in South Vietnam. Military Advisor to the U.S. Delegation at the Paris peace talks from 1968 to 1970. Deputy Commander of MACV from 1970 to 1972. Replaced General Creighton Abrams as Commander of MACV from 1972 to 1973. U.S. Army Chief of Staff from 1974 to 1976.

HISTORICAL DATES AND EVENTS RELATED TO VIET-NAM

B.C.

2879 to 258

- Legendary but traceable Hong Bang era with the Hung kings, the traditionally recognized ancestors of the Viet people and nation.

257-207

- The Thuc kingdom.

207-111

- The renegade Chinese dissident warlord Trieu Da (Chao To) against the Chinese Emperor. Declared the Kingdom of "Nam Viet" from Canton to central Vietnam (Da Nang); defeated by the powerful army of the Han emperor Wu Ti.

111 B.C. to 39 A.D.

- First period of Chinese rule.

A.D.

40-43

- Rebellion of the Vietnamese Trung sisters.

43-544

- Second period of Chinese rule.

187-226

- Rebellion of Si Nhiep.

248

- Rebellion of Dame Trieu.

399-413

- Rebellion of Lam Ap.

544–602

- The first Ly kings.

602-939

- Third period of Chinese rule.

722

- Mai Hac De rebellion.

791

- Great king Bo Cai.

862

- Nam Chieu-Cao Bien conflict.

906-923

- Khuc family.

938

- Vietnamese General Ngo Quyen defeated the formidable Chinese armada on the Bach Dang River, ending a millennium of Chinese rule, and founded the Ngo dynasty.

938-968

· The Ngo kings.

968-980

· Dinh Bo Linh defeated the 12 insurrecting warlords, reunited the Vietnamese people, proclaimed the Dinh dynasty and the country's new name as "Dai Co Viet".

980-1009

· The Anterior Le dynasty.

1009-1225

· The Ly dynasty.

1225-1400

· The Tran dynasty.

1400-1407

· The Ho dynasty.

1407-1427

· Brief period of Chinese domination.

1418-1428

· Le Loi's insurrection and victory over the Chinese Wu forces.

1428-1527

· The Le dynasty.

1527-1592

· The Mac dynasty.

1533-1592

· The Mac-Le conflict and re-establishment of the Le kings.

1543

- The generals of the Nguyen family began to set up the Le court in the southern part of the country.

1545

- The generals of the Trinh family held power at the Le court in the northern part of the country.

1570-1786

- Period of conflict between the Trinh-Nguyen families (or war between the Inner Family [South] and the Outer Family [North]).

1786-1802

- Revolt of the Tay Son brothers with victorious Nguyen Hue (no relation to the Nguyen family) proclaiming himself Emperor Quang Trung.

1802-1954

- The Nguyen dynasty with Nguyen Anh, survivor of the Nguyen family, who defeated Nguyen Hue, reconquered and reunified the country from north to south. He proclaimed himself Emperor Gia Long in 1802 and reigned until his death in 1819. Succeeded by Emperor Minh Mang (1819-1840), who was followed by Emperor Thieu Tri (1841-1847). His successor, Emperor Tu Duc, died in 1883 and his heir, Emperor Ham Nghi, was not enthroned but arrested by the French government and sent to exile in Algeria where he died in 1925. His son, Nguyen Vinh Thuy, did not become enthroned until in 1932 by the French colonial authority to be Emperor Bao Dai, the last of the Nguyen dynasty and of Vietnamese monarchs.

1862

- In June, the Nguyen Court conceded the six eastern provinces in the south to France.

1883

- In August, the Nguyen Court forced to recognize Cochinchina as a French colony, and Tonkin and Annam as French protectorates.

1884

- In May, China signed the Thien Tan Treaty with France recognizing all agreements covering French rule in Viet-Nam.

1887

- In June, China signed the Peking Convention with France recognizing the border between the French protectorate of Tonkin and China; this was further expanded by another agreement in June, 1895.

Contemporary Period

World War I

- Many *annamites* (Vietnamese) were sent to France to fight in the French forces, and remained there as early Vietnamese immigrants, with the majority becoming workers of the Renault car manufacturer.

1930

- Creation of the Indochinese Communist Party by Ho Chi Minh on February 2; later became the Vietnam Communist Party.

1939

- Outbreak of WWII on September 1.

1941

- On January 8, Ho Chi Minh returned to Viet-Nam at Bac Po for the Eighth Plenum of the Indochinese Communist Party held on May 10. The Vietnam Doc Lap Dong Minh League (Viet Minh) was created on May 19.
- Pearl Harbor attacked by Japan on December 7.

1944

- Allied Forces liberated Paris on August 25.
- Vietnam Propaganda Liberation Troops formed by Ho Chi Minh on December 22 (to become later the PAVN, regular army of North Vietnam [DRV] and of the present Socialist Republic of Vietnam).

1945

- The Yalta Conference (U.S., UK and Soviet Union) on February 4.
- Japanese troops took over Indochina from the French on March 9. On March 11, Bao Dai declared the "Independence of Vietnam" and collaborated with the Japanese occupation forces.
- U.S. Vice-President Harry Truman became President upon the death of President Roosevelt.
- Formation of pro-Japanese government of Tran Trong Kim in Viet-Nam on April 17.
- Conference on and founding of the United Nations in San Francisco, April 25-26.
- Opening of the Potsdam Conference on July 16, during which, on July 24, President Truman accepted the decision to divide Viet-Nam at the 16th parallel for military operations purposes.
- U.S. military dropped atom bombs on Hiroshima and Nagasaki on August 6 and 9, followed by the surrender of Japan.
- Ho Chi Minh in Hanoi on August 25.

- Chiang kai-shek's Chinese troops entered North Vietnam on August 28.
- Bao Dai declared his abdication on August 30.
- Ho Chi Minh proclaimed the independence of Viet-Nam on September 2 and the formation of the Democratic Republic of Vietnam (DRV); Japan signed the act of surrender on the Missouri.
- Arrival of the first units of Chinese troops in Hanoi on September 3.
- Arrival of the first units of British and French troops in Saigon on September 6.
- Arrival of the Indian 20th Division and French 5th RIC on September 12.
- London Agreement between France and the UK on October 9 giving France full rights over Indochina south of the 16th parallel.
- Ho Chi Minh formed the Provisional Coalition Government on December 24 with Nguyen Hai Than and Vu Hong Khanh.

1946

- Ho Chi Minh proclaimed general elections throughout Viet-Nam on January 6, and then held the first session of the National Assembly on March 2 with the formation of the Resistance Coalition Government—with Bao Dai in the capacity as a citizen (no longer emperor) Nguyen Vinh Thuy, Supreme Adviser.
- France and China signed the Chong Qing Agreement on February 28 for French troops to replace the Chinese troops in North Vietnam beginning on March 31, 1946.
- The DRV and France signed a preliminary accord on March 6 for French troops to replace the Chinese troops in North Vietnam on .March 24. Ho Chi Minh met French Admiral d'Argenlieu in Ha Long Bay.

- The Dalat Conference between the DRV and France held on April 18.
- France announced an autonomous Cochinchina in the Indochinese Federation and the French Union on June 1.
- Meeting held between Ho Chi Minh and French Prime Minister George Bidault on July 2 Fontainebleau Conference between the DRV and France was held between July 6 and September 10. Ho Chi Minh signed a convention with French Minister Marius Moutet.
- Ho Chi Minh again met Admiral d'Argenlieu on the Suffren on October 18 in Cam Ranh Bay, and returned to Hanoi on October 20.
- Ho Chi Minh declared a war of resistance against the French in Indochina on December 19, the beginning of the second French Indochinese War to last 8 years until the 1954 Geneva Agreements.

1947

- Emperor Bao Dai and French High Commissioner for Indochina Emile Bollaert signed the Ha Long Agreement on December 7.

1948

- Bao Dai's Prime Minister Nguyen Van Xuan signed another Ha Long Agreement with High Commissioner Bollaert on June 5.

1949

- Bao Dai signed the Elysees Agreement on March 8 with France.
- Bao Dai declared the formation of the State of Vietnam within the French Union on July 7.
- People's Republic of China founded by Mao tse-tung on October 1.

1950

- In January, recognition of the DRV by the PRC; continuation of the resistance war against French colonial rule in Viet-Nam.
- Outbreak of the Korean War on January 25.

1953

- Death of Stalin on March 5.
- Ceasefire in Korea on July 27.

1954

- Berlin Conference of the four great powers (U.S.,UK, France and the Soviet Union) on January 25, resulting in the agreement to convene the Geneva Conference with participation of China (PRC) on April 26 to discuss the Korean and Indochinese problems.
- Fall of French garrison at Dien Bien Phu to the North Vietnamese troops on May 7.
- Opening of the Geneva Conference on Indochina on May 8.
- Ngo Dinh Diem replaced Prince Buu Loc (Emperor Bao Dai's cousin) as Prime Minister of the State of Vietnam on June 18.
- Conference at Trung Gia between the high commands of France and the DRV for the settlement of military issues on July 4.
- Signing of the Geneva Agreements on Vietnam, Laos and Cambodia on July 20, partitioning Viet-Nam at the seventeenth parallel.
- Creation of the South East Asia Treaty Organization (SEATO) on September 8 by the Manila Treaty to contain the spread of communism.

1955

- President Diem defeated the Binh Xuyen underground War Lords and the Cao Dai and Hoa Hao religious sects in South Vietnam on March 29.

- President Diem formally requested that the U.S. provide American instructors to train ARVN troops on May 10.
- President Diem, on July 20, rejected the proposition that general elections be held in the whole of Viet-Nam, as was provided for by the 1954 Geneva Agreements, on the grounds that no free elections could take place in communist North Vietnam.
- Ngo Dinh Diem organized a referendum, on October 23, to depose Emperor Bao Dai, and proclaimed the creation of the Republic of Vietnam (RVN) with himself as President.

1956

- Ngo Dinh Diem, on October 23, organized general elections in South Vietnam for a constituent assembly to promulgate the constitution of the RVN.
- French withdrawal from Vietnam on April 28, and establishment of the U.S. Military Assistance Advisory Group (MAAG).
- Hanoi, on May 11, requested discussions with Saigon regarding the holding of general elections in Viet-Nam and the reunification of the country as provided by the 1954 Geneva Agreements.

1957

- Renewed proposal, on July 18, by North Vietnam's Prime Minister Pham Van Dong to President Diem for general elections and reunification of Viet-Nam.

1959

- Proposal by the DRV on December 22 for meetings with the RVN to discuss the neutralization of both North and South Vietnam, normalization of movements of people and economic cooperation between the two zones; refused by President Diem.

- Arrival of U.S. military advisers in South Vietnam in May as requested by President Diem.
- In October, President Diem passed the anti-communist law with capital punishment for communists and pro-communist persons.

1960
- Unsuccessful military coup d'état on November 11-12 in Saigon against President Diem.
- Formation of the National Liberation Front of South Vietnam on December 20.

1961
- U.S. Vice-president Johnson and President Diem signed joint Declaration on May 11 for increased U.S. assistance to South Vietnam.
- Fourteen-nation Conference on Laos convened in Geneva on May 16.
- President Kennedy increased military aid to South Vietnam without committing U.S. combat troops, on November 16.

1962
- In February, U.S. military presence in South Vietnam reached 4,000, and the U.S. Military Assistance Advisory Group (MAAG) was reorganized to become the U.S. Military Assistance Command, Vietnam (MACV) under the Command of General Paul D. Harkins.
- Signing of the Geneva Agreement on the neutrality of Laos on July 23.
- Riots in Hue with Buddhist manifestations on May 8, followed by protests throughout South Vietnam.
- From June to August, beginning of immolation suicides by fire of seven Buddhist monks in protest against President Diem's repression.

- Military coup d'état overthrowing President Diem led by General "Big" Minh on November 1-2; Diem and his brother Nhu were killed after their surrender. General Duong Van "Big" Minh assumed leadership in South Vietnam.
- President Kennedy assassinated in Dallas, Texas on November 22. Lyndon B. Johnson became President of the U.S.

1964

- General Nguyen Khanh deposed General "Big" Minh on January 30 in a peaceful coup d'état and replaced him as head of the South Vietnamese political regime.
- General William C. Westmoreland replaced General Paul D. Harkins as Commander of MACV on June 20.
- General Maxwell D. Taylor became U.S. Ambassador in Saigon on July 2 to replace Henry Cabot Lodge.
- The Tonkin Gulf incidents with the USS Maddox and USS C. Turner Joy on August 2-4; on August 5, the U.S. 7th Fleet attacked North Vietnamese naval bases and other military installations; on August 7, the U.S. Congress approved the Tonkin Gulf Resolution enabling President Johnson to take measures to mount counter attacks by U.S. forces.

1965

- The U.S. began the bombing of North Vietnam on February 7.
- The first U.S. combat troops (a Marine battalion) landed in Da Nang on March 8. On April 7, President Johnson declared in Baltimore his readiness to open unconditional negotiations with Hanoi and provide $1 billion to South East Asia, including North Vietnam, for economic development.

- The U.S. Army's 173rd Airborne Brigade landed in South Vietnam on May 3.
- In June, Airforce General Nguyen Cao Ky became Prime Minister of South Vietnam; the presence of American troops in South Vietnam reached 50,000.
- Henry Cabot Lodge returned to Saigon as U.S. ambassador on July 8 for the second time, replacing General Maxwell Taylor.
- In November, anti-war demonstrations were becoming widespread in the U.S. In December , U.S. troops in South Vietnam reached 181,000.
- Christmas bombing of North Vietnam halted by U.S. and 14-point proposal made by President Johnson for the settlement of the war in Viet-Nam.

1966

- U.S. bombing of North Vietnam resumed on January 31 after a pause of 37 days.
- In March, U.S. troops in South Vietnam, reached 215,000.
- In April, first time U.S. bombing of North Vietnam by B-52s
- Seven-nation Manila Conference (U.S., Australia, Thailand, South Korea, New Zealand, the Philippines and South Vietnam) held October 24-25.
- President Johnson's visited U.S troops in Cam Ranh on October 26.
- U.S. troops in South Vietnam reached 385,000 in December.

1967

- Ellsworth Bunker replaced Henry Cabot Lodge as U.S. Ambassador in Saigon on March 15. Robert W. Komer, Deputy Commander MACV for Civil Operations and Rural Development Support (CORDS) appointed on May 4 to carry out the "Pacification Program"; U.S. troops in South Vietnam reached 436,000.

- General Nguyen Van Thieu elected President on September 3 with General Nguyen Cao Ky as Vice-president.
- In August, President Johnson announced that the level of U.S. troops in South Vietnam would be 523,000; in December, U.S. troops in South Vietnam reached 486,000.

1968

- Outbreak of Tet Mau Than general offensive on January 30-31 by the Communist forces on all major cities in South Vietnam which lasted till the end of February with all lost positions regained by the ARVN and U.S. troops.
- My Lai massacre incident on March 16.
- President Johnson announced bombing halt of North Vietnam on March 31, and his readiness to open negotiations with Hanoi to end the war in Viet-Nam; he also announced his decision not to seek a second term of office at the next election.
- Hanoi, on April 3, agreed to meet the U.S. for talks in Paris.
- Opening of meetings between U.S. and North Vietnam in Paris on May 13.
- First of the private meetings between U.S. and North Vietnam's Deputy-Heads on June 26.
- First of the private meetings between the Heads of the U.S. and North Vietnamese delegations on September 8.
- On October 31, President Johnson proposed the convening of the Paris Conference on November 6, but President Thieu refused to attend.
- On November 7, Richard Nixon elected President of the United States.
- In December, U.S. troops in South Vietnam reached 536,000.

1969

- Formal opening of the Paris Conference on January 25, with the participation of the U.S., RVN (Saigon), DRV (Hanoi) and the NLF (Viet Cong).
- U.S. bombing of Viet Cong's sanctuaries in Cambodia, February 23.
- NLF's 10-point proposal presented at the Paris Conference on May 8. President Nixon's 8-point proposal presented on May 14.
- Creation of the Provisional Revolutionary Government (PRG) of the Republic of South Vietnam (Viet Cong) on June 6.
- Richard Nixon's letter to Ho Chi Minh of July 16.
- First secret meeting in Paris between Hanoi's Minister Xuan Thuy and the U.S.'s National Security Advisor Kissinger on August 4.
- Ho Chi Minh's letter replying to Richard Nixon on August 25.
- Death of Ho Chi Minh on September 2.
- "Moratorium" of massive anti-war manifestations in the U.S. on November 15.
- In December, U.S. troops in South Vietnam down to 474,000.

1970

- First private session between Le Duc Tho and Henry Kissinger in Paris on January 21.
- U.S. Congress repealed the 1964 Tonkin Gulf Resolution on April 26.
- In May, outbreak of anti-war demonstrations at hundreds of U.S. colleges with dramatic death of four students shot by Ohio National Guards at Kent State University.
- PRG's 8-point proposal presented at the Paris peace talks on September 17.

- President Nixon's 5-point proposal on October 7 (not demanding that the North Vietnamese troops withdraw from South Vietnam.)
- U.S. troops in South Vietnam reduced to 335,800 by December 31.

1971

- On April 24, 500,000 anti war protestors converged on Washington D.C.
- Revelation of the Pentagon Papers by *The New York Times* on June 13.
- Henry Kissinger's trip to China on July 19 to prepare for Richard Nixon's visit in February, 1972.
- Admission of China (the PRC) to the United Nations on October 25.

1972

- Nixon's visit to China on February 28 and signing of the joint American-Sino Shanghai Declaration.
- General offensive launched by the communist forces in several provinces in South Vietnam on March 30.
- On April 15, resumption of U.S. bombing of North Vietnam.
- On July 19, in Paris, Le Duc Tho and Henry Kissinger began to finalize the draft of the Paris Accords.
- Draft of Paris Accords considered acceptable by Washington and Hanoi on October 13.
- President Nixon's letter on October 20 to Prime Minister Pham Van Dong confirming U.S. acceptance of draft Accords and projecting Henry Kissinger's trip to Hanoi for initial signing of the draft on October 24, and the formal signing of the Accords in Paris on October 30, 1972; this timetable was confirmed by Pham Van Dong's reply letter of October 21 to Richard Nixon.

- President Thieu addressed the Saigon national Assembly on October 24, rejecting the October 20 draft Accords.
- Resumption of Le Duc Tho-Kissinger meetings on November 20 in Paris, continued until December 13.
- Twelve days-and-nights U.S. bombing of Hanoi and Hai Phong (Operation code name Linebacker II) begun on December 18.

1973

- Resumption of Le Duc Tho-Kissinger meetings in Paris on January 8-13. Le Duc Tho and Henry Kissinger formally initialed the draft Accords on January 23 at the Center for International Conferences in Paris.
- President Nixon's letter of January 16 to President Thieu giving assurance that the U.S. would defend the Republic of Vietnam should Saigon agree to sign the Paris Accords.
- Official signing of the Paris Accords on January 27 by the Foreign Ministers of the DRV (Nguyen Duy Trinh), RVN (Tran Van Lam) and PRG (Nguyen Thi Binh) and the U.S. Secretary of State (William P. Rogers.)
- Ceasefire throughout Viet-Nam on January 28.
- President Nixon's letter on January 30 to Prime Minister Pham Van Dong re the U.S. contribution to healing the wounds of war and reconstruction of North Vietnam.
- Henry Kissinger's visit to Hanoi on February 8.
- Convening of the Paris International Conference. February 26-March 3, on Viet-Nam and the signing of the International Act confirming the Paris Accords; signatories included the U.S., the U.K., P.R.C. and the Soviet Union (permanent members of the UNO Security Council), Canada, Hungary, Iran and Poland (the four members of the International Commission of Control and Supervision) and the three Vietnamese parties (DRV,RVN and PRG); the secretary-general of the United Nations was present as observer.

- Total withdrawal of U.S. troops from South Vietnam completed on March 29.
- Release of last American POWs held in North Vietnam on April 1.

1974
- Fierce fighting between ARVN and communist troops continued.
- President Nixon resigned over Watergate affair on August 9 and was succeeded by Vice-president Gerald Ford, with Dr. Kissinger remaining as Secretary of State.

1975
- In January, communist troops launched attacks in Phuoc Long Province, bordering Cambodia, about 50 kms from Saigon.
- In March, North Vietnamese troops captured the highland provinces of Dak Lak and Pleiku.
- On April 12, the U.S. ambassador and embassy staff left Phnom Penh.
- On April 17, Phnom Penh fell to the Khmer Rouges.
- In April, North Vietnamese troops occupied the northern and central provinces of South Vietnam (Quang Tri, Thua Thien, Hue city, Da Nang city, Quang Nam, Quang Ngai, Phu Yen, Binh Dinh, Khanh Hoa, Binh Thuan, and Phan Thiet).
- On April 21, President Thieu resigned. He left Saigon on April 25. Vice-president Tran Van Huong became President of the RVN for the period of April 21-28, then resigned and "passed power" to General Duong Van "Big" Minh.
- On April 30, evacuation of the last Americans (including U.S. Ambassador Graham Martin) from the U.S. Embassy rooftop by helicopters until 7:00 am; North Vietnamese tanks occupied the Saigon Presidential Palace at 11:00am and commanded that "President" General Duong Van "Big"

Minh proclaim the unconditional surrender of the Saigon government. An estimated 150,000 South Vietnamese people fled the country in the last days of Saigon before the arrival of the North Vietnamese troops. Saigon was renamed Ho Chi Minh City and put under military rule with General Tran Van Tra as Military Governor.

- In May 1975, ARVN officers and ranking officials of the former Saigon regime (about 200,000) were sent to reeducation imprisonment.

1976

- Secretary of State Henry Kissinger declared U.S. willing to consider normalization of relations with Viet-Nam.
- General elections in Viet-Nam on April 25.
- First session of the National Assembly of Viet-Nam held on June 24.
- The proclamation of the reunification of Viet-Nam and the Socialist Republic of Vietnam was issued on July 2.
- Vietnam admitted into the International Monetary Fund (IMF) on September 15.

1977

- In March, Hanoi handed to Washington the first twelve bodies of U.S. MIAs
- The South East Asia Treaty Organization dissolved on June 30.
- In September, the U.S. ended its veto so that Vietnam could become a member of the United Nations.
- In December, Vietnamese troops incursion into Cambodia's territory at Parrot's Peak.

1978

- In January, Vietnamese troops occupied Cambodia at border zones.

- In July, about 80,000 Vietnamese troops launched massive offensive into Cambodian territory; the PRC massed 15 divisions of Chinese troops at the Vietnamese northern border zones.

1979

- In February, Chinese military build-up at Vietnamese borders reached 19 divisions; Vietnamese troops continued thrust into Cambodian territory; Chinese troops launched attacks and entered into Vietnamese border zones about 50 miles deep on a fighting front of 720 kilometers.
- In March, the PRC declared ending its "punitive action" against Viet-Nam, and withdrew Chinese troops from Vietnamese territory; Vietnamese troops estimated at 140,000 troops massed at border zones with China.

1980

- Backed by Soviet Union, Viet-Nam continued with occupation of Cambodia and threatening border zones of Thailand; President Carter increased U.S. military supplies and assistance to the Thai government.
- November, Ronald Reagan elected U.S. president.

1981

- In July, Vietnamese government in Hanoi handed to U.S. remains of three Americans.

1982

- In September, Viet-Nam's Foreign Minister Nguyen Co Thach accepts setting up VN-US meetings to resolve problems of American MIAs.
- In October, Vietnamese government handed to U.S. remains of four Americans.

- In November, inauguration of Vietnam Memorial in Washington D.C., attended by 100,000 Vietnam Veterans.
- In November, death of Soviet leader Leonid I. Brezhnev, succeeded by Yuri V. Andropov.

1983

- In June, Viet-Nam handed to U.S. remains of nine Americans, but suspended U.S.-VN meetings on MIA on grounds of provocative declarations by U.S. officials.

1984

- In February, death of Soviet leader Yuri V. Andropov, succeeded by Konstantin U. Chernenko.
- In February, resumption of VN-US meetings on MIAs; Hanoi handed over to Washington remains of five Americans, and eight more remains in July.
- In November, Ronald Reagan re-elected U.S. president, with George Bush as vice-president.

1985

- Death of Soviet leader Chernenko; succeeded by Mikhail Gorbachev.
- Hanoi handed to U.S. remains of American servicemen: 6 in March, 26 in August, 7 in December.

1986

- In April, Hanoi handed to U.S. 21 remains considered to be of American servicemen.

1987

- In January, Washington sets high priority for MIA/POW issues with appointment of former chairman of Joint Chiefs of Staff, General John W. Wessey Jr. as special presidential envoy for talks in Hanoi.

- In December, promulgation of Viet-Nam's Foreign Investment Law.

1988

- In March, exchange of fire between Vietnamese and Chinese troops over disputed areas of the Hoang Sa (Spratly) islands in the South China Sea.
- In November, George H. Bush elected U.S. president.

1989

- In September, complete withdrawal of Vietnamese troops from Cambodia (engaged against Pol Pot's Khmer Rouges since 1978.)

1990

- The European Union (EU) establishes trade relations with Viet-Nam.

1991

- The People's Republic of China (PRC) and Viet-Nam resume diplomatic relations.
- In August, Gorbachev resigns as secretary-general of Communist Party.
- In December, Gorbachev's resignation as president provokes breaking up of Soviet Union.

1992

- In April, the U.S. lifts embargo on telecommunications with Viet-Nam.
- The Vietnamese government claims all former Saigon regime officials had been released from reeducation.
- In November, William Jefferson Clinton elected U.S. president.

1994

- In February, U.S. lifts trade embargo imposed since 1975 on Viet-Nam.
- Estimates released by the U.S. Center for Military History, Reference Division, Washington, D.C., indicate that 8,744,000 U.S. military personnel were engaged in (rotated through) the War in Viet-Nam, resulting in 58,167 deaths and 153,303 wounded. (about 4,000 servicemen were listed Missing-In-Action with 1,500 cases still unresolved).

1995

- In April, the Vietnamese government in Hanoi releases its official figures for North Vietnam's war casualties from 1955 to 1975, claiming a death toll of one million troops and two million civilians. (Figures given by the Saigon government by January 1975 show a total of 1.2 million deaths for the ARVN and civilian population in South Vietnam.) Conservative estimate for total fatal casualties for troops and civilians in both North and South Vietnam during War in Viet-Nam (1955 to 1975) would be at least in the order of 3.5 million.

1996

- In November, Bill Clinton re-elected U.S. president.

1997

- In July, U.S. and Viet-Nam resume diplomatic relations. 1997 U.S. and Viet-Nam begin talks and negotiations for Trade Agreement.

2000

- As of June 30, U.S. investments in Viet-Nam reach a total of 1.48 billion U.S. dollars with 118 projects, making U.S. the 9th largest foreign investor in Viet-Nam; Bilateral trade between the U.S. and Viet-Nam amounted to US$879 million in 1999 compared to US$222 million in 1992.

- In July, Viet-Nam and U.S. completed negotiations on Trade Agreement, bill signed by President Clinton, and awaiting ratification by U.S. Congress and National Assembly in Hanoi.
- George W. Bush elected president of the U.S.
- Three-day visit to Hanoi and Ho Chi Minh City by President Clinton.

ABOUT THE AUTHOR

Nguyen Xuan Phong

Nguyen Xuan Phong. a Vietnamese national from the Mekong Delta in South Vietnam, was educated in Saigon, Paris, London and at Oxford University as an economist. He was a business executive in the oil industry before assuming cabinet level appointments in the Republic of Vietnam from 1965 to 1975 as Labor Minister, Welfare Minister, and Minister at the Prime Minister's Office. He was also Minister of State in Charge of Negotiations/Chief of the Republic of Vietnam Delegation at the Paris Peace Talks when the War in Viet-Nam came to an end with the collapse of the South Vietnamese government on April 30, 1975. Phong returned from Paris to Saigon five days before the fall of the city to invading North Vietnamese forces. He was subsequently interned for reeducation in North Vietnam from 1975 to 1980. After his release, he began work in Ho Chi Minh City as an English teacher. He is now occupied with economic development in matters that include transport, construction, agriculture, banking and finance, foreign trade, tourism, health care and vocational training in science and technology. Nguyen Xuan Phong has written this recollection of historic events, intermingling deep reflections on hope as a factor in the unfolding of the events.

He has been a member of the Advisory Council of the Center for A Science of Hope since 1989.

CENTER FOR A SCIENCE OF HOPE

The Center for A Science of Hope was founded in 1983 to monitor and assess the status of knowledge about the human capacity to hope and to help demonstrate ways to deliberately engage this capacity in resolving critical issues of the times.

Hope is a key element in the capacity of people to mobilize energies to confront life's challenges. It is an observable dynamic found in both individual and societal groupings across many cultures. More than an outcome from internal or external stimulation, hope is a critical precursor to and shaper of events as well. The centrality of hope requires systematic, interdisciplinary study of its nature and dynamics, and efforts to discover ways in which hope can be engendered and sustained as a constructive force in human affairs.

While hope is a powerful energizer in human affairs, specific hope goals, objects or end-results may be ethical or unethical, and may be well-founded or illusory. As history demonstrates, specific hoped-for events or hoped-for results may benefit or harm the individual or the human community. As hope appears to be an essential constituent of all human struggle, there is the need to deepen understanding of this human capacity. Studies abound in which hopelessness is a factor. More needs to be done to understand hope in terms of its positive, energizing character.

The Center for A Science of Hope helps build bridges among and between scholars, practitioners and the general public to accelerate understanding of hope and its meaning in life and work. The Center has established connections with other centers and institutes and with people from around the world who are studying hope's complex interactions, as well as with those who simply are encouraged by knowing that hope, and their hopes, can have a positive impact in their life's endeavors.

The Center for A Science of Hope is an activity center of ICIS, [International Center for Innovation and Synthesis], a not-for-profit 501[c][3] organization which is also affiliated with the United Nations as a non-governmental organization.

In addition to **Hope and Vanquished Reality** by Nguyen Xuan Phong, the Center's other publications include ASPECTS OF HOPE, THE PROCEEDINGS OF A SEMINAR ON HOPE, Lamar Carter, Ann Mische, and David R. Schwarz, Eds., ICIS Center for A Science of Hope, 1993, ISBN 0-9636208-0-0. The Center has also sponsored re-publication of Shlomo Breznitz' MEMORY FIELDS, a remembrance of life as a child in a Catholic orphanage when his parents were sent to Auschwitz. The Center also publishes an occasional newsletter, ***HopeWATCH.***

Center for A Science of Hope
121 Avenue of the Americas
New York, NY 10013
(212) 219-3560 / FAX (212) 254-7342
E-mail: *sciofhope@aol.com*

INDEX

A

B

C

D

E

F

G

H

J

K

L

M

N

P

R

S

T

V

W

X

Printed in the United States
19790LVS00002B/315